Guilds, Society & Economy in London 1450–1800

Guilds, Society & Economy in London 1450–1800

Edited by

Ian Anders Gadd
and Patrick Wallis

Centre for Metropolitan History
Institute of Historical Research
in association with
Guildhall Library (Corporation of London)

2002

First published in the United Kingdom in 2002 by

Centre for Metropolitan History
Institute of Historical Research · School of Advanced Study
University of London
Senate House · Malet Street · London WC1E 7HU
in association with
Guildhall Library (Corporation of London)

ISBN 1 871348 65 X

Printed in Great Britain by Q3 Digital/Litho, Loughborough LE11 1HH

The editors and the Centre for Metropolitan History would like to thank the
following for their generous sponsorship of this publication:

Guildhall Library (Corporation of London)
The Worshipful Company of Brewers
The Worshipful Company of Clothworkers
The Worshipful Company of Cutlers
The Worshipful Company of Drapers
The Worshipful Company of Feltmakers
The Worshipful Company of Fishmongers
The Worshipful Company of Founders
The Worshipful Company of Goldsmiths
The Worshipful Company of Grocers
The Worshipful Company of Haberdashers
The Worshipful Company of Merchant Taylors
The Worshipful Company of Pewterers
The Worshipful Company of Salters
The Worshipful Company of Skinners
The Worshipful Company of Vintners
The Worshipful Company of Wax Chandlers
and The Worshipful Society of Apothecaries

Contents

List of Plates, Figures and Tables

List of Abbreviations

CLRO   Corporation of London Records Office
GL   Guildhall Library
PRO   Public Record Office
Rep.   Repertories of the Court of Aldermen, CLRO
CSPD   *Calendar of State Papers Domestic*
STC   A.W. Pollard and G.R. Redgrave, *A short-title catalogue of books printed in England, Scotland and Ireland and of English books printed abroad 1475–1640*, 2nd edn., 3 vols (London, 1976–1991)
Wing   D. Wing, *Short-title catalogue of books printed in England, Scotland, Ireland, Wales, and British America and of English books printed in other countries 1641–1700*, 2nd edn., 4 vols (New York, 1982–98).

Contributors

Dr Ian Archer, Fellow and Tutor in Modern History at Keble College, Oxford, is author of *The Pursuit of Stability: Social Relations in Elizabethan London* (Cambridge, 1991) and *The History of the Haberdashers' Company* (Chichester, 1991). He is a contributor to *The Cambridge Urban History of Great Britain* and has papers in the press on popular politics, memorialisation, and social networks in early modern London. He is General Editor of the Royal Historical Society Bibliographies on British History and his current research interests included both charity and taxation.

Dr Matthew Davies was employed as a research fellow with the History of Parliament Trust from 1994 until 2002, where his work included a major study of London and its MPs in the fifteenth century. He has recently been appointed to the post of Director of the Centre for Metropolitan History at the Institute of Historical Research, in the University of London. He is currently working (with Ann Saunders) on an official history of the Merchant Taylors' Company. Recent publications include *The Merchant Taylors' Company of London: Court Minutes 1486–1493* (Stamford, 2000).

John Forbes was educated at Birmingham University, graduating in Chemistry in 1938. He is a Liveryman of the Goldsmiths' Company and was Deputy Warden (Head of the Assay Office) from 1953 to 1983. He is the author of *Hallmark: A History of the London Assay Office* (London, 1999).

Dr Ian Gadd is a Research Editor at the *New Dictionary of National Biography*. He received his doctorate from the University of Oxford for a study of the Stationers' Company between 1557 and 1684. For 1999–2000, he was the Munby Fellow in Bibiliography at the University of Cambridge. He is currently editing a volume of the Stationers' Company records, and is working on a history of the Company between 1617 and 1710. He is also co-editor of the *HoBo* website (formerly the History of the Book@Oxford).

Dr Perry Gauci, Tutor in History at Lincoln College, Oxford, is author of *Politics and Society in Great Yarmouth, 1660–1722* (Oxford, 1996) and *The Politics of Trade: The Overseas Merchant in State and Society, 1660–1720* (Oxford, 2001). His work on the livery companies is the result of his research into the political development of the late Stuart town. He came to study London at the History of

Parliament Trust, and his work on merchants formed part of a project completed at the Centre for Metropolitan History.

Dr Ron Homer is a liveryman of the Pewterers' Company, the Company's archivist, and a past President of the Pewter Society. He has written extensively on pewter and the history of the craft, particularly on pewtering in provincial England and medieval London.

Dr Mark Jenner is a lecturer in History at the University of York. The author of articles on various aspects of the cultural and social history of early modern England, he is completing books on English conception of 'cleanliness' and 'dirt' as reflected in the environmental regulations of London *c*.1530–*c*.1700 and on water supply in London *c*.1500–*c*.1830. He is an editor of *Londinopolis: essays in the cultural and social history early modern London* (2001).

Derek Keene is Leverhulme Professor of Comparative Metropolitan History at the Institute of Historical Research, University of London, and the outgoing Director of the Centre for Metropolitan History. He has published on many aspects of the physical environment, economy and culture of English and Continental towns and their hinterlands between the seventh and the nineteenth century. After early works focusing on Winchester, he turned his attention to London. He is now interested in comparing metropolises within the larger systems of which they form part. Recent publications include contributions to *The Cambridge Urban History* and to *The Development of Standard English, 1300–1800* (ed. L. Wright). He is the general editor of the forthcoming new history of St Paul's Cathedral.

Giorgio Riello is completing a PhD thesis in Economic History at University College London on 'The boot and shoe trade in London and Paris in the long eighteenth century', supervised by Negley Harte. He has been a fellow of the Banca Nazionale del Lavoro in Rome, the Einaudi Foundation of Turin, the Royal Ontario Museum, and the Pasold Research Fund. His publications include 'La società del consumo nell'Inghilterra del Settecento: trent'anni di studi', *Richerche di Storia Sociale e Religiosa*, 55 (1999) and 'The art of walking: mobility, urban renaissance and eighteenth-century footwear', *Journal of Psychogeography and Urban Research*, 1 (2001). He is currently a Research Assistant at the Charles Booth Centre of the Open University.

Dr James Robertson is a lecturer in the History Department at the University of the West Indies, Mona, Kingston, Jamaica. His doctorate focused on London's roles as a 'capital city' between 1580 and 1642, and was supervised by Derek Hirst at Washington University, St Louis. He was a visiting assistant professor at Beloit College in Beloit, Wisconsin before being appointed to his current post. He has just completed a two-year University Fellowship from the U.W.I. and the Jamaican Government, writing a history of Spanish Town, the capital of the English colony.

Patrick Wallis is a lecturer in the Institute for the Study of Genetics, Biorisk and Society and the Department of History at the University of Nottingham. He is currently completing his doctorate at Oxford on the trade and regulation of London apothecaries in the seventeenth century and beginning a study of popular and public responses to epidemic disease in England from the sixteenth to the nineteenth centuries.

Dr Joseph Ward teaches History at the University of Mississippi. He is the author of *Metropolitan Communities: Trade Guilds, Identity, and Change in Early Modern London* (Stanford, 1997) and an editor of *The Country and the City Revisited: England and the Politics of Culture, 1550–1850* (Cambridge, 1999) and of *Protestant Identities: Religion, Society, and Self-Fashioning in Post-Reformation England* (Stanford, 1999). He is completing books on cultural exchange in early modern London and on the management of provincial charities by London livery companies.

Preface

As Keeper of Manuscripts at Guildhall Library, it gives me great pleasure to introduce this collection of essays devoted to the history of the 'ancient' livery companies of the City of London. The Manuscripts Section of our library holds the surviving archives of most of these, and as a result much of the historical research in this field involves many hours of study in our reading room. I am also very pleased that Guildhall Library has been able to assist in the publication of this book.

The essays collected here are a welcome extension of the long tradition of scholarship on the history of London's livery companies. However still more remains to be done. Speaking personally, I would like to see more edited texts of company records. Those companies whose records have been published are referenced again and again, while the rest remain conspicuous by their absence. As a result, apart from a handful of diligent scholars, the records of many companies are only ever consulted for genealogical purposes, a valuable but limited aim.

Also, there tends today to be an understandable, but in my opinion unhealthy, gulf between the members of the companies and the members of the universities who study those companies' history. There is enormous interest within the companies in their past, as is shown by their involvement in the conference at which these papers were first presented, and by their generous financial support of this publication. We need to find a way in which this interest can be guided and encouraged. In return, the livery companies themselves may be in a position to help the scholars. Over the last few years, they have willingly contributed to Guildhall Library's costs, for which all users of the library should be grateful. This collection presents us with an opportunity to think further on how the different constituencies interested in the history of London's livery companies can best work, individually or collectively, to benefit such research and its dissemination in the future.

Stephen Freeth
Guildhall Library
September 2001

1.

Introduction

IAN ANDERS GADD AND PATRICK WALLIS

> The best of *Politics* is that *Invention* whereby men have bin fram'd into *Corporations*, *Guilds*, or *Fraternities*.
>
> William Shepheard, Of Corporations, Fraternities, and Guilds
(London, 1659), sig. A3r

> *A Gull Citizen:*
> he is one loves to heare the famous acts of Citizens, whereof the guilding of the Crosse hee counts the glory of this age: and the foure Prentises of London above all the Nine Worthies. He intitles himselfe to all the merits of his Company, whether Schooles, Hospitall or exhibitions, in which hee is joynt benefactor, though foure hundred yeeres agoe.
>
> John Earle, Micro-Cosmographie, Or, A Piece of the World Discovered
(London, 1633), sig. G11v–G12r

London's companies were, according to the pamphleteer and restoration historiographer royal James Howell, the fabric 'whereof the main part of the City may be said to be composed: who for the Industry and Arts, their Inventions, and sundry wayes of Manufactures, may be compared to so many *Hives of Bees*, the emblems of sedulity and diligence'.[1] Howell's 1657 encomium to the guild would have resounded dully among others of his contemporaries: the critic of the Stationers' Company, Richard Atkyns, in 1664 saw companies as 'petit-states' and censured them for being technologically inhibitive, economically parasitic and accountable to no-one; Sir Thomas Wilson, later keeper of the records at Whitehall, in his analysis of the state of England in 1600 did not even think them important enough to notice.[2] London's livery companies have long excited competing opinions. The terms have largely mellowed since the sixteenth century, but debate continues. The papers collected here explore aspects of the London companies between the mid-fifteenth and the end of the eighteenth centuries. They reflect the current liveliness of interest in companies among historians of London, but – like the conference at which they originated – they also seek to address a broader audience; as indicated by the amount of library-shelving that their histories take up, the companies continue to fascinate a wide variety of people.

Beginning with John Stow, writing in 1598, historical accounts of the companies have accumulated over the centuries. The pace of production grew exponentially in the nineteenth century, when, as a product of developing civic consciousness and pious self-justification by the companies in the face of hostile investigation by Parliament, the corporate archives of London began to be opened to outside scholars.[3] Over the following hundred and fifty years a small mountain of volumes and articles have been dedicated to London's companies. As their numbers expanded certain genres emerged. From the nineteenth through to the early twentieth century, histories ranged from well-intentioned antiquarianism to urgent political treatises.[4] Most crucially, the leading thinkers of the new economic history turned their attention to guilds. William Cunningham in his *Growth of English Industry and Commerce*, and then George Unwin, in both his *Industrial Organization in the Sixteenth and Seventeenth Centuries* (1904) and *The Gilds and Companies of London* (1908), put guilds at the centre of their investigations of the transition from medieval to capitalist society. For them, the crucial question was whether or not guilds – and indeed capitalism itself – were economically 'a good thing'? Were they monopolistic cartels exploiting artisans for the benefit of proto-capitalists, or alternatively socially beneficial economic regulators – proto-trades unions? The social use of guilds was a question that interested other early twentieth-century writers, notably including R. H. Tawney and Emile Durkheim, who saw in the corporate tradition a possible means to overcome the anomie of industrial life.[5] It is a measure of their influence that while the subject itself soon became a backwater of economic history as a whole, in many later studies of guilds these approaches remained central.

The chronological structure of English guild studies has its roots in the late nineteenth century. Unlike much of mainland Europe, where in many states guilds were closed down in the late eighteenth century, English guilds were never directly abolished. Without an obvious crisis to explain the companies' fall from economic grace into apparent 'old corruption', historians have sought succour in anthropomorphic images of their growth, maturity, sickening and decline. Unwin saw the apotheosis of the guilds, and particularly the London companies, in the fifteenth and sixteenth centuries, and whilst he identified the late sixteenth and particularly the seventeenth centuries as a time of fundamental change, he characterised them as period of general decline. Historians have offered revised dates for the onset and symptoms of corporate wasting. However, the idea of a general 'rise' and 'fall' remains, though it not only fails to account adequately for the histories of *individual* companies, but also seldom defines how the health of the English guild system as a whole might be measured or explains how it is that companies continue to exist today.[6] The 350 years covered by the essays collected here saw a particular flourishing of the London companies, socially, economically and politically. It was also a period that saw a series of profound challenges to all London's companies, from the specific crises of the reformation, the civil war, the great fire, and the purges and charter surrenders of the 1680s to the more general shifts in terms of London's size, social structure and economy. While the companies were often deeply affected by such events, their responses helped shape the development of London's economy and society. Thus, while not ignoring the issue of why the companies 'rose' or 'declined', we should also be addressing a more fundamental question: how did they manage to endure at all?

As questions of urban crisis and stability came to centre stage in the 1970s, notably through the work of Paul Slack and Peter Clark, attention to the companies expanded in new directions.[7] In the work of Valerie Pearl and Robert Ashton, London companies took on new clothing as *political* organisations, implicated in the stresses and conflicts of pre-civil war London.[8] The general revival in historical work on the capital in the 1980s produced a renewal of interest in the London companies which matched the broader renaissance in work on European and British guilds. Following academic fashions, traditionally formulated political and economic concerns were replaced by issues of power and community. In a modern reconfiguration of the political interest in 'guild socialism' of the early twentieth century, Anthony Black argued that, through their rhetoric of community and fraternity, European guilds were important reservoirs of cultural traditions that formed precursors of civil society.[9] In contrast, Heather Swanson in her work on York, provocatively if problematically, revived the idea of English guilds as imposed administrative systems independent of artisan's interests.[10] Questions of social stability remained important, but in the hands of Steve Rappaport and Ian Archer, examination of these issues became a lens through which a far clearer image of the London companies could be made visible. Rappaport's exhaustive statistical investigation highlighted some of the individual choices that membership of a London company could bring: from the runaway apprentice to the aspiring journeyman, from the 'stranger' and 'foreigner' to the company officers.[11] Archer broke new ground by contextualising the companies against other London institutions in order to show how the companies operated in urban society at an individual and corporate level.[12] Meanwhile, research into artisan and urban work on the European mainland was revealing more complex economies and less isolated corporate systems, reviving the question of their economic utility, while also drawing new attention to the cultural and ceremonial fabric of guild life.[13] Even more recently, studies have begun to challenge assumptions about the parochial nature of the London companies, demonstrating how membership and active regulation could stretch to accommodate the city's suburbs, and how as patrons of charities their influence could extend to the provision of welfare or education across the country.[14]

Often existing at arm's length from the historiography outlined here, another tradition of histories of companies – single-company histories – has developed and flourished. Largely executed as 'house' histories and deliberately limited in focus, such studies have nevertheless often proved invaluable for historians working on the London companies more generally, not least as it is to these kinds of projects that we owe many important published editions of company records, from Edward Arber's *A Transcript of the Registers of the Company of Stationers 1554–1640 AD* (1875–94) and C. M. Clode's *Memorials of the Guild of Merchant Taylors of the Fraternity of St John the Baptist* (1875) onwards. The separation of this genre from the academy can be over-stated: from Sylvia Thrupp in the 1930s to Ian Archer and Michael Berlin in the 1990s, professional historians have also produced a significant number of such studies.[15]

From the early fourteenth century, to be a freeman of London – to be an economically and politically active citizen – one needed to be a member of one of the companies which represented and regulated various trades and crafts in the city. In short, a freeman was a company-man.[16] Arguably, by the mid-eighteenth century the edges of the system were fraying, but large numbers of Londoners remained enveloped in the fabric of company life. In this, London was much like any other European city. Guilds were the most familiar economic institution in the towns of Western Europe between the thirteenth and the end of the eighteenth centuries. Throughout these centuries, craftsmen and tradesmen grouped together (or were grouped by others) to provide themselves with a range of social, economic, and often religious benefits, organising themselves by individual trades or crafts in larger towns, more arbitrarily and more heterogeneously elsewhere. Often guilds became prominent enough within the town or city to receive formal recognition from either the urban or national authorities (or indeed both) that legitimated their corporate authority. The social prestige and economic privileges this brought came at the price of corporate obligations; normally it meant the guild becoming part of the financial and administrative machinery of town and crown, often providing money for the state in the manner typical of early-modern governance.[17] Membership of the guild also frequently became linked with political rights as a local citizen. Moreover, the process of seeking recognition encouraged institutional conformity and imitation: in spite of significant economic differences from one trade to another, guilds sought to 'fit in' by modelling themselves on existing guilds and fraternities. It was a cross-pollination that led to institutions with remarkably similar structures. London was just one European urban centre that conformed to this model.

Unlike most English towns, London developed a large number of separate, often single-craft, companies. The earliest appeared in the twelfth century.[18] From the fourteenth century they grew in numbers and importance, and by the late sixteenth century, there were perhaps as many as seventy such companies recognised by the city authorities. Many had already sought royal recognition through the grant of a charter of incorporation, formalising the corporate personality of the company at law; even more had already acquired the more material trappings of a meeting place and common property. The origins of many of the oldest such companies lay with primarily religious fraternities such as the Fraternity of St John the Baptist from which the Merchant Taylors' Company developed. By the reformation, they had become sufficiently distinct from these that, for the most part, they survived the Edwardian legislation that annihilated religious guilds across the kingdom.[19] The extent of their influence over London's economy and society varied from company to company and from trade to trade, but taken together by the fifteenth century the companies formed the largest and most important network of urban institutions after the parish. In terms of numbers alone, perhaps as many as three-quarters of the males in mid-sixteenth-century London were members of a company and, although the proportion seemed to decline from that date in the face of London's ever-rising population, by the end of the seventeenth century at least one-half of all male Londoners remained companymen.[20] Of course, membership could mean very different things to different people – indeed a number of the papers in this collection (most notably those by Robertson, Gauci and Riello) consider this very issue – but the London companies nevertheless exerted an undeniably powerful presence in early modern London.

Incorporation may have effectively conferred upon companies a legal immortality that superseded the brief span allocated to their members, but such perpetuity masked a remarkably changeable reality.[21] A company was quite simply unable to exist, let alone function, without the active participation and belief of its members. Charters, ordinances, meetings, officers, halls and records all helped to structure the relationship that the members had with their company and provided a sense of permanence and antiquity. But a company's forms and procedures were endlessly reshaped and rewritten by the immediate concerns of its members in a rapidly changing metropolitan context.[22] Even familiar and long-standing practices such as apprenticeship or search were subject to subtle but profound shifts in response to changing social and economic conditions both within and outwith the company and the trade. Companies were recreated at every court meeting and every quarter day; they were in a real sense social structures in motion. Although it proved a great strength in terms of survival, such fluidity was inevitably a source of profound worry. Companies were ever fearful of actions or events that might threaten to 'dissolve' them; some companies did indeed fade away leaving only a hall or less behind them.[23] The derivative processions, ceremonies, fur-and-velvet pomp and circumstance that even the newest companies adopted were – like the urgency with which halls were built (and rebuilt after the fire) – driven by this sense of insecurity.

In contrast to the impression given by the consolidated archives and magnificent edifices they produced, companies were neither monolithic nor impersonal. They ranged from the magnificence of the Grocers or Mercers to the marginal existence of some of the lesser companies who spent much of the period borrowing accommodation and were eternally strapped for cash; similarly even the largest companies rarely numbered more than a few thousand members at any one time, while most had only a few hundred freemen.[24] There was no single 'type' of company; nor, for that matter, was there a single 'type' of member. Nor, indeed, were incorporated companies the sum total of guild-style institutions in London. Incorporation allowed a company to acquire property in perpetuity, provided it with a legal identity, and consolidated and confirmed its rights, privileges and jurisdiction. However, not every company succeeded in gaining such a charter, nor did all try: the trajectories of organisation within different crafts were diverse, often for individual and political reasons as much as economic. [25] The political and financial costs of obtaining a charter were for long periods beyond some, such as the Horners' and Paviours' companies which, despite medieval origins, were not incorporated until 1638 and 1672 respectively. Those groups which did eventually succeed sometimes took decades to reach their goal: it cost the Pewterers' Company at least twenty years and almost £200 spent on lobbying to secure its charter in 1474.[26] Even when the incorporation was being sponsored by powerful patentees, as in the case of the Distillers, the process could be extended and complex, often because of opposition from the Court of Aldermen and existing companies.[27] Freemen encompassed a huge diversity of wealth, status, ambition and opportunity, from the jobbing journeyman to the most senior alderman, from the most active and aspirant city-dweller to the passive suburban or provincial member content simply to pay his quarterly dues. Moreover, as the name-calling and beard-pulling that could interrupt the peace of court meetings remind us, relationships within the company were often intensely personalised; indeed the highly ritualised and formal nature of the meetings and the responsibilities of office acted as an important counterweight to potential personal conflicts, many of which derived from the complexity of personal, business and financial relations that existed outside the bounds of the company hierarchy.

Above all, however, we need to recognise the distinction between the company 'system' and the company members and their work. It is all too easy to slip into eliding the official actions made by the company's rulers in the company's name with the opinions and behaviour of its other members. Freemen did not necessarily agree with the opinions or activities of the courts of assistants; nor did all members of the courts of assistants inevitably have a common position. At times such discontent might demonstrate itself in a dramatic confrontation at a meeting and so come down to us carefully mediated by the clerk, but equally, disaffection could develop into silent disillusionment and alienation.[28] Appreciating this separation of company and member is not just a question of understanding contemporary politics and urban communities; the issue was also a personal one. Freemen's divergent life-paths can be (and have been) conceptualised in terms of success and failure, but to do so is to define the realities of life for many, perhaps most, freemen as deviating from a pre-determined career path. Like the large proportion of apprentices who never became freemen, the variations of an individual's career were as integral a part of the company system as the feasting and processions of the courts of assistants; company history is as much about exclusion as inclusion. Similarly, it is important to emphasise that, although they were largely established by artisans for their own purposes, the relationship between company and trade (or craft) was at best loose and at worst almost non-existent. Members of the Grocers' Company might well not be grocers; not all tailors might be members of the Merchant Taylors' Company. And even if they were, the realities of business, the overlapping boundaries of trades, and the complexity of production and retail bore little relation to the 'ideal-type' artisan framed in company ordinances, although this need not mean companies had no economic value to their members.[29]

It is worth underlining that even the most nuanced investigation of those named as freemen in company minute books can only produce a pallid and disjointed impression of the urban economy. Servants, lodgers, transient migrants and the numerous journeymen, artisans and labourers outside the companies would be largely notable by their omission from the records, but probably the most striking absence from such a picture would be women. As Maureen Bell has argued, in corporate records 'the existence of the man effectively blots out any record of activity by the woman'.[30] Although the household economy of early modern craft production relied on the participation of all members of the family, particularly wives, and although women could be found working outside companies, they are largely absent from the records of guilds and companies, generally only appearing when the male head of the household is for some reason absent (most usually through death). Women's work is a particular victim in views of London's economy drawn from the company perspective. London had no equivalents to the female guilds found in parts of the continent, and largely excluded women from entering apprenticeships or becoming independent masters unless they were widows of freemen. Even then they could face additional restrictions from company officers uncomfortable with the idea of an economically independent female.[31] Indeed, the formalisation of guild structures – bastions of homosociality – from the middle ages onwards appears to have been one of the factors diminishing the independence and visibility of women's work.[32] But their case serves as a reminder that inside and especially outside the walls of the city much economic activity – if taken as the sum of what those people actively working were doing – existed beyond the direct grasp of the companies. The essays here are concerned with the core of the corporate system, but they are composed with an awareness that the accounts they contain need to be read as only one of many histories of London, just as guilds need to be appreciated as only one among many sources of solidarity and community – alongside parishes, families, neighbourhoods and circles of friends. As Gervase Rosser has pointed out, the very complexity of work created a need for a 'range of associational ties'.[33]

Awareness of such differentiation, however, does not inevitably consign to failure more ambitious attempts to understand the companies collectively: rather, it makes the need for such efforts even more pressing. The history of companies may tend to become fragmented by the boundaries between companies or periods or archival resources, but this is not inevitable. More of a balance needs to be struck between the close investigation of single corporate bodies and the development of wider interpretations of their place in the city.

The following chapters have been developed out of a series of papers presented at a conference hosted by the Centre for Metropolitan History at the Institute of Historical Research of the University of London on 13 April 2000. They form a diverse collection of work and although the authors hold no common position on the debates discussed above, they share a sense that the study of London companies remains an exciting and important part of historical scholarship. The chapters are followed by responses from three other scholars involved in the field, Joe Ward, Mark Jenner and Derek Keene, who formed a panel of discussants at the original conference; here they offer further thoughts on the concerns and questions raised in these essays and seek to highlight areas of further research.

Market regulation has long been an area of interest to historians of guilds. As four of the papers in this collection illustrate, search was the most obvious way in which London's companies exerted their influence over the crafts and trades they governed and it is also a major concern apparent in many of their surviving records. As the fist in the corporate glove, the meaning, extent and effectiveness of search is arguably the key to understanding the nature of the companies' hold over the metropolitan economy. Search was undoubtedly a key function of companies, yet it was far from being standardised nor was it the be-all and end-all of corporate policing. Matthew Davies and Patrick Wallis devote their attention to the metropolitan experience of company power. Davies examines the *practices* of power in the fifteenth-century Merchant Taylors' Company, emphasising that this is a very different subject to the formal role of the company expressed in its ordinances. Examining the full range of company activities, not just search, he demonstrates how the court of assistants reacted to economic pressures and changes in the marketplace with a clear sense of priorities that aimed to maintain the formal structures of the craft, while taking a pragmatic and flexible approach to aliens and strangers and related crafts, such as botchers. Strikingly, although it was at this time largely composed of members active in the trade, the company was not overly concerned with issues of quality control; the nature of goods remained largely an issue for customers and retailers to negotiate in the marketplace. Through an analysis of patterns of policing within two companies in the seventeenth century, Wallis demonstrates the frequency and extensive social and institutional reach of the searches and the punishment they led to. The sheer extent of these companies' regulatory activity, the volume of offending, and the nature of the punishments imposed, he argues, bears close comparison to the re-integrative emphasis of early modern legal processes at large, underlining the need to link work on guilds with broader analyses of early-modern social and institutional forms.

Taking different companies as their foci, Ronald Homer and John Forbes both analyse an aspect of London guilds which has largely gone unnoticed: their direct provincial influence. Homer demonstrates both the surprising extent of the Pewterers' searches and the technical and social processes the search involved. Search served to underwrite metal quality, while price regulation by the company further limited competition in the market for pewter. His portrait of a London corporate power operating on a national scale – securing legislation and exercising a strong influence in the supply of raw materials – has parallels with Forbes' discussion of the Goldsmiths' Company. The Goldsmiths stand out as an example of corporate survivalism, with their role in hallmarking maintaining their effectiveness as a regulatory body to modern times. Nonetheless, as Forbes shows, securing statutory backing (rather than royal proclamation) for their activities in provincial search and controlling alien craftsmen was a long-term problem for the company.

Recognising the flexibility and fluidity of guilds also means that monocausal analyses of rise or decline become problematic. Considering the weakening of guild economic regulation in the eighteenth century (itself a gradual and partial process, as Michael Walker has shown) as signalling the wholesale marginalisation of the companies ignores their ability to adapt to changed circumstances.[34] What companies actually *did* changed constantly over the centuries. While some of their functions might at times cease or at least become moribund, others might develop or come to the fore, as Perry Gauci argues here. As both he and Giorgio Riello suggest, companies still had several very active functions into the eighteenth century. Their work suggests that London companies were more comparable with European guilds in this period than has often been thought.[35] Far from a barren desert, the eighteenth century appears to have witnessed adaptation and indeed occasional revival, rather than absolute decline. We need to recognise the less visible attractions that guilds possessed as centres of sociability offering opportunities for productive networking and guarantees of character and identity. As Gauci shows, companies provided merchants with forums in which they could successfully further their businesses. Irrespective of their regulatory or craft role, companies served both as aids to defining creditworthiness and as talking-shops, clearing houses for gossip and information, and places to develop the loose networks of sociability and association which allowed the mercantile economy to function, a particular concern in London which was very late in providing exchanges for merchants. In his examination of a very different company and section of the population, Riello highlights the relationship of the company, with its traditional ordering of apprentices, journeymen and masters, to the family economy in a gradually changing economic environment. Drawing productively on recent studies of rural economic systems, he highlights the way the Cordwainers' Company continued to play a role in the organisation of the shoemaking trade until provincial competition finally sank the metropolitan craftsman toward the end of the eighteenth century. It was, as he emphasises, a world in which even ostensibly 'weak' companies could have a great influence.

One aspect long associated with the 'decline' of the companies was a shift in their formal purpose from the regulation of craft and trade to the governance of charitable funds. In his chapter, Ian Archer takes up the question of the nature and extent of corporate charity in a range of companies in the sixteenth and seventeenth centuries. Through an extensive analysis of charitable funds and company accounts, Archer challenges the traditional picture of their transition to a philanthropic role in the late seventeenth century. In its place, he shows that charitable giving by the companies was, if anything, declining at that time as companies struggled with repairing the damage from the great fire at a time of falling real incomes: the heyday of charity was between 1550 and 1650.

The impact of the metropolitan companies was not just a matter of their material wealth or regulatory power. As the papers by Ian Gadd and James Robertson show, image was fundamental to their influence. Gadd draws our attention to the construction and diffusion of two of the media by which corporate identity was promulgated: the company histories disseminated in antiquarian works on London in the late sixteenth and seventeenth centuries; and the more ephemeral collections of their arms printed as broadsides over the same period. These were, as he shows, not merely influential upon later historians. They acted to constitute a sense of the composite nature of urban life and the pre-eminence of the guilds within the fabric of London society and government for contemporaries. The target audience of the story Robertson takes up was very different. The various histories of Dick Whittington that were produced in verse, drama or chapbook prose during the seventeenth century were, he argues, forces in shaping the views of provincial immigrants and commentators on London. They created, however, not a reliable guide to the metropolis but a myth of metropolitan experience which compared favourably to the harsh experiences of most newcomers. The riches and fame attained by Dick through his cat – and his luck – were nevertheless still potent symbols. Robertson's analysis reminds us that, although in theory the companies were omnipresent, for many even basic membership was far too high a target.

NOTES

We would like to thank S.R. Epstein, Derek Keene, and Margaret Pelling for their comments on earlier versions of this introduction.

1. J. Howell, *Londinopolis: An Historicall Discourse or Perlustration of the City of London* (London, 1657), p. 41.
2. R. Atkyns, *The Original and Growth of Printing* (London, 1664), p. 19; T. Wilson, 'The State of England Anno Dom. 1600', in F. J. Fisher (ed.), *Camden Miscellany*, 16 (London, 1936).
3. G. D. Ramsay, 'Victorian Historiography and the Guilds of London: The Report of the Royal Commission on the Liveries Companies of London, 1884', *London Journal*, 10 (1984), pp. 155–66; 'City of London Livery Companies Commission: Report and Appendix in 5 parts', *Parliamentary Papers*, 39 (1884).
4. See W. Herbert, *The History of the Twelve Great Livery Companies of London* (London, 1834–7) for an example of the former and G. Renard, *Guilds in the Middle Ages* (London, 1918), especially G. D. H. Cole's introduction, for an example of the latter. See also L. Brentano, *The History and Development of Gilds and the Origin of Trade-Unions* (London, 1870).
5. E. Durkheim, *The Division of Labour in Society*, trans. G. Simpson (London, 1933), pp. 26–7; R. H. Tawney, *The Acquisitive Society* (London, 1921), pp. 127.
6. A number of the companies, such as the Goldsmiths and Apothecaries, still exercise certain statutory rights – see 'Corporations', *Halsbury's Laws of England*, 4th edn, 9/2 (1998), §1212. See also: J. R. Kellett, 'The Breakdown of Gild and Corporation Control over the Handicraft and Retail Trade in London', *Economic History Review* 2nd ser., 10 (1957–8), pp. 381–94.
7. P. Clark and P. Slack, *Crisis and Order in English Towns, 1500–1700: Essays in Urban History* (London, 1972).
8. V. Pearl, *London and the Outbreak of the Puritan Revolution* (London, 1961); R. Ashton, *The City and the Court, 1603–1643* (Cambridge, 1979); V. Pearl, 'Change and Stability in Seventeenth-Century London', *London Journal*, 5 (1979), pp. 3–34.
9. A. Black, *Guilds & Society in European Political Thought from the Twelfth Century to the Present* (London, 1984). In his review of Black's book, Peter Riesenberg described the work as 'an extended if not massive justification for social democracy as recently revived as a political force in Britain by the S.D.P.' (*Speculum*, 61 (1986), pp. 900–1).
10. H. Swanson, *Medieval Artisans: An Urban Class in Late Medieval England* (Oxford, 1989).
11. S. Rappaport, *Worlds Within Worlds: Structures of Life in Sixteenth-Century London* (Cambridge, 1989).
12. I. W. Archer, *The Pursuit of Stability: Social Relations in Elizabethan London* (Cambridge, 1991).
13. M. Sonenscher, *Work and Wages: Natural Law, Politics and the Eighteenth-Century French Trades* (Cambridge, 1991); J. R. Farr, *Hands of Honor. Artisans and Their World in Dijon, 1550–1650* (Ithaca and London, 1988); J.-P. Sosson (ed.), *Les Metiers Au Moyen Age*

(Louvain-la-Neuve, 1994); C. R. Hickson and E. A. Thompson, 'A New Theory of Guilds and European Economic Development', *Explorations in Economic History*, 28 (1991), pp. 127–68; C. Poni, 'Local Market Rules and Practices', in S. Woolf (ed.), *Domestic Strategies: Work and Family in France and Italy, 1600–1800* (Cambridge, 1991), pp. 69–101; S. Cerutti, *La Ville Et Les Metiers: Naissance d'un Language Corporatif (Turin, 17ᵉ–18ᵉ Siècles)* (Paris, 1990); S. Cerutti, 'Group Strategies and Trade Strategies: The Turin Tailors Guild in the Late Seventeenth and Early Eighteenth Centuries', in Woolf (ed.), *Domestic Strategies*, pp. 102–47; S. R. Epstein, 'Power, Resistance and Authorities. Craft Guilds and Technological Change in Pre-Industrial Europe', in B. H. A. Ransom (ed.), *Guild-Hall and Government: An Exploration of Power, Control and Resistance in Britain and China* (Hong Kong, 1997), pp. 46–63.

14. See, in particular, the work of J. Ward: *Metropolitan Communities: Trade Guilds, Identity, and Change in Early Modern London* (Stanford, 1997); and 'Godliness, Commemoration, and Community: the Management of Provincial Schools by London Trade Guilds', in M. C. McClendon, J. P. Ward, and M. MacDonald (eds.), *Protestant Identities: Religion, Society, and Self-Fashioning in Post-Reformation England* (Stanford, 1999), pp. 141–57.

15. S. Thrupp, *A Short History of the Worshipful Company of Bakers of London* (Croydon, 1933); I. W. Archer, *The History of the Haberdashers' Company* (Chichester, 1991); M. Berlin, *The Worshipful Company of Distillers: A Short History* (Chichester, 1996).

16. 'Guild', as a term, has had a contentious history. As Derek Keene has pointed out, 'guild' was originally used to mean any association that required subscription payments. However, a few historians have felt it should only be used to describe the religious fraternities from which many of the London companies developed as opposed to the companies themselves. In spite of this, many modern English historians have co-opted *guild* as a generic term to describe craft and trade organisations to the extent that its use has become ubiquitous. Both the strength and weakness of *guild* as a term as opposed to *company* lies in the universality with which the former can be applied, as it allows comparisons, generalisations and abstractions to be made that cross local, regional and national boundaries and serves as a pragmatic solution to the problems of cataloguing, indexing and translating. As a result, in this introduction, we use 'guild' in a generic sense, and 'company' to mean specifically the London companies. On the usage of 'guild' in particular, see E. Coornaert, 'Les Ghildes Médiévales (Vᵉ–XIVᵉ Siècles): Définition – Évolution', *Revue historique*, 199 (1948), pp. 22–55, 208–43 (esp., pp. 29–31: 'Le mot'); G. Rosser, 'Crafts, Guilds and the Negotiation of Work in the Medieval Town', *Past and Present*, 154 (1997), pp. 3–31 (pp. 3–4); S. Reynolds, *An Introduction to the History of English Medieval Towns* (Oxford, 1977), pp. 165–66; S. Reynolds, *Kingdoms and Communities in Western Europe, 900–1300*, 2nd edn. (Oxford, 1997), pp. 71–3; M. J. Walker, 'The Extent of the Guild Control of Trades in England, c.1660–1820: a study based on a sample of provincial towns and London companies' (unpublished PhD thesis, University of Cambridge, 1985), p. 393. On notions of freedom, see J. Barry, 'Bourgeois Collectivism? Urban Association and the Middling Sort,' in J. Barry and C. Brooks (eds.), *The Middling Sort of People: Culture, Society and Politics in England, 1550–1800* (Basingstoke, 1994), pp. 84–112.

17. S. Hindle, *The State and Social Change in Early Modern England, c.1550–1640* (Basingstoke, 2000), pp. 10–11, 21–3.

18. M. Davies, 'Artisans, Guilds and Government in Fifteenth-Century London', in R. H. Britnell (ed.), *Daily Life in Late Medieval England* (Stroud, 1998), pp. 125–50; E. Veale, 'The "Great Twelve": Mistery and Fraternity in Thirteenth-Century London', *Historical Research*, 64 (1991), pp. 237–63.

19. Veale, 'The "Great Twelve"'; Archer, *Haberdashers*, pp. 32–45; C. J. Kitching, 'The Quest for Concealed Lands', *Transactions of the Royal Historical Society*, 5th ser., 24 (1974), pp. 63–78; C. J. Kitching (ed.), *London and Middlesex Chantry Certificate 1548*, London

Record Society, 16 (London, 1980); P. Cunich, 'The Dissolution of the Chantries', in P. Collinson and J. Craig (eds.), *The Reformation in English Towns 1500–1640* (Basingstoke, 1998), pp. 159–74; S. Brigden, *London and the Reformation* (Oxford, 1989).

20. These figures include journeymen who were, by definition, freemen. Rappaport, *Worlds Within Worlds*, pp. 49–53 (this estimate has been queried: see C. M. Rider, 'Our City and Chamber of London: the relationship between the City of London and the Crown, 1547–1558' (unpublished PhD thesis, University of Wales, Bangor, 1992), pp. 11, 20 n. 44); V. Pearl, 'Change and Stability', pp. 3–34 (pp. 13–14, 30 n. 23); J. P. Boulton, *Neighbourhood and Society: A London Suburb in the Seventeenth Century* (Cambridge, 1987). From 1556, London set a minimum age of 24 for apprentices gaining the freedom of the city (although sons of freemen could be freed by patrimony at the age of 21); from 1563, the same age restriction for apprentices was applied nationwide – CLRO, Letter Book S, ff. 97v–99r; Rappaport, *Worlds Within Worlds*, pp. 322–9; 5 Eliz 1, c.4.

21. S. Reynolds, 'The History of the Incorporation or Legal Personality: A Case of Fallacious Teleology', in *Ideas and Solidarities of the Medieval Laity: England and Western Europe* (Aldershot, 1995), pp. 1–20.

22. Sonenscher, *Work and Wages*, pp. 2, 99; S. R. Epstein, *Wage Labor and Guilds in Medieval Europe* (Chapel Hill, 1991), p. 102.

23. In 1684, 'N. H.' suggested that the halls of the Girdlers' and Fletchers' Companies (whose 'Trades thereof are quite lost and gone, there being none of either of them') be taken over by the linendrapers, a trade at that time without a corporate structure: *The Compleat Tradesman: or, the Exact Dealers Daily Companion* (London, 1684), sig. C5r.

24. These figures include journeymen but not apprentices. See Pearl, 'Change and Stability', p. 30, n. 24; Rappaport, *Worlds Within Worlds*, p. 215 and *passim*.

25. The rise of new technologies and trades, from printing to gunmaking, from soapmakers to distillers, produced a number of new London companies at the same time as some of the older companies, such as the Woolmen, declined. See also: S. Cerutti, 'Group Strategies and Trade Strategies', p. 102; M. Howell, 'Achieving the Guild Effect without Guilds: Crafts and Craftsmen in Late Medieval Douai', in Sosson, *Les Métiers Au Moyen Age*, pp. 109–28.

26. J. Hatcher and T. C. Barker, *A History of British Pewter* (London, 1974), pp. 149–51.

27. Berlin, *Distillers*.

28. J. R. Farr, 'Cultural Analysis and Early Modern Artisans', in G. Crossick (ed.), *The Artisan and the European Town, 1500–1900* (Aldershot, 1997), pp. 56–74; Sonenscher, *Work and Wages*, p. 25.

29. See Gauci in this volume.

30. M. Bell, 'Women in the English Book Trades 1557–1700', *Leipziger Jahrbuch zur Buchgeschichte*, 6 (1996), pp. 14–16.

31. M. Wensky, 'Women's Guilds in Cologne in the Later Middle Ages', *The Journal of European Economic History*, 11 (1982), pp. 631–50; M. Howell, *Women, Production, and Patriarchy in Late Medieval Cities* (Chicago, 1986).

32. M. A. Clawson, 'Early Modern Fraternalism and the Patriarchal Family', *Feminist Studies*, 6 (1980), pp. 368–91; K. Honeyman and J. Goodman, 'Women's Work, Gender Conflict, and Labour Markets in Europe, 1500–1900', *Economic History Review*, 44 (1991), pp. 608–28; D. Herlihy, *Medieval Households* (Cambridge, Mass., 1985), p. 101; Epstein, *Wage Labor*, pp. 121–4. Although see also: E. Musgrave, 'Women in the Male World of Work: The Building Industries of Eighteenth-Century Brittany', *French History*, 7 (1993), pp. 30–52; M. Weisner, *Working Women in Renaissance Germany* (New Brunswick, 1986); P. J. P. Goldberg, *Women, Work, and Life Cycle in a Medieval Economy* (Oxford, 1992), esp. pp. 330–7.

33. G. Rosser, 'Workers Associations in English Medieval Towns', in Sossons, *Les Metiers Au Moyen Age*, p. 284; G. Rosser, 'Crafts, Guilds and the Negotiation of Work in the Medieval

Town', *Past and Present*, 154 (1997), pp. 3–31; Farr, *Hands of Honor*; Boulton, *Neighbourhood and Community*.

34. Walker, 'The Extent of the Guild Control'.

35. Sonescher, *Work and Wages*; S. Cerutti, 'Group Strategies and Trade Strategies', pp. 102–47; S. Cerutti, *La Ville et les Metiers*; M. J. Neufeld, *The Skilled Metalworkers of Nuremberg: Craft and Class in the Industrial Revolution* (New Brunswick, 1989).

2.

The Livery Companies and Charity in the Sixteenth and Seventeenth Centuries

IAN W. ARCHER

Among the dominant themes in the history of charity in England in the early modern period are the displacement of informal by formal means of support, and the concentration of relief on the civil parish. The parochial basis of relief enabled the English state to reconcile local élites to the principle of taxation for the support of the poor, and the increasing availability of public relief resulted in a decline in traditions of 'hospitality', and (more controversially) neighbourhood assistance.[1] Although the significance of these developments cannot be denied, preoccupation with them may have diverted historical attention away from the continuing role of corporate bodies lying outside the parochial framework in relieving the poor and in supporting broader charitable projects. It is true that the reformation witnessed a major onslaught on the confraternal life of the religious guilds, and it was briefly feared that the trade guilds would be swept away alongside them.[2] However a strong case can be made for regarding the period 1560–1640 as the golden age of the London livery companies, as their membership increased dramatically and their continuing vital role in trade regulation was supplemented by a growing involvement in the provision of welfare; their property portfolios swelled and their status as charitable trustees was enhanced.[3] Proper appreciation of the role of the companies is rendered difficult by the extraordinarily fragmented nature of research upon them. The effect of individually-commissioned company histories, often works of *pietas* or corporate legitimation, has been the ghettoisation of the subject. There is a crying need for works of synthesis and comparison.[4]

The distribution of charity became increasingly important in the self-representation of the livery companies during the early modern period. Although the degree to which, and the processes by which, the companies became detached from the regulation of their respective trades varied enormously from one company to another, in all cases an increasing proportion of their rulers' time was spent in the distribution of charity. The larger companies in particular came to command impressive portfolios of charitable endowments, each involving the wardens in making multiple payments. One sympathises with the remark of the

Ironmongers' Company in a letter to Oriel College in Oxford in 1621 in which they acknowledged their obligation 'to discharge our consciences in performing the will of the dead by whose legacy we reap no benefit but much trouble and hazard'.[5] That was perhaps not quite true because these charitable resources also represented an enormous reservoir of patronage which company rulers did not hesitate to use, nominating candidates for vacant almsrooms, sponsoring young tradesmen with whom they were connected for loan stocks, and participating in the choice of recipients of cash hand-outs at the quarter days.

But however mixed the rulers' motives may have been, there is little doubting the centrality of the rhetoric of charitable action within the livery company sphere. Members were exposed to the recitation of the wills of benefactors at quarter meetings; they could read about charitable benefactions on boards about their halls; they saw benefactors commemorated in heraldic glass, portraits, company plate and even statuary. Around the hall complexes there were often almshouses inhabited by almsmen in gowns bearing rebus commemorating their benefactors and their sponsoring companies; the almsmen themselves would attend regular services at which they would be required to give thanks for the goodness of their benefactors. Distributions of charity were often incorporated into ritual frameworks which served to emphasise the vertical relationships articulated in acts of charity. They might be accompanied by commemorative sermons celebrating the munificence of the donor or by dinners for the wardens which underscored the ways in which the exercise of charity brought élite Londoners together.[6] The charity of the London companies was a key element in the city's identity as a godly city. Andrew Willet's survey of London charity in 1613 sought to prove that sixty years of the gospel had brought forth more good works than twice as many years of popery. He stressed in particular the role of the companies through their contribution to loan stocks for 'poor occupiers' and to university education. In 1658 the fellows of Pembroke Hall flattered their Draper benefactors:

> It is a manifest truth for which you and the Nation in you, and for you, have much Reason to bless God that your large hearts and public spirits particularly celebrated for the universal patronage of these two most public interests of all others, Religion and Learning, have from time to time furnished us with more real arguments wherewith to confront the Romish brags of their good works, than any Protestant City in the world besides.[7]

Nevertheless, the task of the historian in recovering the scale of the companies' contribution is not assisted by their reticence in divulging information to investigators like Willet who, in spite of instructions from the lord mayor to assist him in his enquiries, had found the companies 'too nice and scrupulous'. Willet opined, no doubt with justice given the predatory attentions of courtiers to lands supposedly concealed from the chantry commissioners, that 'it is for that many vulturs eyes are in these catching dayes, too much prying in every corner for their prey'.[8]

An accurate assessment of the role of the companies in charity depends on distinguishing between several forms of assistance, both in terms of the source of relief and in terms of the form in which it was distributed. Some relief was informal: courts of assistants, when faced with a petitioner for relief, might simply call for a whip-round among those present.[9] They might alternatively draw upon the resources of the poor box which contained voluntary contributions and sometimes the proceeds from fines.[10] It is important to realise that in both these eventualities the amounts given are unlikely to be recorded in the company accounts; these practices were more common in the craft-based guilds and in earlier periods. The records might therefore lead to some underestimation of the role of the companies particularly in the years before 1550. But, as the élites became increasingly insistent on the need to discriminate among the recipients of relief and as pressure on resources increased in the course of the sixteenth century, so the drive to record, enumerate, and account for charitable expenditures was more evident. The companies made regular contributions to the poor from their own corporate resources, that is, the receipts from quarterage dues, fees for apprenticeship presentments and freedoms, fines, and the surplus on rental income beyond any specified trusts. Such payments from corporate resources, or the 'house' as they were sometimes referred to, should be distinguished from payments made by the companies under specified endowed trusts. These trusts might be directed towards the benefit of the company's own poor, or they might be directed to charitable ends outwith the company, and often beyond the bounds of the city.[11] Likewise, in considering the charity directed at members we need to distinguish between the different ways in which the relief was distributed. First, regular cash pensions might be provided either as a form of outdoor relief analogous to that provided in the parishes or as part of package which included accommodation in company-run almshouses. Second, companies might make one-off 'casual' payments to those in particular distress, such as to those seeking relief from debt, or to victims of plague.[12] Occasionally such gifts were made in the form of work materials, like the metal given to Stephen Barrow, pewterer, 'being in great poverty'.[13] Third, they might make grants of fuel and clothing, usually from specific trusts and often supplementing payments to those in almshouses.[14]

Although the bulk of this chapter will be concerned with the companies' expenditures on the support of their own members, it has to be remembered that the companies played a key role in supporting charitable objects beyond the confines of their own membership, both in London and in the rest of the kingdom. W. K. Jordan showed that in the period 1480–1660 Londoners invested no less than £584,711 in charities outside London and Middlesex as compared to £1,304,500 in the metropolitan area, and much of this provincial charity was administered through the companies. The Haberdashers, for example, ran schools at Bunbury, Monmouth, and Newport on the Welsh borderlands; they supported lecturers at Newland in the Forest of Dean, Monmouth and Bunbury; they owned the impropriated tithes of Leiston in Suffolk, Wigston Magna, Bitteswell, and Diseworth in Leicestershire, Albrighton in Shropshire, and Awre in Gloucestershire; and they made distributions to the poor of several other parishes in the provinces. As Joe Ward has recently argued, the widespread charitable interests of the London livery companies made them key agents of national integration because the management of these charities gave the companies a reservoir of provincial patronage and involved them in the mediation of local disputes.[15]

Was there anything new about charitable provision by the companies in the sixteenth and seventeenth centuries? The provision of charity had always been a key component of guild activity as the returns to the commission of enquiry into guilds in 1388–9 indicate, with many of the features we associate with the early modern period already present in the provision of almshouses, the existence of endowed charities, and the payment of regular pensions.[16] Thus, Matthew Davies has demonstrated how the Tailors provided alms of about £30 per annum in the period 1400–1440, falling to less than £20 per annum in the 1460s and 1470s; and from 1415 the company had a set of seven almshouses financed by charitable grants from John Churchman and the bishop of Norwich. The Goldsmiths had seventeen almsmen in 1423 who received grants totalling £42 per annum, although like the Tailors they seem to have cut back their provision in the later fifteenth century. It is difficult to compare these figures with the later sixteenth-century data because of changes in accounting procedures and the problem of inflation. By the 1590s the Merchant-Taylors (as the Tailors had become) were spending £201 per annum on their poor from corporate and trust sources combined: that is, between six and seven times as much as in the early fifteenth century. To this figure should also be added the £84 per annum that was being spent by the yeomanry organisation for which we do not have comparable fifteenth-century data. The Goldsmiths appear to have been spending £186 per annum in the 1590s – four to five times as much as in the early fifteenth century. The performance of the Merchant Taylors and Goldsmiths does appear much less impressive when the four-fold inflation and the enormous increase in the size of the companies of the intervening period is taken into account, but it does seem to be the case that, if as Davies has suggested the companies granted less charity in the later fifteenth century, they staged a recovery from the mid-sixteenth century. In the case of the Grocers' Company which hitherto had supported just six almsmen at the hall, it was only in the 1550s that the payment of regular pensions in outdoor relief began, and by the 1590s they were providing pensions to twenty persons at an annual expenditure of £60 per annum. The recovery may have been still more pronounced in the case of the smaller companies whose charitable activity (at least as reflected in their accounts) was at a fairly low level in the mid-sixteenth century, but rose thereafter. Expenditure by the Carpenters' Company rose from £1–£2 per annum in the 1550s to £13 per annum in the 1590s.[17]

The ability of the companies to respond to the needs of their members depended ultimately on the health of their finances. The finances of city institutions in this period are a murky subject demanding historians' attention, but there is a reason to suppose that in the period 1560–1640 the companies prospered. They had survived the crisis of the reformation when it had seemed that they might be swept away in the 1547 holocaust of institutions that underpinned chantries and obits, although their subsequent financial position was undermined by the repurchase of the properties which had been previously used to support superstitious uses. But their rent rolls swelled in the years thereafter, both as demand for property increased and as they accumulated more endowments. Thus the Drapers' rental income rose from a total of £277 per annum in 1547 to £2,127 per annum in 1687. Of this, the income free from specified trusts (and therefore free to be spent as the assistants saw fit) increased from £93 per annum to £717 per annum.[18] In the mid-1630s the Drapers were enjoying a total income of approximately £1,776 per annum. Rents accounted for £917 and entry fines for a further £812, so that property accounted for a striking 97% of annual income. Annual expenditure on charity totalled £937 (excluding overhead payments to company officials) – some 53% of the company's total annual income – with £659 supporting specified trusts and the remaining £278 coming from the surplus of corporate resources. The company's property portfolio, and in particular the income from entry fines, was critical in enabling expenditure on this scale.[19]

The example of the Drapers also makes clear another of the changes since the later medieval period, namely the growing importance of the companies as charitable trustees. There were antecedents for this in the earlier period as many of the obits and chantries with which the companies had been entrusted incorporated payments to the poor. Several almshouse foundations, notably those of the Taylors and the Whittington charity, had been secured by endowments. From the closing years of the fifteenth century, the companies came to be entrusted with funds for the provision of schools. Among the earliest were Sir Edmund Shaa's school at Stockport (1488) managed by the Goldsmiths, Sir John Percival's school at Macclesfield (1503) entrusted to the Taylors, and Dean Colet's St Paul's (1510) under the Mercers. [20] But there were further changes in the sixteenth and seventeenth centuries. First, as the table of charitable expenditures in several of the leading companies makes clear, there was a huge surge in the volume of endowed charity, reflecting both the need for alternative forms of commemoration in the post-reformation decades and a response to the growing problem of poverty (see Table 2.1 below, p. 24). Second, as W. K.

Jordan explained, there were new forms of endowed charity in this period. Loan stocks, aimed at assisting young tradesmen in the acquisition of credit to kick-start their businesses, began in the early sixteenth century with six donations with a capital value of £1,352 2s 0d in the years before 1530, a further £2,320 in the period 1530–1560, and £18,795 in the next forty years. The capital value of the loan stocks administered by the Merchant Taylors rose from £600 in 1580 to £4,500 in 1645; the number of tradesmen who might enjoy them at any one time rose from 20 to 110.[21] Most of these loan stocks bore modest interest payments which were used to support other charitable objects. Interest in the provision of work for the poor was reflected in the beginnings of apprenticeship funds in Elizabeth's reign and in the provision of stocks to set the poor on work which became increasingly popular in the seventeenth century. The reformation established its own set of priorities, with the need for an effective preaching clergy reflected in the growing numbers of exhibitions for study at the universities offered through the companies. The companies funded several of these from their own resources, acting under pressure from the ecclesiastical hierarchy, commencing in 1551 and revived in 1564 at the instigation of Bishop Grindal. Others were supported by endowments which accelerated in volume through the Elizabethan and Jacobean decades.[22] Likewise, the resources released by Londoners to support parish lectureships (most of them channelled through the companies) grew from £3,803 in the period 1561–1600, to £10,000 in the period 1601–20, £11,000 in the 1620s, and £12,000 in the 1630s.[23]

What was the relative importance of the parish and company in the charitable calculations of Londoners? Patterns of testamentary giving can help answer this question. Of the 218 freemen whose wills were proved in the Prerogative Court of Canterbury in the years 1570–3, 72% left some kind of bequest to the poor, while in 1636–8 52% of the 383 freemen whose wills were proved in that jurisdiction made a charitable bequest. Whereas in 1570–3 13% of testators in the sample left money for charitable purposes in their livery companies, the proportion for the 1636–8 sample is only 10%. There was, however, in both periods a sizeable number of additional testators who, while not making a charitable donation to their companies, left them a piece of plate or money for a funeral dinner. In 1570–3 there were an additional 51 testators in this category (23%), in 1636–8 an additional 40 (10.4%). This suggests that the companies were never as central to the charitable impulses of Londoners as their parishes: even those who recognised their personal obligations towards their company at the time of making their wills did not necessarily think of a charitable bequest first. Moreover, the companies seem to have exerted a diminishing hold on the loyalties of their members, even in the years before the civil war. However, for the wealthier citizens the companies remained important in their charitable calculations because of the centrality of the companies as managers of endowed charities.[24]

In the sixteenth and seventeenth centuries the livery companies became the favoured trustees for the bulk of the endowed charities of London merchants and tradesmen, including those that they established in the provinces. The incorporated status of the companies was attractive to those seeking to establish charities in perpetuity, and they offered more security than groups of parochial feoffees. The enjoyment of a legal personality meant that the companies could sue and be sued in the courts, an important consideration for donors who wanted insurance against fraudulent executors and protection against legal challenges to title. Moreover, the companies had an accumulated stock of experience in the administration of charity; their governors were well connected with London lawyers and knew the workings of central government apparatus; and the donors knew personally the men who would be administering their benefactions. These attractions were highlighted by Samuel Middlemore, a clothworker who gave his company £800 in 1628 to establish a charity which would provide £40 per annum for the purchase of clothes and coals for the poor of St Clement Eastcheap:

> I desire ... to enlardge my selfe towards the releif and succour of the poore haveinge had worthy presidents of good men even of this Company that have led the way before in this kinde. And for that in such cases some trusty and sure friends are therein more especially to be made use of. And knoweing none more fitt or more worthy and on whose love I may presume and depend than this worshipfull Company of Clothworkers whereof I am a member.[25]

These issues of trust may have been given added edge in the case of the large number of charities administered by Londoners in the provinces, for in the later sixteenth and seventeenth centuries the godly values of the London donors may have been at odds with the religious conservatism of the local élites in the 'darker corners of the land'. The situation may have been changing in the early seventeenth century, as London merchants became more willing to entrust their charities directly to parishes and to provincial corporations, probably a sign of the greater integration of the local and London élites and also of the consolidation of the power and duties of parish vestries as their grip over poor relief tightened.

As for the overall volume of relief directed to the poor in parishes and companies, this remains a difficult question because of our ignorance about the size of the poor rate in early modern London and the problems of reconstructing the overall contribution of the livery companies from fragmentary evidence. In *The Pursuit of Stability*, I attempted to calculate the relative importance of the various sources of poor relief in London in the Elizabethan period. This showed that, by the mid-1590s, the companies were supporting at least 200 almsmen and almswomen backed by pensions amounting to £600 per annum. These resources were supplemented by endowments yielding £250 per annum exclusively for the support of the poor in the companies. Companies in addition contributed a sum of £800 per annum from their corporate resources in pensions and casual payments. Total expenditures on the company poor therefore amounted to £1,650 per annum. That compares with a total of £2,825 per annum distributed through the parishes, comprising £1,425 from the poor rate, £251 in the yield from endowments, £523 in cash legacies, and the equivalent of £626 in gowns.[26] How the position changed in the early seventeenth century is less clear. The poor rate doubled in 1598 and a much lower proportion was siphoned off to Christ's Hospital, but the figures in Table 2.1 show that resources available through the companies surged forwards, particularly as a result of accumulating endowments. The relatively healthy state of company finances allowed much more to be spent on pensions from house stock. Although their resources were never adequate to the problems they faced, it is striking that the Clothworkers were able to support 113 pensioners in 1639–40 compared to 20 in the later 1590s.

In default of a global measure of charitable resources, it may be helpful to compare resources in individual companies and parishes. *Per capita* company resources can be calculated by multiplying the estimated figures for company membership according to household size of 4.5. These can then be compared with *per capita* levels of parochial expenditure on the poor (incorporating both the income from the rates and from legacies). Thus, the Grocers were spending 10*d* per person per annum in the 1630s, the Merchant Taylors 6.5*d* per person per annum, and the Clothworkers just 4*d* per person per annum. In comparison, the suburban Westminster parish of St. Martin-in-the Fields was spending 7*d* per person per annum, the poor riverside parish of St. Andrew Wardrobe 9.5*d*, and the wealthy inner-city parish of St. Antholin 3*s* 10*d*.[27] In both companies and parishes there was a marked disparity in provision between wealthier and poorer groups. While the companies were hardly in the same league as the wealthier parishes, their contribution was not insignificant.

The comparison of company and parochial resources is, however, a rather artificial exercise because they were each concerned with different types of poor. The parishes concentrated on the absolutely destitute while the companies paid much more attention to relative poverty, showing particular concern for those of formerly high status (especially those who had borne office in the company) who had since fallen on hard times. No less than 10% of the liverymen of the Merchant Taylors received some form of assistance from the company in the early seventeenth century. Large sums could be swallowed up by individuals: in 1608, for example, the Drapers agreed to pay a pension of £30 per annum to Sir Thomas Pullison, a former lord mayor on account of his 'antiquitie and charges passed in this Company and the Citie'. This is not to say that company charity passed by the problems of the struggling tradesmen, but it does help us to understand their periodic complaints about the distribution of charitable resources between livery and yeomanry.[28]

Probably at no time in their history was charity so important to the companies' role as during the century between 1550 and 1650. In the first forty years of the seventeenth century, expenditures on the company poor increased four-fold in the three companies considered in Table 2.1. However, the situation changed in the later seventeenth century. Expenditure on the company poor fell by one third, chiefly because of the companies' mounting financial problems. At the root of these problems was the burden of debt inherited from the civil war, while hopes that their creditors might be satisfied in the Restoration period through the windfall gains of entry fines were dashed by the great fire which destroyed forty-four company halls, and wiped out much of their property portfolio. Rents fell from £1,257 13s 5d to £584 10s 2d in the Drapers, from £1,271 6s 0d to £231 15s 0d in the Goldsmiths, from £588 11s 8d to £317 12s 4d in the Ironmongers. Rebuilding was financed by means of long leases on lower rents, thereby eroding the companies' financial base.[29] In particular, the cost of rebuilding halls (which members' subscriptions only very partially met) was very high: £13,000 for the Fishmongers, £13,716 for the Mercers, £13,000 for the Drapers (with an additional £1,000 spent on the garden). It was also necessary to replace charitable schools and alsmhouses: the rebuilding of St. Paul's School cost the Mercers £6,190, while the Whittington almshouses cost a further £600.[30]

In these circumstances it became very difficult for the companies to meet requests for charitable assistance during this period. As the Mercers put it in 1670:

> this Company is in no condition at present to bring a further charge upon themselves, because their loss by the late dreadful fire and their charge since upon several public buildings in this City hath not only exhausted their stock but set them much in debt and thereby rendered them incapable not only of remoter acts of charity but of relieving even their own distressed members.[31]

Table 2.1, while showing clearly the collapse in giving from corporate resources at this time, underestimates the seriousness of the problem. Comparison of the 1639–40 data with that from 1679–80 conceals some of the decline from pre-fire levels of giving because new charitable foundations had been established in the interim. The data from the Grocers, which allows a comparison between the immediate pre-fire period and the later 1670s, shows more clearly the scale of the problem. Expenditure from corporate funds on the poor fell dramatically, and overall expenditure on the poor within and outwith the company was halved, the brunt of the cuts being borne by the company's own poor.[32] Although the Grocers' problems were extreme, other companies

TABLE 2.1

Charitable expenditures of Grocers, Merchant Taylors, and Clothworkers, later 1590s, later 1630s and later 1670s compared (£ p.a.)

	Grocers				Merchant Taylors			Clothworkers		
	1590s	1630s	1664-5	1670s	1590s	1630s	1670s	1590s	1630s	1670s
	£ s d	£ s d	£ s d	£ s d	£ s d	£ s d	£ s d	£ s d	£ s d	£ s d
Company poor: corporate	67 10 0	218 15 0	87 9 0	24 13 11	89 7 9	158 11 6	78 15 0	48 17 6	182 7 8	11 0 0
Company poor: trust	12 11 4	23 18 0	145 5 4	44 0 4	114 12 10	827 2 1	692 5 0	37 5 4	107 0 0	187 10 0
Company poor: total	80 1 4	242 13 0	232 14 4	48 14 3	201 0 7	985 13 7	771 0 0	86 2 10	289 7 8	198 10 0
Non-Company poor: corporate	—	—	—	—	4 0 0	4 0 0	2 0 0	—	6 0 0	5 19 6
Non-Company poor: trust	22 5 4	145 16 11	377 4 7	305 7 10	29 0 2	393 2 9	356 8 5	49 6 8	201 17 6	271 16 8
Non-Company poor: total	22 5 4	145 16 11	377 4 7	305 7 10	29 0 2	397 2 9	358 8 5	49 6 8	207 17 6	277 16 2
Schools: corporate	34 13 4	6 5 0	—	—	10 0 0	40 13 4	1 2 6	30 0 0	12 9 0	7 0 3
Schools: trust	—	60 0 0	108 0 0	205 0 0	90 0 0	317 3 4	95 0 0	—	36 0 0	38 0 0
Schools: total	34 13 4	65 5 0	108 0 0	205 0 0	100 0 0	357 16 8	96 2 6	30 0 0	48 9 0	45 0 3
Universities: corporate	22 0 0	39 13 4	—	—	19 3 4	40 3 4	—	10 0 0	34 0 0	1 17 6
Universities: trust	—	65 0 0	75 0 0	27 10 0	—	28 0 0	44 0 0	13 13 4	17 10 0	25 0 0
Universities: total	22 0 0	104 13 4	75 0 0	27 10 0	19 3 4	68 3 4	44 0 0	23 13 4	51 10 0	26 17 6
Religion: corporate	—	—	10 0 0	2 0 0	—	—	—	—	24 13 4	—
Religion: trust	3 17 4	3 17 4	—	—	—	34 0 0	12 0 0	14 13 4	49 10 8	73 2 10
Religion: total	3 17 4	3 17 4	10 0 0	2 0 0	—	34 0 0	12 0 0	14 13 4	74 4 0	73 2 10
Other: corporate	2 0 0	2 0 0	6 0 0	—	7 0 0	21 0 0	—	—	—	—
Other: trust	—	—	—	—	—	—	—	—	8 0 0	—
Other: total	2 0 0	2 0 0	6 0 0	—	7 0 0	21 0 0	—	—	8 0 0	—
Company size (in 1630s)		1260				8000			3900	
Per capita expenditure on company poor (pence per person)[1]		9.6d				6.48d			3.84d	

Sources: GL, MSS 11571/8, accts. for 1596–8; 11571/12, accts. for 1638–9; 11571/15, accts. for 1664–5; 11571/16, accts. for 1679–80; Merchant Taylors' Company, accts. for 1596–8, 1638–9, 1679–80; Clothworkers' Company, accts. for 1596–8, 1639–40, 1679–80; Parliamentary Papers 1884, XXXIX, parts 1–5; V. Pearl, 'Change and Stability in Seventeenth-Century London', *London Journal*, 5 (1979), pp. 30–1.

[1] Compare per capita parochial expenditures (pence per person): St Martin-in-the-Fields, 7.2d; St Andrew Wardrobe, 9.6d; St Antholin, 45.6d.

faced similar cutbacks. Where receipts from rents fell, charitable expenditures were often cut back proportionately. Loan stocks often disappeared into general funds, although there were efforts to maintain the charitable payments which had been made from the interest.[33] The Grocers had debts of £24,000 in 1670, and were reduced to hand-to-mouth payments to the importunate recipients of their charitable trusts, granting money 'for a present supply until by the advance and coming in of more money a further payment may be appointed'.[34] Unsuccessful in their efforts in 1670 to secure from parliament the power to raise monies for the payment of their debts by assessment on the company membership, they found themselves entangled in multiple Chancery suits, and from 1673 their hall was sequestrated as lengthy negotiations for composition with their creditors proceeded.[35] Failure to meet their charitable obligations also rendered the companies extremely vulnerable to law suits from the intended recipients of their charities. The Grocers' attempts to settle were further complicated by litigation with Christ's Hospital, and by repeated threats from recipient parishes; in 1698 the Haberdashers were sued by the inhabitants of Newland for their failure to appoint specific lands to their charity after the sale in 1675 of the manors in Huntingdonshire which had previously supported the charity.[36]

Those historians who would argue that the loss of economic functions by the companies was compensated for by a diversification of their social roles need to confront the implications of the very serious financial problems faced by most companies in the later seventeenth century, and one of the purposes of this chapter is to suggest that historians must pay proper attention to the financial basis of the companies, which remains under-researched. It is particularly noticeable that the companies' own members bore the brunt of the cutbacks in charitable expenditures. Expenditure on pensions and university exhibitions to the sons of members out of house stock was curbed (a process, which if the Grocers are a guide, had begun before the fire) and, in the case of the Clothworkers (a company with a very large and turbulent artisan body), it was virtually abandoned altogether. Where difficulties were encountered in meeting trust obligations, it was those directed at company members which suffered most. This was probably because the companies were less fearful of litigation from their own members than from non-company recipients. But the patience of members was showing signs of real strain. In the 1690s the Merchant Taylors faced litigation from their yeomanry over the non-payment of charities that the latter thought were due to them.[37] If charity was one of the means by which loyalty to the companies was sustained, those loyalties were seriously frayed in the later seventeenth century. By the end of the seventeenth century the heyday of the companies' role in charity had passed, and the misfortunes of the funds entrusted to their care may have contributed to the decay in posthumous giving that was a feature of this period.[38]

NOTES

1. S. and B. Webb, *English Local Government from the Revolution to the Municipal Reform Act, Volume 1: The Parish and the County* (London, 1906); P. Slack, *Poverty and Policy in Tudor and Stuart England* (London, 1988); J. Walter, 'The Social Economy of Dearth in Early Modern England', in J. Walter and R. Schofield (eds.), *Famine, Disease and the Social Order in Early Modern England* (Cambridge, 1989); F. Heal, *Hospitality in Early Modern England* (Oxford, 1990); I. K. Ben-Amos, 'Gifts and Favors: Informal Support in Early Modern England', *Journal of Modern History*, 72 (2000), 295–338; B. Kumin, *The Shaping of a Community; the Rise and Reformation of the English Parish, c. 1400–1650* (Aldershot, 1996); S. Hindle, *The State and Social Change in Early Modern England, c. 1550–1640* (Basingstoke, 2000); M. J. Braddick, *State Formation in Early Modern England, c. 1550–1700* (Cambridge, 2000), chapter 3.

2. S. Brigden, *London and the Reformation* (Oxford, 1989); C. M. Barron, 'The Parish Fraternities of Medieval London', in C. Harper-Bill, and C. M. Barron (eds.), *The Church in Pre-Reformation Society: Essays in Honour of F.R.H. du Boulay* (1985), pp. 13–37; M. K. McIntosh, 'Local Responses to the Poor in Late Medieval and Tudor England', *Continuity and Change*, 3 (1988), pp. 209–45; B. McRee, 'Charity and Gild Solidarity in Late Medieval England', *Journal of British Studies*, 32 (1993), pp. 195–225.

3. S. Rappaport, *Worlds Within Worlds: Structures of Life in Sixteenth Century London* (Cambridge, 1989); I. W. Archer, *The Pursuit of Stability: Social Relations in Elizabethan London* (Cambridge, 1991); J. P. Ward, *Metropolitan Communities: Trade Guilds, Identity, and Change in Early Modern England* (Stanford, 1997).

4. I have, of course, been a collaborator: I. W. Archer, *The History of the Haberdashers' Company* (Chichester, 1991). The historiography of the companies also needs its historian. For some suggestive beginnings, see G. D. Ramsay, 'Victorian Historiography and the Guilds of London: the Report of the Royal Commission on the Livery Companies of London, 1884', *London Journal*, 10 (1984), pp. 107–34, but the flurry of studies in the 1990s also deserves scrutiny: do these works represent the latest attempt at corporate re-invention?

5. E. Glover, *A History of the Ironmongers' Company* (London, 1991), p. 80; compare with GL, MS 15201/1, p. 112.

6. I. W. Archer, 'The Arts and Acts of Memorialisation in Early Modern London', in J. Merritt (ed.), *Imagining Early Modern London: Perceptions and Portrayals of the City from Stow to Strype, 1598–1720* (Cambridge, 2001), pp. 89–113.

7. A. Willet, *Synopsis Papismi* (London, 1614), p. 1219; A. H. Johnson, *The History of the Worshipful Company of Drapers of London*, 5 vols. (1914–22), vol. 3, p. 248.

8. Willet, *Synopsis Papismi*, p. 1233. Compare with J. Stow, *A Survey of London*, C. L. Kingsford (ed.), 2 vols (Oxford, 1908), vol. 2, pp. 247–8.

9. GL, MS 7090/2, ff. 130v, 229, 254; MS 11588/1, f. 48; Clothworkers' Hall, Clothworkers' Company, Court Minutes, 1581–1605, ff. 19, 92v; GL, Merchant Taylors' Company, Court Minutes, 1562–74, p. 673.

10. GL, MS 15201/2, p. 8; Clothworkers' Hall, Clothworkers' Company, Court Minutes, 1558–81, f. 90v; 1581-1605, ff. 98, 152, 169v.

11. They are surveyed in *Parliamentary Papers, 1884, XXXIX*, parts 1–5, Report of Her Majesty's Commissioners Appointed to Inquire into the Livery Companies of the City of London.

12. Clothworkers' Hall, Clothworkers' Company, Court Minutes, 1581–1605, f. 135v; GL, Merchant Taylors' Company, Court Minutes, 1562–74, p. 760; GL, MS 15842/1, ff. 18v, 25, 115, 123.

13. GL, MS 7090/2, f. 130v; MS 7090/3, f. 33v.

14. The best examples are the elaborate provisions made for the almsmen and women of the Merchant Taylors' Company in the early seventeenth century under the charities of Robert Dowe, John Vernon, William Parker, John Hide, and Robert Gray.

15. W. K. Jordan, *The Charities of London, 1480–1660* (London, 1960), pp. 20–7, 308–18, 421 n. 1, 423–30; Archer, *Haberdashers' Company*, pp. 71–3; J. P. Ward, 'Godliness, Commemoration and Community: the Management of Provincial Schools by London Guilds', in M. C. McClendon, J. P. Ward, and M. MacDonald (eds.), *Protestant Identities: Religion, Society, and Self-Fashioning in Post-Reformation England* (Stanford, 1999), pp. 141–57; J. P. Ward and N. E. Key, '"Divided into Parties": Exclusion Crisis Origins in Monmouth', *English Historical Review*, 115 (2000), pp. 1159–83.

16. J. T. Smith and L. T. Smith (eds.), *English Gilds: the Original Ordinances of more than One Hundred Early English Guilds,* Early English Text Society, original series, 40 (London, 1870); McRee, 'Charity and Gild Solidarity'.

17. M. Davies, 'The Tailors of London and their Guild, *c.* 1300–1500' (unpublished D.Phil. thesis, University of Oxford, 1994), pp. 69–75; M. Davies (ed.), *The Merchant Taylors' Company of London: Court Minutes, 1486–1493* (Stamford, 2000); T. F. Reddaway, *The Early History of the Goldsmiths' Company, 1327–1509* (London, 1975), pp. 5, 111, 135, 147–8; Archer, *The Pursuit of Stability*, pp. 121–4; N. V. Sleigh-Johnson, 'The Merchant Taylors' Company of London, 1580–1645, with Special Reference to Politics and Government' (unpublished Ph.D. thesis, University of London, 1989), pp. 273–80.

18. Johnson, *Drapers*, vol. 2, p. 123, vol. 4, pp. 348–9.

19. Johnson, *Drapers*, vol. 3, p. 205, vol. 4, pp. 125–8.

20. C. J. Kitching (ed.), *London and Middlesex Chantry Certificate, 1548*, London Record Society, 16 (London, 1980), pp. 81–95; J. Imray, *The Charity of Richard Whittington: A History of the Trust Administered by the Mercers' Company, 1424–1966* (London, 1968); Davies, 'Tailors', pp. 69–75; Jordan, *Charities of London*, pp. 206–10.

21. Jordan, *Charities of London*, pp. 172–6; Sleigh-Johnson, 'Merchant Taylors', p. 65.

22. Jordan, *Charities of London*, pp. 251–2; Rep. 12, ff. 324, 327v, 330, 337v, 344; Rep. 15, ff. 356, 385r–v; Mercers' Hall, Mercers' Company, Court Minutes, 1560–1595, ff. 57v, 64r–v.

23. Jordan, *Charities of London*, pp. 284–92.

24. PRO, PROB 11/52–55, 11/167–178.

25. Clothworker's Hall, Clothworkers' Company, Book of Deeds and Wills, p. 326. Compare with GL, Merchant Taylors' Company, Court Minutes, 1636–54, ff. 101r–v; Johnson, *Drapers*, vol. 3, p. 334.

26. Archer, *Pursuit of Stability*, pp. 178–81.

27. Westminster City Archives, St. Martin-in-the-Fields Overseers' Accounts, 1638–40; R. W. Herlan, 'Poor Relief in the Parish of Antholin's Budge Row, 1638–1664', *Guildhall Studies in London History*, 2 (1977), pp. 177–99; GL, MS 2088/1.

28. Archer, *Pursuit of Stability*, pp. 121–3; Johnson, *Drapers*, vol. 3, p.110; Sleigh-Johnson, 'Merchant Taylors', pp. 273–80.

29. Johnson, *Drapers*, vol. 3, p. 279; W. Prideaux, *Memorials of the Goldsmiths' Company*, 2 vols. (London, 1896), vol. 2, p. 160; Glover, *Ironmongers*, p. 72. Compare with Archer, *Haberdashers' Company*, pp. 89–95; I. Doolittle, *The Mercers' Company, 1579–1959* (London, 1994), pp. 81–3, 96–110.

30. P. Metcalfe, *The Halls of the Fishmongers' Company* (London, 1977), p. 71; Johnson, *Drapers*, vol. 3, p. 287; Doolittle, *Mercers' Company*, pp. 75, 76.

31. Doolittle, *Mercers' Company*, p. 82.

32. The expenditure on schools in 1679–80 is artificially inflated because the company paid off some of its salary arrears in that year.

33. Archer, *Haberdashers' Company*, pp. 109–111.

34. W. Ravenhill, *A Short Account of the Company of Grocers* (1689); GL, MS 11588/5, pp. 76, 78, 94, 111, 112, 128, 132, 194, 253.

35. GL, MS 11588/5, pp. 103–4, 128, 138–9, 158–9, 162–3, 164–5, 165–7, 199, 200, 202, 204, 208, 213, 222, 253a, 258, 263–4, 333, 346, 349, 350, 368, 371, 373, 394, 397, 398, 421, 429.

36. GL, MS 11588/5, pp. 256–7, 259, 263, 266, 284–5, 289–90, 292, 300–1; Archer, *Haberdashers' Company*, pp. 112–13.
37. Sleigh-Johnson, 'Merchant-Taylors', pp. 347–8.
38. D. T. Andrew, *Philanthropy and Police: London Charity in the Eighteenth Century* (Princeton, 1989), pp. 45–9.

3.

Early Modern Printed Histories of the London Livery Companies

IAN ANDERS GADD

Hauing thus much not without trauaile, & some charges noted for the antiquitie of these Vintners, about two yeares since or more I repayred to the common hall of that company, and there shewed, and read it in a court of Assistance, requiring them as being one of the principall companies in this cittie (of whome I meant therefore to write the more at large) if they knew any more which might sound to their worship or commendation, at their leysure to send it me, and I wold ioyne it to my former collection: at which time I was answered by some that tooke vpon them the speech, that they were none of the principall, but of the inferiour companies, and so willing me to leaue them I departed, and neuer since heard from them which hath somewhat discouraged me any farther to trauail amongst the companies to learn ought at their hands.

[*Marginal note*:] The Vintoners. one of the *12*. principall companies[.] The readiest to speak not alwaies the wisest men.

John Stow, The Survay of London (1598), sig. N8v

John Stow's extraordinary meeting with the Vintners' Company in the mid-1590s represents the first recorded encounter between a historian and a London livery company. We should perhaps be sceptical of Stow's characterisation of 'some that tooke vpon them the speech' as utterly ignorant of their own corporate rank as it seems unlikely that a company presumably well used to processing in at least eleventh position for civic events would make such an apparently elementary mistake.[1] Anne Crawford in her 1977 history of the Vintners' Company wondered why the Company displayed 'such a remarkable feeling of corporate inferiority' at this meeting but it seems more likely that the company was actually attempting to discourage Stow from his historical investigations.[2] If so, the company succeeded – at least in part. Stow had relatively little further to say about the company; and in the 1603 revised edition this passage criticising the company was omitted altogether.[3] Nonetheless, despite such setbacks, the *Survey* was one of the very first printed works to consider the London livery companies as entities worthy of historical examination.[4]

This chapter charts two of the main ways in which the London companies were collectively represented in print between the late sixteenth and early eighteenth centuries. In particular, it is concerned with accounts of the companies given in Stow's *Survey* and that work's successors through to John Strype's *Survey* of 1720, and with the visual and textual representation of the companies' coats of arms from Benjamin Wright's broadside engraving of 1596 through to Richard Wallis's sumptuous *London Armory* of 1677. The rise and proliferation of 'surveys' of London from Stow onwards has been explored elsewhere; however, although historians have long relied upon them for contemporary evidence about the companies, there has been no study of how these publications specifically treated the companies.[5] Similarly, while early-modern heraldry has been the subject of twentieth-century studies and depictions of the appropriate coats of arms invariably grace single-company histories, the heraldic catalogues of London livery companies printed during the sixteenth and seventeenth centuries have not been explored in detail.[6]

None of the works discussed in this chapter seem to have been officially sponsored or endorsed by the companies themselves.[7] However, this is not to say that the printing press was not actively harnessed by the companies in other ways. From the late sixteenth century onwards, material as diverse as invitations for meetings, parliamentary petitions and ordinance books was regularly being printed on behalf of the companies, a consequence of print offering a cheap alternative to scribal copying.[8] Two companies may also have been directly involved in the production of what seem to be the only published works in the period that focus solely on the history of a single company. Ravenhill's *The Case of the Company of Grocers* (1682; reprinted 1686 and 1688) offered a robust account of the Grocers' Company's recent financial plight following both the civil wars and the fire in a deliberate attempt to assuage the company's creditors and to encourage its own members to invest in their company's financial future. Winstanley's *The Honour of Merchant-Taylors* (1668), later rewritten as *The Honour of the Taylors, or the Famous and Renowned History of Sir John Hawkwood, Knight* (1687), in contrast spliced chivalric adventures with the Merchant Taylors' corporate values of 'Loyalty, Ingenuity, Heroick Atchievement [and] Charity' in order to bolster the morals of the city's youth, closing his accounts with details of the company's charitable foundations.[9] Nevertheless, the apparent lack of corporate interest in contemporary historical and heraldic endeavours to capture the companies collectively in print suggests not only that the works discussed below were produced for a wider and more diverse market than simply the companies themselves but also that such printed representations of the companies were not overtly 'official'.

'Of great antiquity'

John Stow's position at the head of the historiography of the London companies may not seem surprising given his *Survey*'s well-known significance for London history in general. Following contemporary usage, Stow indicated the corporate affiliation of many of the Londoners that he mentioned, underlining the companies' importance as a social marker and a source of social identity and solidarity to the London citizenry as a whole. Their role in managing the bequests of individual citizens was also often highlighted. More significantly, Stow accorded the companies a status equivalent to other worthy citizens, locating their halls, marking their contribution towards a civic project and even sometimes noting their altercations with other companies.[10] As with his accounts of notable individuals, Stow might occasionally pause in his perambulatory narrative (invariably outside the company hall) in order to provide some further historical detail about the company, ranging from a simple note about the date of a company's incorporation to lengthier comments about a company's past activities.[11] His disappointment at the hands of the Vintners' Company was both a notable and unusual example: only here did Stow appear to venture inside the corporate hall, and only here did he attempt to engage directly with contemporary corporate life.[12] Just once, however, were the companies considered collectively in a wider historical context, and significantly this took place outside the central picaresque frame of the text. In an appended section describing the city's 'Temporall Government', Stow supplied a list of some sixty companies who had attended a mayoral feast during Henry VIII's reign.[13] He gave no explanation for why he included this particular feast – his antiquarian nature would suggest that he did so simply because he had a record of it – but he immediately followed the list with a brief passage about how

> [t]hese Companies seuerally at sundry times purchased the kinges fauour and licence by his Letters Patentes, to associate themselues in Brotherhoodes with maister and Wardens for their gouernment, many also haue procured Corporations with Priuileges, &c...[14]

He then offered his opinion that the oldest companies in the city were those of the Weavers, and the Taylors and Linen-Armourers; the last two, as Stow mentioned elsewhere in his text, later combined and eventually formed the Merchant Taylors' Company of which Stow himself was a member. Stow's tone in this section, or indeed his purpose in including this material as almost an appendix to his main text, is difficult to judge. He gets his history wrong: his dating of the Henrican feast to 1531 is at odds with the inclusion of the companies of Shearmen and Fullers which had amalgamated in 1528 to form the Clothworkers' Company, and his distinction between letters patent and incorporation seems a trifle artificial. His admission that he was 'neuer [a] feastfolower' seems to indicate a lack of interest about such formal corporate conviviality (or perhaps personal pique given his own relatively lowly status within his own company), whilst his use of words such as 'purchased' and 'procured' in describing the ways in which he believed that companies gained royal favour implies a certain distaste for hard-nosed politicking.

Novel though this brief passage in Stow's *Survey* was, its significance in the historiography of the London companies would be relatively insubstantial were it not for what it eventually precipitated. The 1618 edition of the *Survey*, revised by Anthony Munday following Stow's death in 1605, did include updated material about the companies and their halls in the main body of the text, but it did not alter or expand Stow's original text on 'Temporall Government'.[15] However, Munday's further revisions for the 1633 folio edition, completed by Humphrey Dyson and published after the death of both men, involved a dramatic substitution of Stow's original list of feasting companies with a forty-five page illustrated catalogue of the London companies in order of rank.[16] The 'Great Twelve' companies and the ten merchant companies were each given a whole page, followed by fifty lesser companies two to a page; in each case, a woodcut of the company's coat of arms surmounted a very brief note about the company.[17] However, this bold development was somewhat undercut by the very conservative nature of the historical detail. The accompanying descriptions usually only gave a company's date of incorporation, perhaps supplemented by a date for its grant of livery; very rarely was the associated craft or trade even mentioned.[18] Companies, it seems, were only to be known by their charters, livery and heraldry.

Nevertheless, through a close examination of these gnomic corporate blurbs, it seems possible to highlight some of the tonal and thematic continuities and changes in the descriptions, particularly between the formal accounts of the great twelve and the occasionally more discursive descriptions of the lesser companies. For example, it was only in the latter group of companies that the 'author' himself (presumably Munday) occasionally 'appeared': of the possible separate existence of the Bottlemakers and Horners, he explained that 'I finde no Record that they were at any time Incorporated'; the Marblers' antiquity was 'unknowne to me; nor can I finde them to bee incorporated'; whilst from the Loriners, he had 'received a note' regarding their corporate appearance before the Court of Aldermen in Henry VII's reign.[19] More omnipresent than the 'author' in these descriptions, however, was the repeated emphasis placed upon corporate antiquity. Practically every company was described as 'of ancient continuance', 'very ancient', 'of very ancient standing', 'of great priviledge of antiquity', 'of large and very memorable antiquity', 'of larger antiquity then leasure will admit to be delivered' or, most simply and frequently, 'of great antiquity'. Antiquity (as much of the rest of the *Survey* also demonstrated) was the highest compliment that could be paid to any institution in early-modern England, all the more so when a company's documented history, as represented by its incorporation, was relatively recent; it also provided a fundamental basis upon which customary and legal rights could be justified. As Edward Bonahue has recently noted in his more general work on 'citizen histories', history provided early modern Londoners with

> an extremely powerful means of representing and, thus, gaining some control over their unfamiliarity. By positioning new social and commercial phenomena within familiar historical scenes, or by connecting them to an extensive historical tradition, London writers could offer a discursive and rhetorical containment of almost any city problem.[20]

The companies may not have been a 'city problem' in quite this sense (although the ambivalent attitude of London and suburban residents to corporate affiliation at this time may have been seen as such), but the repeated emphasis on corporate antiquity allowed more upstart companies, such as the recently-formed Society of Apothecaries and Silkthrowers' Company, to be represented as constituent members of a long and flourishing corporate tradition. This heritage was not a wholly exclusive one: the inclusion of *merchant* companies (such as the Merchant Adventurers) between the major and minor companies suggests both a desire to laud all the key economic institutions in the city and a belief in a wider corporate identity within the capital.[21] Moreover, the length and visual impact of the catalogue as a whole marked out the companies as civic institutions worthy of distinctive and special treatment, with the generous amount of textual 'white space' accorded to the companies underlining their significance to the revisers of the 1633 *Survey*.[22]

The motives behind the inclusion of such a catalogue are unclear, but it seems likely that it owes much to Munday who, himself a member of the Drapers' Company, had written city pageants on behalf of a number of London companies during his literary career. However, as only 45 pages within a revised work of over 900, it would be wrong to overstate the significance of such a section, and whilst Munday may have been well used to producing corporate encomium to order, the brevity of textual description suggests that the companies were themselves not active promoters of this particular section. Even the heraldic woodcuts were not especially innovative as such: numerous coats of arms belonging to previous lord mayors were also illustrated in the 1633 *Survey* and, as we shall see, visual collections of London corporate arms had first appeared in print in the 1590s. Nonetheless, this section of the 1633 *Survey* evidently set an important precedent, as no seventeenth-century successor or rival to the *Survey* seems to have failed to include some sort of section specifically on the companies. Very similar catalogues, often reproducing verbatim the text given in the 1633 *Survey*, appeared in James Howell's *Londinopolis* (1657), Nathaniel Crouch's *Historical Remarques and Observations of the ancient and present state of London* (1681), and Thomas Delaune's *The Present State of London* (1681).[23]

Significant development in the way that the companies were collectively handled by writers on London had to wait until the eighteenth century. Edward Hatton, for example, in his *A New View of London* (1708), returned to Stow's original perambulatory model by including a special thirty-page meander through the corporate and financial buildings of London.[24] Hatton placed the companies within the main body of his work albeit as a separate chapter and, like Stow before him, Hatton used each company hall as an opportunity for a digression about the building and the company's charters and arms. However, he went far further than Stow in providing valuable contemporary details about the actual number of company members, its rules regarding apprenticeship, and the cost of taking its livery. Fold-out plates illustrating the companies' coat of arms prefixed this chapter and the title-page of the second volume. By grouping the companies together with London's new financial institutions, by integrating them textually within London's whole yet marking them out as significant, and by providing important practical information about the costs and benefits of corporate membership, this section of Hatton's book seems to aim at the institutionally-mobile and status-conscious mercantile class that Perry Gauci discusses elsewhere in this collection – anticipating some of the concerns of later advice books on apprenticing children such as R. Campbell's *The London Tradesman* (1747).

This apparent new-found interest in the London companies as contemporary institutions was paralleled by renewed attention to their historical side. If, as seems likely, Stow was one of the first writers to consider the companies as worthy of any historical examination at all, it was with Stow's successor, the antiquarian scholar John Strype, that the companies found their first true historian. In Strype's fully revised 1720 edition of Stow's *Survey*, the companies retained their separate status within the work as an appended section but the catalogue as a whole underwent dramatic expansion, extending to some seventy-five double-columned folio pages.[25] Strype's debt to the 1633 *Survey* was obvious and explicit: each corporate entry began with a reproduction of the relevant 1633 text, headed by a similar (if somewhat smaller) woodcut of the corporate arms.[26] However, his catalogue differed in several significant ways, not least in that the generous white-space of the 1633 *Survey* was replaced with a much more textually-dense page layout. Strype omitted the merchant companies but added a number of London companies – both long extinct and newly incorporated – that had not been included in the 1633 edition. Stow's original feast-list was restored, and a new section concerning company precedence was appended.[27] Most important of all, in each entry Strype sought, wherever possible, to give as much historical detail about the company as possible. In a few cases, he was unable to add anything to the 1633 description, but for the most part, he provided a great deal of new material about the company's history and trade, often transcribing statutes, proclamations and other pertinent texts. One of the longest accounts, for example, concerned the Stationers' Company.[28] An amalgam of narrative history and documentary anthology extending for almost ten columns of text, it detailed the sixteenth-century development of English printing and, although nearly all the text can be traced back to primary sources (most notably the Lansdowne papers), Strype's extensive use of indirect quotation and sophisticated interweaving of different citations constructed a remarkably coherent account. Indeed, the primary sources that he consulted in this particular case are still considered to be among the most significant by modern historians of the Stationers' Company and the book trade. Strype's scholarship was all the more impressive given that, with some exceptions, he seems not to have had access to any of the city's corporate archives.[29]

With all these 'surveys' of London from Stow through to Strype, we need to be wary of assigning too much meaning to the inclusion of collective descriptions of the London companies. The compilers of these books evidently felt that an account of London ought to include some kind of consideration of the companies, with the revised catalogues included in the 1633 and the 1720 *Survey* being the most notable examples of this. Yet the brevity of the information provided in all the pre-1700 catalogues seems at odds with the apparent desire to draw attention to the companies in the first place. This lack of historical detail, the relatively little attention paid to the companies in terms of the length of the overall work (only Crouch's *Historical Remarques* and Hatton's *New View* mentioned the companies on their title-pages), and the cost of the works themselves (a new unbound copy of the 1633 *Survey* cost five shillings whilst Strype's *Survey* retailed for a massive six guineas) all emphasise that we cannot assume that every reader of any of these books had a specific (or even a passing) interest in the companies or even that the accounts of the companies these works provided were 'popular' in any sense or widely read.[30]

'Ornamental for closet or house'

The extent of 'popular' contemporary interest in the companies, however, *can* be better gauged by examining the development in printed catalogues of corporate coats of arms over the same period. Primarily visual rather than textual, usually ephemeral and hence cheaper, and almost wholly focused on the companies, these works did not need to rely on a reasonably literate, reasonably wealthy and reasonably historically-minded readership in the same way as a Stow or Strype did. Indeed, the evidence of numerous editions of such heraldic catalogues as will be discussed below suggests that they may in fact have prompted the addition of corporate heraldic illustrations to the 1633 *Survey* and its successors; they may even have encouraged the inclusion of separate sections on the companies in such works in the first place.[31] For example, the ranking of the companies in the 1633 *Survey*, along with its careful inclusion of the evidently defunct Marblers' Company, seems to derive directly from these printed heraldic catalogues. Either way, it seems clear that there was a market – or at least a perceived market – for printed representations of corporate heraldry throughout the period.

There was, of course, a more general interest in heraldry; as Michael Maclagan claims: 'the sixteenth and seventeenth centuries probably saw the most widespread and general use and understanding of heraldry which has been known to this realm'.'[32] However, such 'use and understanding' was not the consequence of mere idle curiosity; rather, heraldry was indissolubly linked with social status. A coat of arms was the badge of a gentleman, the visible confirmation of an individual's distinguished lineage. The 'professional guardians' of this were the heralds, who from 1530 had been authorised by Henry VIII not only to grant new coats of arms to 'men of good honest reputacyon' but also to police the right to bear existing coats of arms through periodic 'visitations' across the country.[33] Most counties were visited by the heralds at least once every 40 years between 1530 and the formal abeyance of the procedure in the late 1680s and, when challenged by the heralds, armigerous families could be expected to provide the relevant evidence of their gentle pedigree. For most of this period, these exercises in heraldic verification were thorough and effective, not least in terms of earning fees and social respect for the heralds themselves. Indeed, the visitations of the 1570s produced more formal grants of arms than any decade before the twentieth century.[34] There were notorious cases of abuse ranging from ludicrously faked pedigrees through to bitter feuds between the heralds themselves, but these only underline the intense importance that the English gentry attached to lineage, and hence to heraldry. It was only in the decades after the Restoration, as Felicity Heal and Clive Holmes argue, that the gentry became less bothered about visitations and began to show restraint in their heraldic and genealogical displays; moreover, at the same time, the long-standing heraldic interest of antiquarians (many of them gentlemen themselves) shifted into 'a more detached attitude' that was less susceptible to extravagant claims of pedigree.

Heraldry also formed the subject of a great number of early modern printed books, the most popular being Gerard Legh's *The accedens of armory* (1562), which went through five further editions before 1612, and John Guillim's *A display of heraldrie* (1610/11), new editions of which appeared at regular intervals until 1724.[35] The proliferation and indeed the significance of such works prompted the Commissioners for the executing of the office of Earl Marshal (one of the judges in the Court of Chivalry, the legal court responsible for heraldic matters) to order the Stationers' Company in 1620 not to allow the printing of any book concerning pedigree or heraldry without their specific license, while in 1637 the Earl Marshal was included among the Star Chamber's list of formally appointed licensers of the press.[36] Such heraldic books were invariably illustrated – we have already noted that illustrations of coats of arms for former lord mayors appeared in the 1633 *Survey* – but this form of representation was only a small part of a much wider industry of heraldic iconography. As the full title of Henry Peacham's *The gentlemans exercise* (1612) noted, heraldry supplied work for 'diuers Trades-men and Artificers, as *namly Painters, Ioyners, Free-masons, Cutters and Caruers*'. Heraldic painting in particular was of enough importance to the heralds that the Court of Chivalry regularly prosecuted craftsmen for painting false arms, while the kings of arms were in frequent dispute with the Painter-Stainers' Company over the regulation of heraldic painting from the 1570s until the eighteenth century.[37]

Corporate heraldry – that is, coats of arms granted not to individuals but to corporate bodies such as towns and companies – represents an interesting aspect of heraldry in the period. For a London company, a coat of arms was a significant investment, proof of its permanence and distinguished heritage; it defined a company's membership of London's corporate club at the same time as carefully distinguishing it from its peers. The origin of such grants is unclear; Edmund Bolton, writing in 1629, simply noted that the 'adorning [of] Companies with banners of Armes' had been 'the ancient excellent policie of *England*'.[38] The earliest grant of a coat of arms to a London company, the Drapers' Company, dates to 1438–9; however, the grant to the Pewterers' Company in 1451 not only describes itself as a confirmation of *existing* corporate arms, but notes that it is 'custumed and used every crafte to have clothing by hem self to know oon crafte from another. And also signes of armes for every crafte in banner wyse to be borne conveniently in the worship of the Cyte'.[39] Similar wording was used in other fifteenth-century corporate grants. The modern historian of the arms of the London companies, John Bromley, argues that this shows that the London companies were using coats of arms prior to 1430s, but while this may well have been the case, such evidence may not be wholly reliable. Companies, after all, could not prove gentility in the same way that an individual could, namely through blood lineage and land tenure. Indeed, the fact that, as Bromley notes, more fifteenth-century patents granting arms to companies survive than those granted to individuals underlines the way in which the companies had to rely on more material proof of their heritage.[40] We have already seen how important corporate antiquity appeared to the compilers of the 1633 *Survey*, and corporate antiquity was explicitly emphasised in the heraldic visitation of London in 1590 where the arms of a number of companies were described as 'the Auncient Armes' or 'the Armes of Antiquitie'. It is perhaps in this light then that the claims of some companies to have borne arms prior to a particular grant should be read.[41]

As Edward Bonahue has highlighted, civic rhetoric in the early modern period could combine aristocratic with mercantile or craft terminology to produce social hybrid forms (e.g., 'merchant prince'), and from this perspective it seems that corporate heraldry can be seen as another point of contact, combining a traditionally noble attribute (a coat of arms) with merchants and craftsmen.[42] When applied to an individual London citizen, the right to bear a coat of arms could prove controversial, but the companies themselves seem to have escaped any such disapproval either from the heralds or other contemporaries.[43] In fact, corporate heraldry seems to have been the focus of positive interest throughout the period as the number of surviving catalogues of such arms indicates.[44] Manuscript catalogues of the coats of arms of the London companies can be found as early as the 1530s, although it seems that most were compiled for personal use; a number can be directly linked with the work of a particular herald or painter-stainer.[45] *Printed* collections (usually engravings), on the other hand, first appear in the 1590s, and their continuing reproduction in varying forms through to the end of the seventeenth century indicates that there was a good market for such heraldic representations. Coats of arms were necessarily public images and the reproduction of coats of arms in printed works (mostly with woodcuts) was, as we have noted above, not unusual in the period. However, although heraldic books often reproduced dozens of individual coats of arms, there does not seem to have been any equivalent to these printed catalogues of the London companies.[46]

In 1596, the London map-engraver Benjamin Wright published the first collection of metropolitan corporate heraldry that survives: a large sheet-engraving entitled *The armes of all the cheife corporatons[sic] of England W^t the Companees of London* (see Plates 3.1 and 3.2).[47] Similar works may have appeared earlier. In late 1589, the printer Henry Denham had entered the title 'the Armes of all the Cumpanyes of the worshipfull cyttye of London' into the Stationers' Company register (an act of formal registration which suggests that he believed the work would prove popular and hence was particularly concerned to protect his title from infringement by fellow Stationers), but no work of that title seems to have been forthcoming.[48] Meanwhile in 1593, the coats of arms of the great twelve companies flanked a map of London in the first part of John Norden's *Specvlvm Britanniae*.[49] However, Wright's work appears to have been the first comprehensive engraving. His poster-sized collection of corporate coats of arms measures half a metre high and three-quarters of a metre wide with the body of the engraving consisting of the arms of 60 London companies in six rows of ten compartments (6 cm × 6 cm), each carefully numbered in accordance with the company's place in the order of civic precedence. These compartments are surrounded by a single compartmentalised border containing the arms of

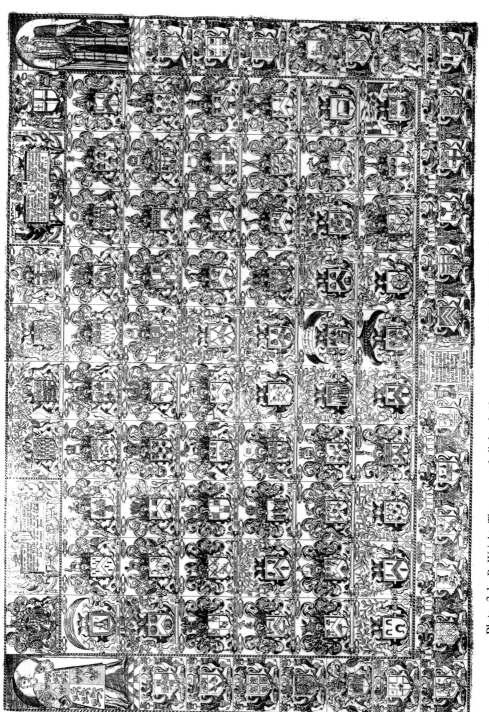

Plate 3.1. B. Wright, *The armes of all the cheife corporatons of England Wᵗ the Companees of London* (1596)
(By permission of the Folger Shakespeare Library)

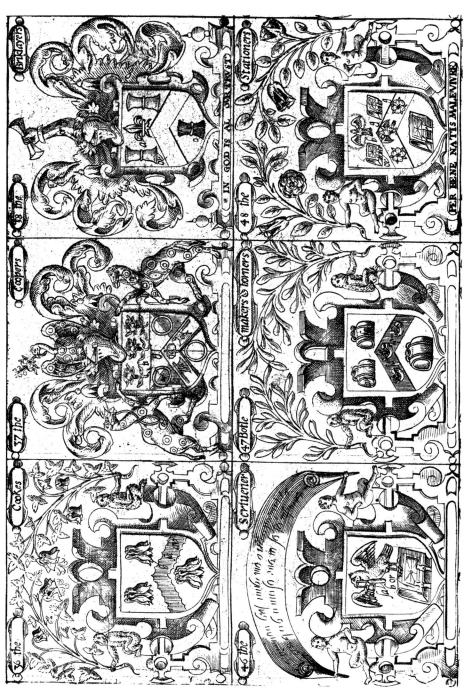

Plate 3.2. Detail of B. Wright, *The armes of all the cheife corporatons of England W^t the Companees of London* (1596) (By permission of the Folger Shakespeare Library)

the Crown, the City of London, four merchant companies, and the 26 cathedral cities. Each company's coat of arms carries letters indicating the appropriate heraldic colours and is flanked by stylised supporters; in many cases, a motto is given underneath. The historian of early modern English engraving, Arthur Hind, noted that 'little is known' about Wright although, by Wright's own admission in the title to this work ('thies first fruits of his Labours'), this engraving represented his earliest work.

It is worth dwelling on the precise format of this engraving as subsequent printed catalogues of London's corporate heraldry, with very few exceptions, followed its style, dimensions and layout very closely. Its sheer size, involving two folio sheets, demanded some sort of display and we must assume that it was aimed primarily at a market who would paste the broadside up on their walls. Consequently, prints of this sort were ephemeral and only a handful of examples of Wright's engraving survive today; a few remain intact, but in at least three cases the engraving has been cut up into its constituent compartments and the resulting fragments have then been pasted into a manuscript book.[50] Such broadsides were obviously cheaper than most printed books but it would be wrong to bracket an engraving such as this with the penny woodcut broadsides that Tessa Watt focuses on in her work on 'cheap print' in the period.[51] Printing from engravings was slower and an engraving could not produce anywhere near as many copies as a woodblock before deteriorating.[52] As a result, an engraved broadside might cost anywhere up to a shilling, prompting Watt to suggest that such works were produced primarily 'for a market of middling Londoners' rather than lowlier or more provincial audiences.[53]

The scope and layout of the work also suggest the kind of audience being targeted. The London companies provided a ready-made group of heraldic subjects that was not only finite and carefully graded in terms of social rank but was also more public than most and concentrated within a single geographical area; presumably, the collection of preparatory sketches was fairly straightforward and did not need to involve any direct engagement with the companies themselves. The prominence and centrality of the companies within the work, carefully buttressed by the arms of more prestigious institutions, provides a remarkably graphic attempt to both define and fix London's society and economy as well as to demonstrate the city's central importance within the realm.[54]

Unlike printed books, new and virtually identical copies of old engravings could of course be made without too much difficulty provided that the plates themselves survived in a serviceable condition; indeed, the relatively high cost of engraving would encourage reuse wherever possible. This makes it bibliographically very difficult to identify later reprints, even if the plates themselves show signs of retouching. As a result, whilst Wright's engraving may have been reissued in the years following 1596, it is not for two or three decades that we find definitive evidence of a new catalogue, and even then many of the heraldic compartments appear to be very closely modelled on Wright's original. During the 1620s and 1630s, copies of something akin to Wright's engraving were being sold by the London print-sellers Francis Williams and William Webb, supplemented with a remarkably lavish engraving of the royal arms and a new compartment containing the arms of the recently formed Society of Apothecaries.[55] In all the surviving copies of this work, the compartments of the original engraving have been cut up which makes reconstructing its original layout and size difficult; however, there seem to be very strong similarities between it and surviving copies of *The Armes Crests Supporters & mottowes of all ye seuerall Companies and Corporations of ye famous Citty of London*, issued by the print- and map-seller Peter Stent (who, like Stow, was a Merchant Taylor) from the 1650s, and reissued, following Stent's death in 1665, by the Stationer John Overton.[56] Although much the same size as Wright's engraving, the layout of these engravings is rather different; their dimensions are, unlike the 1596 engraving, longer than they were broad. The focus on London heraldry is even more striking in that, aside from the royal arms taking up the central top portion of the engraving, the compartments consist wholly of the coat of arms of London, the Merchant Adventurers' Company, the Turkey Company, the East India Company and then 61 livery companies; the arms of nine further merchant companies appear in a very reduced form at the base of the title cartouche. Nevertheless, those compartments bearing the arms of the livery companies are clearly derived from Wright, following closely his ranking and titling of each company, as well as his inclusion of crests, supporters, mottoes and the appropriate letters indicating tincture. In his modern catalogue of Stent's engravings, Alexander Globe noted that this particular title was re-advertised at least five times before the end of the seventeenth century, and argued that the engraving had probably been originally produced during James I's reign, suggesting that there may even have been an earlier version than that associated with Williams and Webb. Overton, who succeeded to Stent's business, continued to sell and advertise what appears to have been the same engraving under the title *The Tradesmen's Arms*; a 1676 advert priced copies at a shilling.[57]

Stent and Overton's engraved catalogues were not the only works of this kind on the market in the third quarter of the seventeenth century. During the 1660s, the famous engraver Wenceslaus Hollar (who worked for both Stent and Overton) produced new engravings of the coats of arms of 61 livery companies that differ slightly (in terms of size and design) from previous versions.[58] About the same time, a new version of Wright's engraving was issued by the printer and print-seller Robert Walton, with the arms of the Society of Apothecaries squeezed into the bottom border where Wright's title had originally been located.[59] However, Walton evidently felt that, even with this addition, the 1596

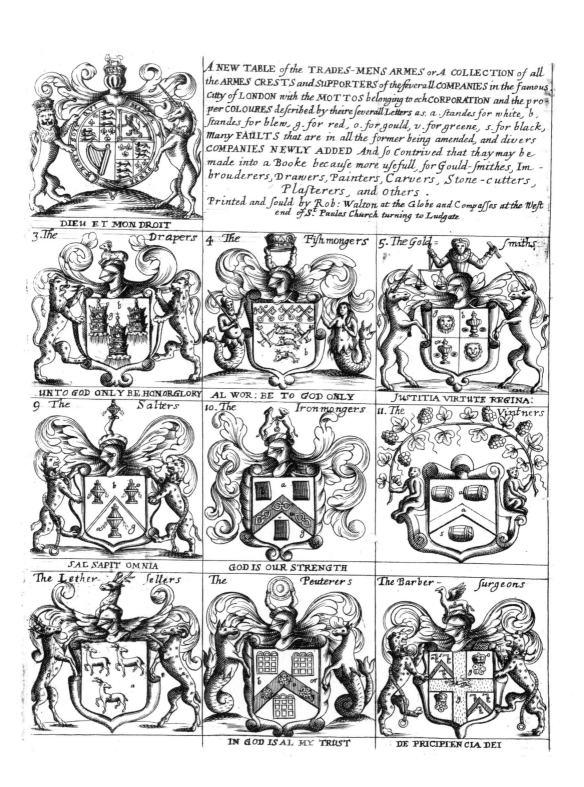

Plate 3.3. R. Walton, *A NEW TABLE of the TRADES-MENS ARMES* (n.d.), f. 1r.
(By permission of Guildhall Library, Corporation of London)

Plate 3.4. Title-page of R. Wallis, *Londons Armory* (1677)
(By permission of the Syndics of Cambridge University Library)

original was proving a deficient model; in 1673, he advertised a new version, *A NEW TABLE of the TRADES-MENS ARMES* (a rather impertinent appropriation of the title of Overton's competing engraving), at 3*s* 6*d* 'if coloured' (see Plate 3.3).[60] The surviving copy in the Guildhall Library is incomplete (and uncoloured), and is cut into five fragments; nevertheless, it is clear that, although the compartments remain the same size as in previous engravings, the overall layout is rather different. Gone are the arms of non-London bodies; instead, the engraving consisted of the arms of the crown and the city, and at least nine merchant companies and 68 livery companies. Walton claimed in his title that 'Many FAULTS that are in all the former being amended, and diuers COMPANIES NEWLY ADDED'; accordingly, the coat of arms of each company has been newly engraved (resulting, in at least one case, in the emendation of a company's motto), and arms for the newly-incorporated Glovers', Distillers', Clockmakers', Silkthrowers', Feltmakers', Soapmakers' and Glassmakers' companies have been added.[61] Even so, Walton failed to take the opportunity to correct anachronisms present in earlier engravings, retaining the arms for the extinct Marblers' Company as well as for the Whitebakers' and Brownbakers' companies in spite of their amalgamation as the Bakers' Company in the 1640s.

In a 1659 catalogue of maps and prints, Walton had advertised his wares as 'being very neat ornaments for houses, gentleman's studies and closets, and useful for divers callings, as Painters, Embroyders, &c'.[62] His *New Table* was similarly aimed at this dual market, as a work able both to decorate and to instruct. It was 'so Contrived that thay [i.e. the arms] may be made into a Booke because more usefull, for Gould-smithes, Imbrouderers, Drawers, Painters, Carvers, Stone-cutters, Plasterers, and Others', but '[a]lthough in a Booke these are most convenient for some, yet for others not, because in broadsheets more Ornamental for closet or house'.[63] Walton's claims were dramatically upstaged by the publication in 1677 of Richard Wallis's *Londons Armory* (see Plate 3.4).[64] The contrast with earlier broadside engravings could not have been more profound. Thirty engraved plates, each measuring approximately 45 cm wide by 35 cm high, reproduced the arms of the Crown, the City of London, its current Aldermen, and 99 companies, four to a page. Seventy-three of these companies could be classified as livery companies, with the remainder consisting of merchant companies, hospitals and other London corporate bodies such as the Royal Society, the Artillery Company and the Academy of the Muses.[65] Clearly a deluxe work, *London's Armory* could be had, according to an advert of 1679, for 25*s* 'in quires' (that is, ready folded as a book, but unbound) or 'pasted on Cloth and Rolled' (that is, for framing and display) at 35*s* – a far cry from the 1*s* or even 3*s* 6*d* sheets of Stent and Walton.[66]

In dedicating the work to the bookseller and current Lord Mayor Thomas Davies, Wallis, who was himself a Painter-Stainer and hence directly involved in heraldic iconography, explained that his work was to provide 'a Reformation' of the 'manifold Errors and egregious Mistakes' that he had found in the representation of company arms

> committed through the stupidity and careless performances of divers Artificers, (*viz.*) Painters, Plaisterers, Gravers, and Carvers; whose absurdities are of late advanced in the most eminent and conspicuous Places of very beautiful and stately Structures.[67]

In a swipe at the rival publications of Overton and Walton, Wallis claimed that craftsmen had been 'unadvisedly misled by putting faith in false Copies; such as have been lately, and now are, exposed to publick Sale in Graving and Printing'. Moreover, such misrepresentation could have grave consequences for the companies:

> I was much concerned what dishonourable reflections it might cast upon so many Worshipful Companies and Worthy Corporations; and was troubled to think that those Loyal Societies, who have so much Truth in their Hearts, should have so much Error in their Arms.

Although Wallis did not explicitly mention the devastating impact of the great fire of eleven years earlier, his words here were clearly aimed at those companies still in the process of rebuilding and restoring their halls, and who, as a result, might shortly be calling on the heraldic services of a number of London craftsmen – such as Wallis himself.[68]

Like Walton before him, Wallis was also well aware of the decorative potential of his engravings. In his preface, he enthused that:

> [t]he turning over the leaves of this little Volume of Variety proves not only profitable to the Judicious Artists, but also delightful to all those Persons of Qualitie, who sometimes are pleased to advance Heraldry into the honour of their Recreations; which indeed is a Contemplation full of pleasing diversities, and agreable[*sic*] to every Noble and Generous Disposition; being in substance the most refined part of Natural Philosophy, while it assumeth also the principles of Geometry, by putting into use almost every Square Angle and Circle. These Sheets being orderly fixt upon fine Canvas, and well framed, may prove Ornamental, when placed in any Magnificent Hall, Gallery, or Beautiful Dining-Room, where the Inquisitive Spectators may be pleasantly entertained with making delightful Comparisons between the Aptitude of the Arms to the Amplitude of any Trade, Science, Art, Mystery, Occupation...[69]

We have already noted how general attitudes to heraldry seem to have changed in the second half of the seventeenth century, and in particular how the desire of the gentry either to acquire or to display their own set of arms seems to have dwindled. However, Wallis's portrayal here of 'Persons of Qualitie' purchasing coats of arms belonging to others, in order to display them ostentatiously as *objets d'art* provides an extraordinary corollary to such developments. In his vision, heraldry becomes fully commodified: a coat of arms that began as a manifestation of a company's desire for elevated social status is reified to such an extent that it becomes divorced from its company and is transformed into an object of desire for those aspiring to an entirely different model of sociability. We do not know how successful Wallis's marketing was, nor indeed whether any of his engravings were actually hung in 'Magnificent' rooms, but with the minor exceptions of the small woodcuts of 76 company arms that frame a city almanac of 1680, and the two sets of engravings, clearly based on Wallis's work, that were issued individually in 1698 and 1701 for each of the great twelve companies, it seems that his *London's Armory* was the very much last word in corporate heraldry during this period – a consequence perhaps of the more general decline in heraldic display that we noted earlier.[70]

Early modern engravings of corporate heraldry have an obviously elaborate and complex history. With the exception of Wallis's 'little Volume of Variety', all the catalogues discussed here appear to have been issued as broadsides. In consequence, there may well have been a number of other rival versions issued during the period for which copies now no longer survive; indeed, the survival of some heraldic engravings seems to have been a direct result of an original readership who, as we have noted, radically reconfigured their copies by using scissors and paste. Moreover, the very nature of engraving – with plates being retouched, re-engraved and passed on from print-seller to print-seller – means that establishing the genealogy of these works is difficult and it remains unclear whether these engravings represent successive attempts to re-market and re-package Wright's original broadside or if they were intended to compete with one another.

As with our discussion of the *Survey* and its successors, we are beset by a series of questions about these engravings that are as yet very difficult to answer. How popular were these works? Who bought them and why? Watt's claim that such 'mid-priced' prints were produced for a London-based middling clientele is one possible answer, but these works may also have appealed to visitors to the capital as something akin to souvenirs. Moreover, it is feasible that such works were disseminated outwith the capital as well.[71] It seems likely that these works also had a practical function in the bespoke world of urban manufactures. Walton's subtitle and Wallis's claims both suggest that such works may also have functioned as pattern books for local craftsmen, especially in the post-fire period. Corporate heraldry could appear on objects as diverse as gowns, funeral palls, guns, buttons, snuffboxes, plate, pottery, glassware and pill tiles.[72] However, even the most reliable evidence of provenance would not necessarily help us to understand *why* people bought these engravings in particular. Was it out of specific personal or even professional interest in the

London companies or a more general one in heraldry? Were such purchases intended for public display or private contemplation? To answer this, we need to understand what kind of public profile the London companies had during the early modern period: did these prints simply reflect a visual knowledge of the companies already shared by much of London (and, perhaps, beyond), or did they educate and inform a populace that otherwise knew little about the companies as a whole?

This last question highlights an important paradox about the companies themselves. The London companies were simultaneously public and private bodies whose decisions and activities could impinge on the lives of many of the city's population and yet whose meetings and records were kept resolutely confidential.[73] The companies were not unusual in that respect; institutions, whether modern or early modern, are rarely transparent. Yet, if the heraldic engravings and the company sections in the *Survey* and its successors are to be believed, there was an increasing public interest in the companies from the 1590s onwards. The origins of such an interest, however, are unclear. Were the companies perceived as active components of a contemporary conception of the city itself, or were they seen as objects of mere curiosity, remnants of an old civic order at a time of rapid social and economic change?

On the surface, the evidence discussed in this chapter appears too slight to be able to offer answers to these questions. The insights offered by Stow and his seventeenth-century successors were rather limited and, if anything, much greater attention seems to have been paid to representing corporate coats of arms than providing historical detail. Nonetheless, it does seem possible that for the readers of these works, these representations in fact reduced the companies from dynamic members of London society into objects principally of historical and heraldic interest. Taken together, the works do not seem to change or develop significantly in their representation of the companies over the period; rather, the repeated emphasis on antiquity and orderliness combined with an essentially identical reiteration of the same material in edition after edition and engraving after engraving reinforce an impression of corporate continuity. From John Stow's musings outside company halls to the 'delightful comparisons' made the 'Inquisitive Spectators' of Richard Wallis's engravings, the companies appear as conversation pieces, as objects to be talked *about* rather than subjects to be engaged *with*. Reified and historicised, the companies are increasingly disassociated and distanced from their own immediate contexts. From this perspective, the Vintners' Company refusal to converse with John Stow and the fact that Richard Wallis alone seemed to be worried about the misrepresentation of corporate coats of arms are symptoms of a wider lack of *corporate* interest in how the companies were represented in print – an apathy or disdain distinctly at odds with the sustained public interest in corporate history and corporate heraldry over the period.

Yet it would be wrong to assume that the companies of early modern London did not care how they were represented or perceived. Without some sense of how to control its corporate identity, a company would have found it much harder to enforce loyalty from its members, to regulate their activities or even to make the authorities listen to its complaints.[74] Clothing, feasts, barges, processions and halls all underlined their interest and investment in presenting a particular image of corporate authority, permanence and wealth. The care and expense they took over the acquisition, preservation and display of their important documents and insignia suggests that, for their members, antiquity and heraldry were important aspects of this sense of corporate identity. However, in these contexts, the intended audience was profoundly local and conservative. As I noted in my introduction to this chapter, the companies were becoming aware of the power of the printing press, yet throughout this period, it does seem that they were generally uninterested in how contemporary printed works were being employed to disseminate those same attributes that they valued so highly. The companies preferred parochial and traditional forms of representation at the same time as their histories and identities were being read and discussed in studies and coffee-houses across London and beyond. As a result, our expanding knowledge of the realities of corporate behaviour needs to be balanced by an awareness of how the companies and their activities were perceived, not only by their officers and their members but also by other contemporaries – including those who may have bought, read or viewed the works examined in this chapter.

NOTES

I am very grateful to Patrick Wallis and Helen Moore for their detailed and probing comments about this paper.

1. M. C. Burrage and D. Corry, 'At Sixes and Sevens: Occupational Status in the City of London from the Fourteenth to the Seventeenth Century', *American Sociological Review*, 46 (1981), pp. 375–93 (especially Table 1).
2. A. Crawford, *A History of the Vintners' Company* (London, 1977), p. 53. The Vintners' court minutes for this date do not survive.
3. J. Stow, *A Survey of London, reprinted from the text of 1603*, C. L. Kingsford (ed.), (Oxford, 1908), vol. 1, p. xxxviii; vol. 2, pp. 247–8.
4. However, Stow's account of London was anticipated in manuscript by William Smythe who produced 'A Brief Description of the Royal City of London, Capital City of this Realm of England' in 1575 (GL, MS 2463; a later version survives as BL, Harleian MS 6363); it includes a short general account of the livery companies and brief descriptions of the company halls, along with illustrations of company arms. Stephen Freeth, to whom I am grateful for drawing my attention to the Guildhall manuscript, observes that references within the work suggest that it was intended for formal publication.
5. J. J. Morrison, 'Strype's Stow: The 1720 Edition of *A Survey of London*', *London Journal*, 3 (1977), pp. 40–54; M. J. Power, 'John Stow and his London', *Journal of*

Historical Geography, 11 (1985), pp. 1–20; W. K. Hall, 'A Topography of Time: Historical Narration in John Stow's *Survey of London*', *Studies in Philology*, 88, no. 1 (1991), pp. 1–15; I. W. Archer, 'The Nostalgia of John Stow' and L. Manley, 'Of Sites and Rites', in D. L. Smith, R. Streier and D. Bevington (eds.), *Of Sites and Rites* (Cambridge, 1995), pp. 17–34, 35–54; E. T. Bonahue Jr, 'Citizen History: Stow's *Survey of London*', *Studies in English Literature 1500–1900*, 38 (1998), pp. 61–85; J. F. Merritt (ed.), *Imagining Early Modern London: Perceptions and Portrayals of the City from Stow to Strype* (Cambridge, 2001).

6. Charles Welch's useful annotated bibliography of such works appended to his facsimile edition of Wallis is only a partial exception to this neglect: *Coat-Armour of the London Livery Companies* (London, 1914). On heraldry, see: M. Maclagan, 'Genealogy and Heraldry in the Sixteenth and Seventeenth Centuries', in L. Fox (ed.), *Genealogy and Heraldry in the Sixteenth and Seventeenth Centuries* (London, 1956), pp. 31–48; A. R. Wagner, *Heralds and Heraldry in the Middle Ages: An Inquiry into the Growth of the Armorial Function of Heralds* (Oxford, 1956); E. Elmhirst, 'The Fashion for Heraldry', *The Coat of Arms*, 4 (1956–57), pp. 47–51; A. R. Wagner, 'The Fashion for Heraldry: Dr Elmhirst's View Reviewed', *The Coat of Arms*, 4 (1956–57), pp. 119–20; G. D. Squibb (ed.), *The High Court of Chivalry: A Study of the Civil Law in England* (Oxford, 1959); J. Bromley, *The Armorial Bearings of the Guilds of London* (London, 1960); J. F. Day, 'Trafficking in Honor: Social Climbing and the Purchase of Gentility in the English Renaissance', *Renaissance Papers* (1987), pp. 61–70; J. F. R. Day, 'Primers of Honor: Heraldry, Heraldry Books, and English Renaissance Literature', *Sixteenth Century Journal*, 21 (1990), pp. 93–103.

7. There is one slight exception to this: in August 1602, John Stow received £3 and 40 complimentary copies from the Stationers' Company 'for his paynes in the booke called the survey of London'. However, as he also received 20 shillings and 50 complimentary copies for his *Summarye of the chronicles of England* at the same time, this may have been more to do with corporate encouragement of a poor author rather than official sponsorship of his research into the London companies; after all, the Stationers' Company itself merited only very passing reference in the first two editions of the *Survey*.

8. See, for example, the section on London in *STC* (16768.4–16787.14). However, in comparison with the church and the state, the London companies seemed relatively slow in discovering the bureaucratic advantages of print: see A. J. Slavin, 'The Tudor Revolution and the Devil's Art: Bishop Bonner's Printed Forms', in D. J. Guth and J. W. McKenna (eds.), *Tudor Rule and Revolution: Essays for G.R. Elton from his American Friends* (Cambridge, 1982), pp. 3–23.

9. Wing R323–25; W3064; H2599. I am grateful to Patrick Wallis for drawing my attention to two similar 'corporate' histories which appeared at almost exactly the same time: T. Sprat, *The history of the Royal-Society of London* (London, 1667) and C. Goodall, *The Royal College of Physicians of London* (London, 1684).

10. See, for example, Stow, *Survey* (1603), vol. 1, pp. 10, 33, 106–16 *passim*, 125, 151, 154, 174, 192, 202, 220, 272–3; vol. 2, p. 158. For a later account that noted in passing the charitable contributions of the London companies, see A. Willet, *Synopsis Papismi* (London, 1634), sig. 5N2r–5(N)8r, especially sig. 5N4v–5N5r.

11. Stow, *Survey* (1603), vol. 1, pp. 170–1 (Parish Clerks), 181–2 (Merchant Taylors), 213–15 (Fishmongers), 230–1 (Skinners), 240–2 (Vintners), 244–5 (Cutlers), 263–4 (Grocers), 269–70 (Mercers), 285–6 (Weavers), 305–6 (Goldsmiths), 315–16 (Barber Surgeons), and 351–2 (Cordwainers).

12. Here I mean Stow as author and historian rather than Stow as London citizen; in the latter capacity we must assume that he visited at least the Merchant Taylors' Hall on occasion.

13. Stow, *Survey* (1603), vol. 2, pp. 190–2.

14. Stow, *Survey* (1603), vol. 2, p. 192. Interestingly, this section (along with a general description of the city's offices that immediately preceded it and an account of the liveries of notable citizens that immediately followed it) does not appear in the 1598 edition; Kingsford, however, does not seem to have noticed that the 1603 edition was at variance here with the earlier edition.

15. J. Stow, *The Svrvay of London...continued, corrected and much enlarged [by Anthony Munday]* (London, 1618) (*STC* 23344), sig. 3Q8r–3R1r.

16. J. Stow, *The Survey of London...now finished by...A[nthony] M[unday,] H[umphrey] D[yson] and others* (London, 1633) (*STC* 23345–45.5), sig. 3E6r–3I5r. The previous editions had been produced in the smaller quarto format.

17. The ten merchant companies were: the Merchants of the Staple, Merchant Adventurers, Merchants of Russia, of Elbing, of Levant, of Spain, and of East India, new French Merchant Adventurers, Company of French Merchants and the Merchants of Virginia. In its single-page juxtaposition of woodcut and accompanying text, the catalogue bears some similarity to *A view of all the right honourable the Lord Mayors of London* (1601), attributed by *STC* (as 14343) to the printer and bookseller William Jaggard.

18. Of the minor companies, explicit reference to a craft or trade was made in only five cases: Stow, *Survey* (1633), sig. 3H5v–3H6r, 3I2r, 3I5r (Bowyers, Fletchers, Stationers, Marblers and Watermen).

19. Stow, *Survey* (1633), sig. 3I1v, 3I2r, 3I3r.

20. E. T. Bonahue Jr, 'The Citizen Histories of Early Modern London' (unpublished PhD thesis, University of North Carolina, Chapel Hill, 1996), p. 11.

21. However, this interpolation did not reflect the realities of civic processions in which the merchant companies do not seem to have taken part.

22. As the purchase of paper was the most expensive part of printing an early modern book, the amount of 'white space' accorded to the companies would have had a noticeable impact on the printer's costs.

23. J. Howell, *Londinopolis; An Historicall Discourse* (London, 1657) (Wing H3090), sig. G1r–G3v; R. Burton [N. Crouch], *Historical Remarques and Observations of the Ancient and Present State of London* (London, 1681) (Wing C7329), sig. D8v–E2r; T. Delaune, *The Present State of London* (London, 1681) (Wing D894), sig. O10r–P9v. Later editions of Crouch's and Delaune's works did not make any changes to the companies section. Howell only described the companies' heraldry, but both Crouch and Delaune provided small illustrations of each company's coat of arms (they seem to have used the same woodcuts as each other), supplemented with brief text.

24. E. Hatton, *A New View of London* (London, 1708), vol. 2, sig. 2P1r–2Q7v. In contrast with Stow, Hatton's route was not a geographical one, but instead proceeded in strict alphabetical order.

25. J. Strype, *A Survey of the Cities of London and Westminster*, 2 vols. (London, 1720), book V, pp. 173–247; see also Strype's Appendix II, p. 14. On this edition, see Morrison, 'Strype's Stow', pp. 40–54.

26. Among the expenses allowed Strype by his publishers was 2*s* 6*d* for a second-hand copy of the 1633 *Survey*: D.R. Woolf, *Reading History in Early Modern England* (Cambridge, 2000), p. 249.

27. Strype, *Survey*, book V, pp. 165, 247–9. It was followed by a section (pp. 249–56) on the companies' concealment of lands following Edward VI's chantries legislation.

28. Strype, *Survey*, book V, pp. 221–2.

29. Morrison notes that a few companies set up committees to assist Strype's research activities: 'Strype's Stow', p. 43.

30. Woolf, *Reading History*, pp. 45, 292. A friend of Strype lamented that the price of Strype's *Survey* 'frightens all but wealthy Citizens in the country'.

31. Strype's expenses for the 1720 *Survey* included 1*s* for a copy of the arms of the London companies; the price suggests this was for a printed heraldic catalogue such as discussed below rather than a specially commissioned report: Woolf, *Reading History*, p. 249.

32. M. Maclagan, 'Genealogy and Heraldry', p. 31.

33. This paragraph is indebted to (and the quotations are taken from) F. Heal and C. Holmes, *The Gentry in England and Wales, 1500–1700* (Basingstoke, 1994), pp. 20–47. I am grateful to Tim Wales for this reference. See also Squibb, *High Court of Chivalry*; Day, 'Trafficking in Honor'; Day, 'Primers of Honor'. On the role of the heralds up to 1530, see Wagner, *Heralds and Heraldry*.

34. Elmhirst, 'The Fashion for Heraldry'; Wagner, 'The Fashion for Heraldry'.

35. T. Moule, *Bibliotheca Heraldica Magn? Britanni?: an analaytical catalogue of books on genealogy, heraldry, nobility, knighthood, & ceremonies...* (London, 1822); Day, 'Primers of Honor', p. 97.

36. Squibb, *High Court of Chivalry*, p. 143; *A decree of Starre-Chamber concerning Printing* (London, 1637), sig. B3v. See also W. W. Greg, *Licensers for the Press, &c to 1640* (Oxford, 1962), pp. 6–7, 31–2, 46, 70, 83–4, 97–8.

37. Squibb, *High Court of Chivalry*, p. 141.

38. E. Bolton, *The cities advocate, in this case or qvestion of Honor and Armes; Whether Apprentiship extinguisheth Gentry?* (London, 1629), sig. D4r.

39. Bromley, *Armorial Bearings*, pp. xviii–xix.

40. That said, thirteen of the companies whose modern arms Bromley includes in his book could not provide evidence of a grant.

41. H. S. London, *Visitation of London 1568*, S. W. Rawlins (ed.), (London, 1963), pp. 125–34.

42. Bonahue, 'Citizen Histories', p. 35.

43. Squibb, *High Court of Chivalry*, pp. 176–7; Bolton, *The Cities Advocate, passim.* The fact that the Court of Chivalry never seems to have considered a suit concerning a corporate grant of arms was cited as a defence in the first case brought in the court for over 200 years when, in 1954, the corporation of Manchester sued over the misuse of its arms: Squibb, *High Court of Chivalry*, p. 125.

44. Welch, *Coat-Armour*, pp. 41ff.

45. See, for example, Gonville & Caius College, Cambridge, MS 552/316, ff. 95r–100r; MS 577/452, ff. 131r–133v.

46. One exception is a 1664 single-sheet engraving held by the Guildhall Library of the coats of arms from the windows of Serjeant's Inn in Fleet Street. Although I have made no comprehensive survey of heraldic books in the period, it seems that few if any included the arms of the London companies; for example, while Payne Fisher's *A Synospis of Heraldry* (1682) included descriptions of the coats of arms for all the archiepiscopal and episcopal sees, the universities and colleges of Oxford and Cambridge, and the inns of court and other legal institutions of London, it did not include any of the London companies.

47. *STC* 26018. See A. M. Hind, *Engraving in England in the Sixteenth and Seventeenth Centuries*, 3 vols. (Cambridge, 1952–64), vol.1, pp. 212–15; *STC*, vol. 3, pp. 189. Oddly, Wright's broadside is not included in R. S. Luborsky and E. M. Ingram, *A Guide to English Illustrated Books 1536–1603*, 2 vols. (Tempe, Arizona, 1998). It is possible that Wright's engraving was the realisation of the work envisaged by Denham in his registration in 1589, but there is no evidence of a link between the two men.

48. E. Arber (ed.), *A Transcript of the Registers of the Company of Stationers 1554–1640 AD*, 5 vols. (London & Birmingham, 1875–94), vol. 2, p. 536.

49. *STC* 18635.

50. Intact copies exist at the Folger Shakespeare Library and the British Library; cut-up copies exist in the British Library, the Bodleian Library and the Huntington Library (where the coats of arms have been coloured in): Hind, *Engraving*, vol. 1, p. 215; Welch, *Coat-Armour*,

pp. 42–43; *English Short-Title Catalogue* (http://eureka.rlg.org); Bodleian Library, Oxford, MS Rawl D.944 ('William Rymill his book').

51. See Tessa Watt, *Cheap Print and Popular Piety, 1550–1640* (Cambridge, 1991), pp. 131–253 for a general study of broadsides during this period; however she specifically does not include heraldic prints in her analysis (p. 351).

52. Watt, *Cheap Print*, pp. 140–6. Watt's figures of only a few hundred copies for an engraving may be conservative: contemporary continental accounts of print-making claimed that 1000–2000 impressions could be drawn from the same plate without retouching: D. Landau and P. Parshall, *The Renaissance Print 1470–1550* (New Haven, 1994), pp. 30–2.

53. Watt, *Cheap Print*, p. 3.

54. Bonahue's model of a 'citizen history' is again instructive here: 'citizen history involves a process of reappropriating traditional kinds of historiography for the interests of the citizens themselves...The story of citizen history, then, is a story of historically central figures [*i.e. monarchs and nobles*] becoming marginal, while marginal figures [*i.e. civic heroes*] are brought to the center...': 'Citizen Histories', pp. 38, 42.

55. *The Emperiall achieuement of our dread Soueraigne King Charles together wth ye Armes Crests Supporters & mottowes of all ye seuerall Companies & Corporations of ye famous Citty of London as they now beare them* (London, c.1635?) (*STC* 5022). Welch, *Coat-Armour*, pp. 45–6; *STC*, vol. 3, pp. 180, 183. Copies survive in the British Library (MS Harl 1049, ff. 1r–7r, Harl 2167, ff. 188v, 249v–54r) and the Victoria and Albert Museum. *STC* suggests the 1635 date; however, it only records the work under Webb's imprint, whilst Welch noted a variant title-page bearing Williams's name.

56. A. Globe, *Peter Stent London Printseller circa 1642–1665* (Vancouver, 1985), pp. 121–2; See also Hind, *Engraving*, vol. 2, pp. 399–400; S. Tyacke, *London Map-Sellers 1660–1720* (Tring, Herts., 1978), pp. xii, 130–4, 143; L. Rostenberg, *English Publishers in the Graphic Arts 1599–1700* (New York, 1963), pp. 35–42, 80–90. Virtually intact copies bearing Stent's and Overton's imprints survive in the Bodleian Library as MS Wood 276a (65) and MS Rawl A170, f. 6 respectively.

57. E. Arber (ed.), *The Term Catalogues, 1668–1709 A.D.* (London, 1903–6), vol. 1, pp. 254, 275; Welch, *Coat-Armour*, p. 47.

58. *Armes of the Twelve Chief Companies out of which the Lord Maior is Yearlie chosen* (n.p., n.d); *These are the Armes of all other Worshipfvll Companies of the Honourable City of London* (n.p., n.d.); Welch, *Coat-Armour*, pp. 46–7. Copies exist in the British Library and Guildhall Library.

59. *The Armes, Crests, and Supporters of all the Citties in England, and of all the Severall Companies of the Famous Cittie of London, with the Severall Mottoes belonging to each Corporation* (London, n.d.); Tyacke, *London Map-Sellers*, pp. 145–6; Rostenberg, *English Publishers*, pp. 43–50. A slightly mutilated copy survives in the Guildhall Library. Walton was also a Merchant Taylor by company and had possibly been a co-apprentice with Stent.

60. *A NEW TABLE of the TRADES-MENS ARMES or A COLLECTION of all the ARMES CREST and SUPPORTERS of the severall COMPANIES in the famous City of LONDON with the MOTTOS belonging to ech CORPORATION and the proper COLOURES described...Many FAULTS that are in all the former being amended* (London, n.d.); Arber, *Term Catalogues*, vol. 1, p. 152; Welch, *Coat-Armour*, p. 47.

61. The motto of the Stationers' Company appeared as 'per bene natis male vivre' in Wright's 1596 engraving and its successors; Walton changed it to 'verbum domine manet in aeturnum'. The change seems to have been noted by at least one contemporary, Chester herald painter Randle Holme, who cited 'the new table' as his source for the new motto: R. Holme, *The Academy of Armory*, I. H. Jeayes (ed.), (London, 1905), vol. 2, p. 409. It is not clear whether the emendation indicates a deliberate change of motto by the company or an

original error on the part of Wright, but a piece of plate given to the company by the widow of a former Master in 1674 was engraved with arms bearing the 'old' motto: J. G. Nichols, 'Mottoes of the Stationers' Company', *Notes and Queries*, 2nd ser., 11 (1861), pp. 389, 438. Further detailed comparison between Walton's *New Table* and previous versions remains to be made.

62. Appended to *A compendius view...of the whole world*, 1659, and quoted in H. R. Plomer, *A Dictionary of the Booksellers and Printers who were at work in England, Scotland and Ireland from 1641 to 1667* (London, 1907), p. 188.

63. This may mean that the five fragments surviving at Guildhall Library were in fact sold as a 'book' rather than a pasted-together broadside.

64. Wing W620; reprinted in facsimile in Welch, *Coat-Armour.* Wallis was keen to secure control of his published text: the work was entered by the Stationer Robert Clavell in the Stationers' Company register in January 1677; and in May Wallis obtained from the crown a fifteen–year monopoly over its printing, reproducing the text of his patent in the prefatory material of the work itself: G. E. B. Eyre, *A Transcript of the Registers of the Company of Stationers from 1640–1708 A.D.*, 3 vols. (London, 1913–14), vol. 3, p. 31; *CSPD, 1677–78*, pp. 124–5; Wallis, *Londons Armory*, f. 4r.

65. Wallis retained the Marblers' Company, but did replace the Brownbakers' and Whitebakers' separate arms of earlier prints with that of the Bakers' Company.

66. Arber, *Term Catalogues*, vol. 1, p. 360.

67. Wallis, *Londons Armory*, f. 5r.

68. Ironically, Wallis later proved himself to be a source of such heraldic 'Error'; in 1687, he was fined £20 by the Court of Chivalry for painting false arms at a funeral: Squibb, *High Court of Chivalry*, p. 92.

69. Wallis, *Londons Armory*, f. 6r.

70. Philip Lea, *London Almanack for XXX years* (n.p., 1680); Welch, *Coat-Armour*, pp. 48–50.

71. Initial attempts to discover the provenance of these surviving prints have so far proved inconclusive.

72. I am very grateful to Hazel Forsyth of the Museum of London for this information. See also G. W. Whiteman, *Halls and Treasures of the City Companies* (London, 1970); J. L. Nevinson, 'Crowns and Garlands of the Livery Companies', *Guildhall Studies in London History*, 1, no. 2 (1974), pp. 68–81; A. Ray, *English Delftware* (Oxford, 2000). A number of pill tiles beautifully decorated with the arms of the Society of Apothecaries survive in such a condition that there is some debate over whether the tiles were designed to be displayed on the wall rather than used for pill rolling; see J. K. Crellin, *Medical Ceramics in the Wellcome Institute*, 2 vols. (London, 1969), vol. 1, pp. 145–6.

73. Paul Griffiths, 'Secrecy and Authority in Late Sixteenth-Century and Seventeenth-Century London', *Historical Journal*, 40 (1997), pp. 925–51.

74. The implications of how one early modern London company was represented and perceived are explored in I. A. Gadd, '"Being like a field": Corporate Identity in the Stationers' Company 1557–1684' (unpublished DPhil thesis, University of Oxford, 1999).

4.

The Adventures of Dick Whittington and the Social Construction of Elizabethan London

JAMES ROBERTSON

From medieval times until the eighteenth century at least, obtaining the freedom of London opened a cornucopia of privileges. These were re-affirmed in successive royal charters and then shaped and interpreted through the Custom of London.[1] The freedom was primarily open to individuals who had served an apprenticeship to a citizen of London, a process that was regulated through the guilds.[2] Residence did not, in itself, a Londoner make. For the majority of those who migrated to London – and who sought to become citizens – the freedom of the City needed to be earned. Would-be citizens had to surmount elaborate barriers to gain admittance, and individual guilds set the height of the bar. The procedures for admission to the freedom established by London custom were distinctive, but they proved far less well known than the privileges citizenship entailed. To understand successfully the significance of the guilds within both the metropolitan and the more widely diffused constructions of Londoners' civic identity, we need to appreciate the widespread contemporary misapprehensions of these companies and their various roles. In this chapter, I examine one significant source of such misunderstandings: the story of Richard Whittington, the international merchant, future Lord Mayor, knight and civic benefactor, who had sprung from 'a sordid scullery' and 'by the prosperous venture of a Cat/Clim'd to the Chair of Londons Magistrat'.[3] Through an analysis of this story, its recasting by seventeenth-century authors, and the ways in which it dealt with many of the barriers that faced everyday migrants, I uncover some of the tensions between the expectations and experiences of aspirant Londoners.

Misconceptions about London were not, however, the sole property of the throngs of country boys and girls who continued to arrive there every year – and who would largely succeed in adopting the city's customs. Even the ruling élites of major provincial towns could remain profoundly ignorant of the roles that the livery companies played in London. In the 1530s, Exeter's worthies demonstrated their unfamiliarity when they drafted a wish-list for the city's Members of Parliament to incorporate into a Parliamentary bill that would give Exeter a single Merchant Guild, with a Hanse and the usual rights appertaining to it – 'just as the Mayor, Sheriffs and citizens of London have'.[4] The bill failed, but these remarkable hopes demonstrate a striking lack of appreciation of the parts that London's many guilds played in municipal life, even as they testify to the city's predominance within the English economy. A century later, during the 1630s, London was invoked again as a model for other cities. On this occasion, the example of the metropolis was being urged on the burgesses of Edinburgh to encourage them to establish merchant companies, because without them 'all persounes indistinctlie run to trade without ordour'.[5] This time it was Charles I who was incorrectly invoking London's practices, demonstrating his ignorance of the Custom of London and the privilege that it offered to citizens in mercantile trades to deal in any branch of merchandise.

So how might would-be Londoners and their provincial kinsfolk come to understand the elaborate civic *cursus honorum* that organised the ways that individuals rose from apprentice to citizen, and then potentially on up through the ranks of municipal and corporate hierarchies to liveryman, warden, Master; member of the city's Common Council, Sheriff, Alderman and, possibly even, Lord Mayor? For London's modern historians, the city was a place where an individual's luck and effort flourished against the odds of high death rates, late marriages, and, on average, low reproduction rates.[6] For contemporaries, I will argue, assumptions about the openness of London society were epitomised by the story of Richard Whittington.

For generations, the myth of Dick Whittington offered potential urban migrants a literary template for accommodating themselves to a complex urban society with remarkable opportunities. The life of Whittington, who died in 1423 after serving as Lord Mayor under Richard II, Henry IV and Henry V, was one of a group of stories about Londoners that were recast and widely diffused through the country as part of the literary repertoire during Elizabeth's last years, at a time when 'citizen comedy and London history attracted the best of the second-string playwrights in London'.[7] A play – since lost – *The history of Richard Whittington, of his lowe byrth [and] his great fortune*, was entered for publication at Stationers' Hall in 1605 'as yt was plaied by the prynces servantes'. Five months later a ballad, *The vertuous Lyfe and memorable Death of Sir Richard Whittington mercer sometymes Lord Maiour of the honorable Citie of London*, which is also lost, was entered.[8] The earliest texts that have survived are Richard Johnson's *A Song of Sir Richard Whittington, who by strange fortune, came to be thrice Lord Maior of London, with his bountifull guifts and liberallity given to this honourable City,* to be sung to the tune of 'Dainty, Come thou to Me,' published in an anthology of ballads in 1612, and T.H. – probably Thomas Heywood's – *The famous and remarkable history of Sir Richard Whittington* (1636?), which exists in several mid-seventeenth-century reprints, indicating the durability and popularity of the tale.[9]

Plate 4.1. Dick Whittington bringing his kitten to be consigned as his venture on Alderman Fitzwarren's voyage.

The good ship Unicorn is in the left-hand corner. From T.H., *The Famous and Remarkable History of Sir Richard Whittington, Three Times Lord Mayor of London... with all the remarkable passages and things of note which happened in his time, with his Life and Death* (London, 1656), sig. A3v. The woodblock was reused in subsequent reprints.

(By permission of The Huntington Library, San Marino, California)

Plate 4.2. Title-page of a later *Famous and Remarkable History* (London, 1686–8).
Note the Swordbearer preceding the Lord Mayor. This block was reused from the 1656 edition.
(By permission of The Huntington Library, San Marino, California)

In these works, the fifteenth-century Mercer's career is adapted very freely to fit the civic conventions current among Londoners in the late sixteenth and early seventeenth century, with most of the additions to the account concentrated in the early stages of Dick's career.[10] The basic story begins with a poor young Dick Whittington coming up to London where he finds a post in the household of a London merchant. He is miserable there and runs away, but after he hears the bells tolling out some variant of:

> Turn againe, Whittington,
> For thou in time shall grow
> Lord Maior of London

he reconsiders and returns 'with speed' to his master's house – and here the ballad temporarily forgets young Dick's status as a scullion

> A prentise to remaine,
> As the lord had decreed[11]

Dick's big break comes through trading away a kitten. When his master sends out a trading vessel to 'a land far unknown', he generously encourages all his servants to consign some trade goods on their own account. As the only thing that young Dick possesses is his cat, it is sent off on the voyage as his venture (Plate 4.1). In the event, the ship reaches 'a land/ Troubled with rats and mice', and the 'nimble' cat is sold for 'Heaps of gold'.[12] When the ship returns, Dick's wealth is such that he can set up as a merchant, marry his master's daughter and go on to become a London tycoon. In time, he becomes Lord Mayor as the bells had predicted, serving three times, and at his death, Whittington endows a long list of civic charities. All in all, these stories of a succession of 'happy' chances offered heady images for any aspiring young Londoner, besides providing models of suitably modest conduct within a well-regulated household and, indeed, for proper responses to divine providence – all oft-repeated themes in their own right.[13]

This chapter, however, will pay less attention to Dick's initial run of lucky breaks and focus instead on the less familiar final sections of the story which describe how Richard Whittington, citizen and Mercer, went on to become sheriff and then 'thrice Mayor of London'. These were promotions for which – except in fiction – specific qualifications were required: particularly the freedom of London and membership in a London guild. How, in this widely-read text, was the route to the top of the civic hierarchy represented, and where were the guilds in the depiction of these successive transitions?

The magnificence of his new wealth allows Dick to surmount social boundaries: in a boldly unspecific move he is simply 'offered' the citizenship and then marries Mistress Alice Fitzwarren.[14] Even this fictionalised sequence of events still highlights important realities about becoming a Londoner. First,

Dick does have to obtain the freedom: possessing considerable capital alone will not allow him to advance. The offer of citizenship to the former scullion is a literary gesture, especially at a time when access to the freedom was becoming sufficiently restricted that even noble patronage might not be sufficient to sway the Court of Aldermen. These growing restrictions are exemplified by the case of John Dawes, who in the 1580s persuaded 'one Myller a freeman of the Company of Drapers being a very poor man' to sign off on an apprenticeship indenture and then, seven years later, for a further 'piece of money' to swear to the completion of Dawes's apprenticeship before the City Chamberlain. When this 'forgery and afterwards perjury' was discovered, both were disenfranchised. Even two years later, in 1595, the Lord Mayor was unwilling to consider re-enfranchising Dawes. A letter from Lord Buckhurst supporting Dawes was rebuffed with the reply that 'John Dawes not to be made free for he never served his years'.[15] The perjury effectively outweighed Lord Buckhurst's letter, which might otherwise have proved effective in securing a candidate the more limited rights of freedom by redemption. At this time, service was necessary for the full privileges of citizenship. Dawes was supposed to become a member of a company in order to acquire the citizenship: he could not be a company member because he had not undertaken the necessary apprenticeship. Such scruples were very different from the widespread assumption among gentry visitors apparent, for example, in John Manningham's 1602 *Diary* that 'almost any man for some 40£ may buy his freedom'.[16] The fictional Dick's luck evades any need to set such assumptions against the citizens' own re-affirmation of their traditional criteria – especially since Alderman Fitzwarren's humble servant would not have been apprenticed and hence would hardly have been eligible to become a citizen, never mind thrice Lord Mayor.

Secondly, the ballad and *History*'s narratives are correct in resorting to such an invention concerning the freedom, since marriage to a wealthy Londoner's daughter was not in itself a route to the freedom of the city. This convention was unusual, and meant that the preliminary drudgery of apprenticeship could not be leapfrogged through marriage to a citizen's widow or daughter, as was possible in many other towns. London's distinctiveness in this matter would be clear enough to any apprentices in, for example, Bristol, England's third trading city, who might see the play, hear the ballads or read T. H.'s *History*. Stories circulating in seventeenth-century Bristol about how John Whitson, seventeenth-century Bristol's own great civic benefactor, achieved his start might have suggested to them a different route to advancement. Whitson had finished an apprenticeship with old Alderman Vawr before the Alderman died, but had yet to take out his freedom – in itself hardly unusual in a city with even worse odds for apprentices than London (around 66% of Bristol apprentices failed to complete their term or take up their citizenship).[17] As a handsome journeyman, this future Jacobean merchant was wooed by his former master's widow who, in the version John Aubrey later recorded, called him 'into the wine-cellar and bad[e] him broach the best butt in the cellar for her; and truly he broach't his Mistresse, who after married him.' Whitson then took out his freedom, and took over his former master's business – all in the interval before their first child was born. The story, with its ribald *double entendre*, could be expected to 'last perhaps as long as Bristol is a city,' shaping Bristolian apprentices' understandings of the way to thrive.[18] Variants on this theme would be familiar enough to contemporaries in Edinburgh or, indeed, in the great cities of Germany or North Italy, where marrying into the merchant élite was often the only option open to an ambitious outsider.[19]

Mistress Alice Fitzwarren would have been very unwise to get involved with young Dick, the handsome scullion, before he became a freeman of London. When John Whitson married the widow of a London alderman as his second wife he gained a beautiful bride to take back to Bristol, along with valuable contacts and capital, but not the freedom of London.[20] In other cities, where the dowries of freemen's daughters included citizenship or some rights, good fortune of the scale that Whittington enjoyed would proceed in a very different manner; in London, even Whittington, despite all his luck, was obliged to follow closely defined civic pathways. The *History* described how Whittington's splendid marriage was attended by the Lord Mayor and Aldermen and 'by this means [the bridegroom] had got acquaintance with the best'.[21] Some eighteenth- and nineteenth-century chap-book versions then added to the splendour by having the Stationers' Company attend the ceremony as well, acknowledging the continuing significance of corporate activities for Londoners.[22] Such contacts would be valuable, but in London Dick needed to become a citizen to take full advantage of his good luck.

With Dick's marriage both the early versions of the story and their popular successors change pace. As a citizen, a merchant in his own right, and now a wealthy merchant's son-in-law, Whittington had succeeded in reaching a major plateau in the city's *cursus honorum*. By this stage, his achievements exemplify the ambitions of the majority of the young men and women who came to London to better themselves through taking up an apprenticeship or marrying a freeman: a group whose initial hopes of advancement were particularly likely to be shaped by the categories inherent in just such pamphlets and ballads.[23] Following this social transition, the character of the historical sources that the early biographers depended on for their information change, leaving much less space for invention. How the original Richard Whittington got his start could apparently be re-imagined freely in the sixteenth century. The name of Whittington's wife was carved on their joint tomb in St. Michael Paternoster Royal: the story of 'Dame Alice' the Alderman's charitable daughter, along with her scrupulous father, the great merchant Master Fitzwarren, whose household harboured Dick, his cat and a tyrannical scullery maid, as well as the setting up of such a fortunate trading voyage were all fictional constructs, spun out of the tomb's inscription.[24]

The career path that the chap-books created for Whittington, with his succession of lucky breaks, also demonstrates that institutional milestones were not the only important transitions in Londoners' lives. Dick's attempt to run away proved important in his own development as a great Lord Mayor and, at least in Johnson's *Song of Sir Richard Whittington* where he promises that 'If God so favour me/I will not prove unkind', the incident foreshadowed his role as a munificent civic benefactor. With all the consequences of deserting his master in running off to 'purchase liberty' and, if he had been an apprentice, breaking his indenture, Dick's flight and quick return would hardly be recognised as a stage on the official route towards citizenship. However, as a feature of the lives of newly-arrived Londoners facing the trials of apprenticeship or urban domestic service, Dick's unhappiness was far more widely shared. London's Elizabethan apprentices had a non-completion rate of around 62%; some died, but around 50% of enrolled apprentices appear to have dropped out.[25]

While apprentices' and servants' departures were not always a result of problems faced in service, the years before freedom clearly could offer a multitude of difficulties. A list of ten 'accidents' that Robert Pink, a troubled London apprentice, compiled for a consultation with Richard Napier, a Buckinghamshire clergyman and astrologer, offers us a set of alternative turning-points for a native Londoner. At two years of age, Pink had the small pox; at '5 or 6' he was bitten by a mastiff; then at seven and – twice – at nine years old he was 'taxed' with theft by a goldsmith 'who lived in the house with us' and by his mother. Then 'my mother married when I was about 12 years of age to a barber[,] but my own father was a grocer'. Pink was later apprenticed and 'came to my master aged 14 years 7 months and a fortnight', earlier than most Elizabethan apprentices.[26] Then, 'a year after [he] had the small pox'. He was 'in love [at] about 20 years of age & 3 months'. When Pink was 'aged about 24 years my master died'; he 'stayed with my mistress about 4 weeks & so we parted but I think I had little thanks'.[27] For this Londoner's son, many of the forces that shaped his fortunes were indeed outside his control: epidemics; fierce animals; dealing with lodgers; his father's death, and his mother's remarriage to a member of the less prestigious barber's trade; and, most recently, the death of Pink's master and the subsequent break up of the household in which he had spent the previous eleven years and might well have expected to spend another two years. Dick may have been miserable in Alderman Fitzwarren's kitchen, but he did not have to face the frequent deaths that disrupted many London-born Londoners' lives, or the tensions that might appear within the 'blended households' formed when widows or widowers remarried – transitions that, for Pink, were compounded by social disparagement and accusations of theft within the new families.[28] Furthermore, at the point when Pink consulted Richard Napier, he had yet to establish his own household, although it had been four years since he had – presumably unhappily as apprentices were not permitted to marry – fallen in love. In personal and indeed in public terms, Dick's own marriage to Mistress Alice proved far more successful than Pink's doomed love affair, and allowed Dick to set up a household of his own. For would-be citizens, marriage – at the appropriate moment – proved a key transition, ideally providing some of the capital, connections and the mutual assistance and support which could be so important to establishing a business as well as a household.

Dick not only avoids Robert Pink's pitfalls but achieves remarkable success in municipal government. In dealing with Richard Whittington's splendid municipal career, his sixteenth- and seventeenth-century eulogists could draw on a much fuller record. The published narratives they relied on left less space for invention, but the continuing processes of literary selection as a late-medieval merchant was refurbished as a model Elizabethan benefactor offer further insights into early-modern Londoners' priorities and the role of civic history in shaping newcomers' assumptions and citizens' imaginations. There are few references that allow us to date when the transformation of Whittington's career took shape. The image of London's church bells ringing out a pattern into which a message could be slotted, rather than ringing a series of bells in sequence, appears at the earliest an Elizabethan embellishment, since change-ringing was a post-Reformation development.[29] Similarly, while Whittington's repeated invocations of God and providence do help to hold the *Song* together, and prove congruent enough with mainstream Protestant piety, they are otherwise unspecific. In both the *Song* and the *History*, the historical material clumps in two areas: initially on Whittington's achievement in holding the Lord Mayoralty three times, a remarkable claim in its own right; and then on his charitable bequests in London. Whittington's service as Lord Mayor was not only impressive but impossible to equal as in 1435, twelve years after his death, a city ordinance enacted that no-one who had served twice as Lord Mayor should be called to serve a third time.[30] The sixteenth- and seventeenth-century versions of the story skip over his repeated mayoralties to describe instead a career whose elements might yet be emulated – with a lot of luck. In all the published versions, the image of the bells chiming out that Dick Whittington would be 'thrice Mayor of London' acts more as a memorable slogan rather than a significant factor in the development of Dick's story and career in London.

Being Lord Mayor of London was clearly the highpoint of Whittington's civic career. It may not have been likely for a poor migrant to become Lord Mayor, but this part of the Whittington story served well to exemplify the sheer breadth of London's opportunities. However, once Dick is Lord Mayor his personality is swamped by his office. In the pamphlets and ballads, attention centres on public shows.[31] In Whittington's case, a splendidly lavish gesture provides the climax for a feast where Henry V, his new-crowned Queen, and the royal court are the Lord Mayor's guests. Their host brings in 'a great bundle of Bonds, Indentures, and Covenants' for money borrowed by the king for his French wars, which Whittington then cancels and burns:

> At this the King was much extasi'd, and the rather, because it came so unexpectedly, and from so free a spirit, and inbracing him in his Arms, said unto him, That he thought never king had such a subject: and at his departure, did him all the grace and honour that could descend from a king to a Subject.[32]

It is a generous gesture and presents a magnificent image: 'in kind curtesie/ God did thus make him great.' Whittington's own wealth means that some of the debts were his own and others were owed to his father-in-law, Alderman Fitzwarren, but the *History* then lists further bonds due to the various city companies and to the City of London itself, and in burning these the Lord Mayor acts for London itself.[33] This is not just a very rich Richard Whittington destroying debts owed to his family, but London's splendid Lord Mayor erasing corporate assets in a patriotic gesture. The former scullion lighting this fire has indeed grown to fill his office.

Whittington's prominent seat at the feast celebrating the coronation of Katherine of France as Henry V's Queen then provides an occasion to 'shew to the World, that at these high Solemnities, Inaugurations and Coronations, the Lord Mayor of the City of London, and the Aldermen have place, and their presence is still required', reaffirming the City's national importance as 'the king's Chamber' or strong-room.[34] Under the Tudors and the Stuarts, whose family trees both sprang from Queen Katherine's second marriage with Owain Tudor, citing precedents from this particular royal consort's coronation feast would have particular authority.[35] Nor is this all: T. H.'s *History* then links Henry V's expressions of gratitude to a claim that this exchange is the basis for the Lord Mayor's right to have the City's sword carried in front of royal visitors when they are within the Liberties of the City.[36] In reality, however, the citizens' claims to this honour were only held by prescription rather than a particular royal grant.[37] During Elizabeth's reign, this assertion of civic pride contributed to the squabbling between the citizens and the royal Lieutenant of the Tower of London who objected to the presence of the Lord Mayor's Swordbearer.[38] Under the Stuarts, always sticklers for royal protocol, attempts to have the Swordbearer march in front of royal processions within the City and Liberties, or precede the Lord Mayor and Aldermen when they attended services at St. Paul's Cathedral, provoked even more heat.[39] Yet, if the Whittington pamphlets were to be believed, authority for these contentious civic claims could be traced back to England's greatest medieval king and London's most celebrated Lord Mayor, much in the same way that other significant past events were given renewed topical currency by many of the London city comedies of the period (Plate 4.2).

However, neither his service as Lord Mayor nor his remarkable wealth provided the primary foundations for Whittington's lasting fame. At the end of the sixteenth century, it was Whittington's bequests that loomed much larger in his image as an exemplar for Elizabethan Londoners. The titles of both the lost play and the ballad of 1605 stressed Whittington's 'great fortune' and his 'memorable death', and it was the manner in which he disposed of his 'great fortune' that served to make his death so 'memorable'. His charitable foundations accordingly provide the second focus for the 'historical' component of the popular texts. The description of his generosity illustrates a process of selective memory in which a group of late-medieval charitable donations were re-cast for post-reformation sensibilities.

The problem of tying a long list of benefactions into the general narrative offered a challenge to the authors. Richard Johnson's ballad was more successful in linking Whittington's generosity to his confidence after the city's bells rang out his 'fortune', having Dick promise that:

> If God so favour me,
> I will not prove unkind,
> London my love shall see,
> And my great bounties find.[40]

There was certainly a long list of substantial donations to record. As Johnson put it elsewhere, Whittington:

> began the School of Christ Church in London, he builded Whittington College, with Almes houses for 13 poor men and divine lectures to be read there for ever, he repaired Saint Bartholomewes Hospital in Smithfield, he glazed and paved part of Guild hall, he builded the West gate of London called Newgate.[41]

These commissions included major monuments that were still conspicuous in the Elizabethan city to the extent that even the rawest of newcomers to London would be able to locate them. Furthermore, these listings portray the whole city of London as Whittington's heirs, rather than simply the members of the Mercers' Company or the inhabitants of Vintry Ward, in which both the college of priests and the almshouse stood. Indeed, in the Ward's case Johnson's list omits a remarkable combined 123-seat public lavatory and first-floor parish almshouse, 'Whittington's Longhouse', in Vintry Ward, although this building remained standing until the great fire.[42] Civic piety no longer claimed something that was only a landmark for local residents as a city-wide monument. As a result of these particular selections, future generations of citizens became the final beneficiaries of Whittington's good fortune. All of this meant that popular memories of Whittington could supersede the very specific prerequisites for a career in medieval London.

The recasting of Dick Whittington as a model benefactor for subsequent Londoners presents an appealing image, but more was going on here. The charitable donations of a wealthy medieval merchant were being described in terms more acceptable to a sixteenth-century protestant city. As Richard Grafton, the early Elizabethan chronicler, stated in the conclusion to his version of these lists, 'look upon this ye aldermen for it is a glorious glass'.[43] Although the balladeers' catalogues reflect antiquarian scholarship and enthusiasms, they then use this material to produce thoroughly ahistorical depictions. These descriptions ran counter to some popular views of Whittington's legacies – opinions that led a mid-sixteenth-century vicar to break open Whittington's tomb 'thinking some great riches...to be buried with him'.[44] Furthermore, the pamphleteers' ostensible aim of offering insights into Whittington's character is thoroughly subverted, as his biggest single donation is never mentioned. Whittington's original will focused on the conventional medieval goal of endowing a college of priests who would say masses for his and his wife's souls. This college was suppressed in 1548 under the chantry legislation of Edward VI. The Mercers' Company then re-purchased from the Crown most of Whittington's original charitable endowment, although some properties had to be sold to raise the necessary cash. The former college of priests was not regained from the Crown and after passing through several hands the 'Site of the said late dissolved College of Wittingdon alias Whittington' was subsequently purchased by the Skinners' Company in 1602. It was only at this stage that the 'College' title became applied to the almshouse component of Whittington's surviving bequests.[45] In the late sixteenth-century retellings of Whittington's life, however, the almshouse became the central element of his charity, and by this time it did appear to be the precursor of a large number of charitable bequests left to the care of the London guilds (Plate 4.3). Whittington's final stroke of 'luck' was, therefore, to leave the oversight of his major bequests to his guild. Other fifteenth-century civic benefactors were less fortunate in the survival of their legacies or their fame through the legal challenges of the Reformation.[46] Once redefined as an almshouse, Whittington College appeared as a pattern for protestant charity. Both the ballad and the *History* close with calls for emulation:

> Those bells that call'd him so,
> Turne again Whittington'
> Call you back many moe
> To live so in London.[47]

In tracing these organisational developments, we have moved away from the categories that framed the popular stories of Whittington for national

Plate 4.3. The building of Whittington College.
The work depicted could as easily illustrate Whittington's outlay on Newgate Prison as the college
of priests established in his will. The pamphlet's original readers would have found that the almsfolk
and row of almshouses depicted on the right hand side of the picture presented a more familiar
image of urban charity. From *Famous and Remarkable History*, sig. B4r.

Within the engraving:

VERA EFFIGIES PRECLAR DOMINI RICHARDI WHITTINGTON EQVI AVRATI

Huius *ſparſa viri totiū benefacta per* ... *enſa monſtrant indice qualis er*

The true portraicture of *RICHARD WHITTINGTON thriſe Lord Maior
of London a vertuous and godly man full of good Works (and thoſe famous) he builded
the Gate of London called Newegate.which before was a miſerable doungeon.He builded
Whitington Colledge & made it an Almoſe houſe for poore people Also he builded a
greate parte of ȳ hoſpitall of S.Bartholomewes in weſtsmithfield in London.He alſo
builded the beautifull Library at ȳ Gray Friers in Londō,called Chriſtes Hoſpitall;
Alſo he builded the Guilde Halle Chappell and increaſed a greate parte of the Eaſt
ende of the ſaied halle,beſide many other good workes.*

R. Elſtrack ſculpſit

Plate 4.4. Renold Elstrack, 'Sir Richard Whittington'.

A reworked Jacobean engraving of Sir Richard Whittington. In this revised state Elstrack's initial fairly conventional *memento mori* skull under Whittington's right hand is replaced by a cat, demonstrating what printsellers expected a portrait of Dick Whittington to include.

(By permission of Guildhall Library, Corporation of London)

circulation. Within the City, stories of Whittington served to reaffirm the openness of citizens' own institutions. For their members, London's livery companies were much more than regulatory bodies with a social dimension; besides citing the freedom of the City, Londoners also defined themselves through their membership of City guilds. In such terms, Whittington was not only 'thrice Lord Mayor', he was also a member, and thrice Master, of the Mercers' Company and that guild's own continuing pride in its distinguished former member was demonstrated repeatedly during the later sixteenth century.[48] The company obtained a portrait of the early Tudor grammarian and namesake Richard Wyttington, with a picture of a cat painted on it, so that an apparent portrait of the Mercers' great medieval benefactor could grace their hall in a manner appropriate for a Tudor alderman (Plate 4.4). In 1573 the company added a terracotta bust of Whittington to the hall's decorations, this time as part of a group of seven benefactors to the Mercers' Company. On a similar respectful note, successive generations of Mercers replaced the banners which decorated Whittington's tomb in 1569, 1616, 1654 and 1655, while individual Mercers left bequests in their wills to the Whittington College almshouse.[49] These gestures all mixed institutional pride with individual respect, as well as demonstrating that by the middle of Elizabeth's reign, stories of Whittington and his cat were already circulating in and around Mercers' Hall. Whittington's path into Londoners' corporate memory was extraordinary, but the particular themes emphasised in the sixteenth-century retellings showed how current Whittington's bequests remained.

The London presented in the late sixteenth- and early seventeenth-century Dick Whittington stories was a place defined by institutional continuity yet, at the same time, the demographic lottery and the chances of trade created remarkable opportunities for a lucky few. If they entered the system at the right point, conformed to the right customs, stayed alive and, above all, were extraordinarily fortunate, young men from quite humble backgrounds could still achieve distinction.[50] For such migrants, becoming Londoners required earning membership of a host of overlapping communities: guilds, parishes and wards. In practice, the fifteenth-century Lord Mayor Richard Whittington, had hewed just such a path as a successful Londoner. However, the major achievement of the literary recasting of the Elizabethan Whittington stories was to make his good fortune accommodate the ambitions of a much wider band of migrants. He became far more than a rich Mercer from Vintry Ward; instead, 'Dick' was simply lucky, and so became a great Londoner, who was not only thrice Lord Mayor, but could astound Henry V with his generosity. Hence, it was perhaps *only* in those pamphlets and the subsequent chap-books, written for provincial peddlers' packs or apprentices' garrets, that Whittington's civic career would be summed up through his three terms as Lord Mayor, scissoring him away from his guild.[51] The generations of young people who took the road to London with *Dick Whittington* in their pocket or with verses from the ballad in their ears, might expect that:

> A countrey Boy comes up to town,
> perhaps no cloths to his back ...
> yet he need never lack;
> If that he be just and true,
> and have an honest face,
> And willing any work to do,
> he need not want a place

even if he was not 'known' 'to one creature there'. However, on their arrival these country boys would soon discover the necessity for even the luckiest migrant to enter a formal apprenticeship as a prerequisite to entering the freedom of the city, since, as even the preceding verse of this celebratory ballad noted:

> No Forraigner can set up there,
> [the citizens'] orders are so strong,
> In Shop they must not sell no ware,
> least they the Free-men wrong.

In ballads, at least, the sheer magnificence of the City of London – 'a brave Town,/and a fine City' – could smooth over the divergence between the hopes of these young migrants and the citizens' defence of their privileges.[52] Yet, when it came to eliding this gap at the heart of the popular perception of the freedom of London, the late Elizabethan recasting of the Whittington myth successfully presented a more inclusive view of London, by focusing on the donations that moulded Whittington's lasting fame as a great Londoner. However, this transformation marginalised the network of particular loyalties that shaped individual citizens of London's construction of their own civic identities. These literary priorities flew in the face of the local loyalties that framed most Londoners' social worlds. Indeed, the extent to which these fictions were able to overcome the limitations of Dick Whittington's civic status as a 'Citizen and Mercer of London', was only possible through Richard Whittington's massive generosity *and* Dick's amazing luck.

NOTES

I am grateful to April Shelford, Linda Sturtz and the editors of this volume for their comments on earlier drafts of this essay.

1. The city charters are reprinted in *The Historical Charters and Constitutional Documents of the City of London* (London, 1884). There is little scholarly discussion of the Custom of London, which remained orally transmitted with the Recorder of London interpreting controversial points. For citizens of London, the Custom shaped their understanding of both

what it meant to be a Londoner and their responses to legal questions. *A Breefe discourse, declaring and approving the necessarie and inviable maintenence of the laudable customs of London* (London, 1584) (*STC* 16747), offers a general defence of both the practical utility and the legal authority of their 'many laudable and ancient Customs'.

2. Other routes were open, particularly 'redemption', the purchase of the freedom and 'patrimony', admitting the legitimate sons of freedmen born after their father had been made free. During the sixteenth and seventeenth centuries, however, citizens' sons still tended to undertake apprenticeships to acquire the freedom, which may well have provided them with a wider network of business contacts. As for redemption, while some freedoms were granted by this procedure, since it could resolve hardship cases when individual apprentices were ineligible to complete their terms of service through some misfortune or else through an early marriage, the Court of Aldermen was reluctant to admit large numbers by this route.

3. 'The Mind of the Frontispiece', introductory poem in Francis Kirkman, *The Unlucky Citizen Experimentally Described in the Various Misfortunes of an Unhappy Londoner* (London, 1673) (Wing K638).

4. J. Youings, *Early Tudor Exeter: The Founders of the County of the City* (Exeter, 1974), p. 12.

5. D. Stevenson, *The Scottish Revolution, 1637–44: The Triumph of the Covenanters* (Newton Abbot, 1973), p. 51, citing *Edinburgh Records 1626–41*, xv, p. 179.

6. R. A. P. Finlay and B. Shearer, 'Population growth and suburban expansion', in A. L. Beier and R. A. P. Finlay (eds.), *London, 1500–1700: The Making of the Metropolis* (London, 1986), pp. 37–57; S. K. Rappaport, 'Reconsidering Apprenticeship in Sixteenth-Century London', in J. Monfasini and R. G. Musto (eds.), *Renaissance Society and Culture: Essays in Honor of Eugene F. Rice, Jr.* (New York, 1991), pp. 239–61; M. Bailey, 'Demographic Decline in Late-Medieval England: Some Thoughts on Recent Research', *Economic History Review*, 2nd ser., 49 (1996), pp. 1–19.

7. L. C. Stevenson, *Praise and Paradox: Merchants and Craftsmen in Elizabethan Popular Literature* (Cambridge, 1984), pp. 15–21 'quotation at p. 21'. On the literary construction of Elizabethan and Stuart London: L. Manley, *Literature and Culture in Early Modern London* (Cambridge, 1995), along with essays by I. Archer, D. Bevington, M. Butler, L. Manley and P. S. Seaver in D. L. Smith, R. Strier and D. Bevington (eds.), *The Theatrical City: Culture, Theatre and Politics in London, 1576–1649* (Cambridge, 1995); E. T. Bonahue, 'Social Control, the City, and the Market: Heywood's *If You Know Not Me, You Know Nobody*', *Renaissance Papers* (1993), pp. 75–90, and L. Hutson, *Thomas Nashe in Context* (Oxford, 1989). For the re-writing of Sir Thomas Gresham's career, J. Gasper, 'The Literary Legend of Sir Thomas Gresham', in A. Saunders (ed.), *The Royal Exchange*, London Topographical Society Publication, 152 (London, 1997), pp. 99–107.

8. E. Arber (ed.), *A Transcript of the Registers of the Company of Stationers of London, 1554–1640*, 5 vols. (London, 1875–1894), vol. 3, pp. 282, 296.

9. Richard Johnson, *A Crowne-Garland of Goulden Roses* (London, 1612) (*STC* 14672); expanded edition (1631) (*STC* 14673); reprinted, W. Chappell (ed.), Percy Society 6 (London, 1842), pp. 20–5, quotations here at pp. 22–3. The ballad is also anthologised in L. Manley (ed.), *London in the Age of Shakespeare: An Anthology* (London, 1986) pp. 232–6. T. H., [Thomas Heywood?], *The Famous and Remarkable History of Sir Richard Whittington, Three Times Lord Major of London ... with all the remarkable passages and things of note which hap[pe]ned in his time, with his Life and Death* (London, 1656) (Wing H1780), and H. B. Wheatley (ed.), *The History of Sir Richard Whittington by T. H.*, Villon Society, 5 (London, 1885). A 1686–8 (Wing H1782) reprint of the *History* puts Heywood's name on the title page. The 1636 composition date is argued by E. T. Bonahue: 'Heywood, the Citizen Hero, and the *History* of Dick Whittington', *English Language Notes*, 36 (1999), pp. 33–41.

10. The original Richard Whittington's career is set out in C.M. Barron, 'Richard Whittington: the Man Behind the Myth', in A. E. J. Hollaender and W. Kellaway (eds.), *Studies in London History: Presented to Philip Edmund Jones* (London, 1969), pp. 197–248.

11. Johnson, *Crowne-Garland* (1842), p. 21.

12. Johnson, *Crowne-Garland* (1842), pp. 22–3.

13. Dysfunctional households provided plentiful material for Elizabethan and Jacobean playwrights. On the petty treasons that occurred when women or servants turned on their husbands or masters: F. E. Dolan, *Dangerous Familiars: Representations of Domestic Crime in England, 1550–1700* (Ithaca, N.Y., 1994), and, more generally, V. Comensoli, *'Household Buisness': Domestic Plays of Early Modern England* (Toronto, 1996), pp. 65–109. Disputes between masters and their apprentices were occasionally depicted on stage, C. A. Bernthal, 'Treason in the Family: The Trial of Thumpe v. Horner', *Shakespeare Quarterly*, 42 (1991), pp. 44–54.

14. T.H. *History*, sig. C4r.

15. Lord Mayor to Lord Buckhurst, Remembrancia, CLRO, ii, ff. 17–17v, no. 91, 17 March, 1595.

16. R.P. Sorlien (ed.), *The Diary of John Manningham of the Inner Temple 1602–1603* (Hanover, N.H., 1976), p. 42.

17. P. V. McGrath, *John Whitson and the Merchant Community of Bristol*, Historical Association, Bristol Branch, Pamphlet 25 (Bristol, 1975), p. 8. The dismal completion rate in Bristol is cited in P. S. Seaver, 'A Social Contract? Master Against Servant in the Court of Requests', *History Today*, 39 (September 1989), pp. 50–6 'at p. 50'.

18. A. Clarke (ed.), *'Brief Lives', chiefly of Contemporaries, set down by John Aubrey, between the years 1669 & 1696*, 2 vols. (Oxford, 1898), vol. 2, p. 297. The Victorian editor bowdlerises Aubrey's original punch line. It is given in full in O. L. Dick (ed.), *Aubrey's Brief Lives* (London, 1949), p. 317. McGrath, *John Whitson*, pp. 8–9.

19. On Edinburgh: H. Dingwall, 'The Importance of Social Factors in Determining the Composition of the Town Councils in Edinburgh, 1550–1650', *Scottish Historical Review*, 65 (1986), pp. 17–33; and Florence D. Herlihy, *Women, Family and Society in Medieval Europe: Historical Essays, 1978–1991*, A. Molho (ed.), (Providence, R.I., 1995), pp. 193–214.

20. McGrath, *John Whitson*, pp. 13–14.

21. T. H., *History*, sig. C3v–C4r.

22. Wheatley, *History*, p. v.

23. Compare with I. K. Ben-Amos, 'Service and Coming of Age in Seventeenth-Century England', *Continuity and Change*, 3 (1988), pp. 41–64 and on women's options: V. B. Elliott, 'Single Women in the London Marriage Market: Age, Status and Mobility, 1598–1619', in R. B. Outhwaite (ed.), *Marriage and Society: Studies in the Social History of Marriage* (London, 1981), pp. 81–100.

24. The fifteenth-century ordinances for Whittington's Hospital, the Almshouse at St. Michael Paternoster Royal, did include the names of 'Sir William Whittington knight and Dame Johane his wiff' along with 'Sir Ive FitzWarren & Dame Molde his wife the fadres and moders of ye same Richard Whityngton and Alice his wiff' in the list of people whose souls were to be prayed for, while the genealogy was known to John Stow: J. M. Imray, *The Charity of Richard Whittington: A History of the Trust Administered by the Mercers' Company* (London, 1968), p. 115; J. Stow, *The Survey of London*, C.L. Kingsford (ed.), 2 vols. (Oxford, 1908), vol. 1, p. 242. The ordinances were re-copied after the Reformation and a copy was supposed to be kept at the almshouse, but the absence of a pedigree on Whittington's tomb apparently left space enough for elaboration.

25. The experiences of Nehemiah Wallington, the early seventeenth-century Londoner whose life we now know best, included two attempts to run away to the country – even though

Wallington was a Londoner's son, with his family and social networks all centered on London: P. S. Seaver, *Wallington's World: A Puritan Artisan in Seventeenth-Century London* (Stanford, Cal., 1985), pp. 21–2, 29. On the rapid turn-over among domestic servants in London: B. W. Capp, 'The Poet and the Bawdy Court: Michael Drayton and the Lodging-House World in Early Stuart London', *The Seventeenth Century*, 10 (1995), pp. 27–37. The estimated figures are from Rappaport, 'Reconsidering Apprenticeship', pp. 253–6.

26. See S. K. Rappaport, *Worlds Within Worlds: The Structure of Life in Sixteenth Century London* (Cambridge, 1989), p. 295.

27. 'Robert Pink's account of his own accidents', Oxford, Bodleian Library, MS Ashmole 174, no. 40, ff. 179–180. On Napier, see: M. MacDonald, *Mystical Bedlam: Madness, Anxiety and Healing in Seventeenth-Century England* (Cambridge, 1981). He did not have many London clients.

28. For a discussion of the 'blended' families among the English settlers in the seventeenth-century Chesapeake, which also combined high mortality rates with social opportunities, see: D.B. and A. Rutman, '"Now-Wives and Sons-in-Law": Parental Death in a Seventeenth-Century Virginia County', in T.W. Tait and D.L. Ammerman (eds.), *The Chesapeake in the Seventeenth Century: Essays on Anglo-American Society and Politics* (Chapel Hill, N.C., 1979), pp. 153–82.

29. A. Woodger, 'Post-Reformation Mixed Gothic in Huntingdonshire Church Towers and its Campanological Associations', *Archaeological Journal*, 141 (1984), pp. 269–308. The campanological element of Woodger's argument is not disputed in G. W. Bernard's critique, 'The Dating of Church Towers in Huntingdon Re-Examined', *Archaeological Journal,* 149 (1992), pp. 344–50.

30. A. B. Beaven, *The Aldermen of the City of London, Temp. Henry III – 1908,* 2 vols. (London, 1908–13), vol. 2, p. xxvii.

31. On this tendency: D. J. Woolf, 'Of Danes and Giants: Popular Beliefs about the Past in Early Modern England', *Dalhousie Review*, 71 (1991), pp. 166–209.

32. T. H., *History*, sig. E4v–E5v; Johnson, *Crowne-Garland* (1842), p. 24.

33. T. H., *History*, sig. E4v–E5v.

34. T. H., *History*, sig. E3r.

35. R. A. Griffiths and R. S. Thomas, *The Making of the Tudor Dynasty* (New York, 1985), pp. 25–37, also E. R. Henken, *National Redeemer: Ôwain Glyndwr in Welsh Tradition* (Ithaca, N.Y., 1996), p. 55, for Queen Katherine's marriage, her re-marriage and her grandson Henry's royal lineage.

36. T. H. *History*, sig. E5v–E6r.

37. L. Jewitt, *The Corporation Plate and Insignia of Office of the Cities and Towns of England and Wales*, W. H. St. John Hope (ed.), 2 vols. (London, 1895), vol. 2, p. 100.

38. Lord Mayor to Lord Chancellor, Remembrancia, CLRO, i, no. 432, n.d. [1582]; R. B. Manning, 'The Prosecution of Sir Michael Blount, Lieutenant of the Tower of London, 1595', *Bulletin of the Institute of Historical Research*, 57 (1984), pp. 216–24; J. Stow, *The Svrvay of London...continued, corrected and much enlarged [by Anthony Munday]* (London, 1618) (*STC* 23344), pp. 238–48.

39. Remembrancia, CLRO, vii, nos. 113 (17 April 1633, Privy Council to Lord Mayor and Dean and Chapter of St. Paul's) and 117 (3 May 1633, Order of the Star Chamber). Also, P. E. Jones, 'The Surrender of the Sword', *Transactions of the Guildhall Historical Association*, 3 (1965), pp. 8–15, and Jones, 'Sword and Mace', Appendix C in R. Smith (ed.), *Ceremonials of the Corporation of London* (London, 1962), pp. 177–80.

40. Johnson, *Crowne-Garland* (1842), p. 22.

41. This list is from Johnson, *The pleasant walkes of Moore-Fields* (London, 1607), (*STC* 14690), sig. C3v.

42. P. E. Jones, 'Whittington's Longhouse', *London Topographical Record*, 23 (1972), pp. 27–34.

43. R. Grafton, *Chronicle or History of England*, (1569), quoted in Imray, *Charity of Richard Whittington*, p. 2.

44. Stow, *Survey*, vol. 1, p. 243.

45. Imray, *Charity of Richard Whittington*, pp. 1–53. The Bargain and Sale of the Skinners' purchase of the College uses the older descriptive phrase (quoted here), which they also employed the following April in a lease for part of that property: 'the great messuage, being part of the capital messuage and Site of the late college of Whittington alias Whittington College'. By the late seventeenth century, however, when the Skinners' Company acquired a further plot within this block, the former College's name was only included as one among a list of aliases for 'the Parish of St Michael Pater Noster alias, St Michael in the Old Royall alias Whittington College': Sir John Norris to Skinners (3 Dec 1602), GL, MS 31301/330; Deed of Covenant, Thomas Forman to John Pilkington (12 Apr 1603), MS 31301/331; Sale and Deliverance, James Fairclough to Skinners (20 Apr 1674), MS 31301/333.

46. Whittington's success here can be contrasted with the erasing of the various 'charitable and ecclesiastical institutions prepared to pray for [John Pyel's and Adam Fraunceys's] souls in perpetuity' established by two other late fourteenth-century London merchants who had built up substantial landed estates: S. J. O'Connor, 'Introduction', *A Calendar of the Cartularies of John Pyel and Adam Fraunceys*, Camden Society, 5th ser., 2 (London, 1993), p. 74. Conversely, Colin Burgess suggests how burdensome individual parishes found the massive accumulation of traditional pious commitments that the Reformation then swept away: C. Burgess, '"By Quick and by Dead": Wills and Pious Provisions in Later Medieval Bristol', *English Historical Review*, 102 (1987), pp. 837–58.

47. Johnson, *Crowne-Garland* (1842), p. 25. A.M. Hind, *Engraving in England in the Sixteenth and Seventeenth Centuries*, 3 vols. (Cambridge, 1952–64), vol. 2, pp. 192–3.

48. Barron, 'Richard Whittington', p. 215.

49. The painting is now lost. However, two states of a nineteenth-century copper engraving, along with a lithograph version are held at the Guildhall Library, Print Room, Portraits C. On these corporate conventions, see also: R. Tittler, 'The Cookes and the Brookes: uses of portraiture in town and country before the Civil War', in G. MacLean, D. Landry and J. P. Ward (eds.), *The Country and the City Revisited: England and the Politics of Culture, 1550–1850* (Cambridge, 1999), pp. 58–73. For the terracotta bust: J. Imray, *The Mercers' Hall*, London Topographical Society Publications, 143 (London, 1991), p. 20. On the banners: Imray, *Charity of Richard Whittington*, p. 5 n. 2. There were bequests in 1521, 1563, 1583, 1592, 1598, 1601 and 1647 (Imray, *Charity*, pp. 64–5, and n. 1).

50. On the range of backgrounds of men who became Aldermen at this juncture: R. G. Lang, 'London's Aldermen in Business, 1600–1625', *Guildhall Miscellany*, 3 (1971), pp. 242–64.

51. On the readership and distribution of these kinds of pamphlets: M. Spufford, *Small Books and Pleasant Histories* (Cambridge, 1981); R. Tardif, 'The "History" of Robin Hood: A new social context for the texts', in S. Knight and S.W. Mukherjee (eds.), *Words and Worlds: Studies in the Social Role of Verbal Culture* (Sydney, 1983), pp. 130–145; T. Watt, *Cheap Print and Popular Piety, 1550–1640* (Cambridge, 1991).

52. 'London's Praise, or, the Glory of the City' (1685), in H. E. Rollins (ed.), *The Pepys Ballads* 8 vols. (Cambridge, Mass., 1929–1932), vol. 3, pp. 218–22 at pp. 220, 218.

5.

Governors and Governed: The Practice of Power in the Merchant Taylors' Company in the Fifteenth Century

MATTHEW DAVIES

As part of the ceremonial that accompanied the annual election of the master and wardens of the guild of London tailors (known from 1503 as the Merchant Taylors' Company), each of those chosen was required to swear a lengthy admission oath, in which the numerous and weighty responsibilities of their offices were invoked. Central among these was the promise to 'kepe all the good ordenaunces, custumes and usages of the bretherhode and of the crafte which be not revoked and the which have been made by your predecessours byfore your tyme and truly corecte all theym that breke or disobeye the same'.[1] These officers were aided in their task by a body of 24 senior members of the craft, known as the court of assistants, who met together regularly in order to agree new ordinances, to modify or annul old ones, to punish offenders, and to develop mechanisms and policies for the regulation of London's largest craft. This task was by no means straightforward, and the records generated by the court and by the officers of the company in the course of their duties are particularly revealing about the ways in which regulation was carried out in practice. By drawing upon this valuable evidence, this paper seeks to analyse the approach taken by the company to regulation and to chart the varying relationships between the company's governors and those who practiced the craft of tailoring in London in the fifteenth century.

The problem for historians trying to assess the nature of guild regulation is that the surviving records often reveal more about companies' aspirations than actual practice. Ordinances in particular need to be treated with caution when trying to understand the relationships between crafts and their guilds in the medieval and early modern periods. As Michael Sonenscher has noted with reference to the trades of eighteenth-century Paris, regulations were little more than 'cryptic summaries of a number of extended dialogues: between masters and journeymen, between different groups of master artisans, and between journeymen themselves'. Regulations acted as a normative framework within urban crafts. Indeed, they were drafted in the full knowledge that they could never distil work relationships and productive processes into a few statutes.[2] To take a prime example, in London the 'ideal' career path of a craftsman portrayed a smooth transition from apprenticeship to the freedom, and onto eventual membership of the livery of a craft. But, as a number of historians of London's companies have observed, the proportion of apprentices who completed this journey was small: between half and two-thirds of apprentices in fifteenth- and sixteenth-century London failed even to complete their training and either left the city altogether or drifted off into the world of work on the margins of London's economy.[3]

Similar problems of distinguishing 'ideal' from 'reality' face historians attempting to discover the ways in which guilds and their officers regulated their crafts. A common characteristic of many ordinances is that they only survive as later copies, abstracted from their original context into specially commissioned compilations. The function of such books was to ensure that the customs of the craft were given due prominence, both as a source of guidance for officers and as a means to emphasise the continued relevance of these customs and of the authority which was conferred on those who enforced them. A good example of this is a set of ordinances that was included in an illuminated manuscript book compiled by the Merchant Taylors' Company towards the end of the first decade of the sixteenth century. The book begins with an account of what was termed the 'ghostly treasure' of the company, in other words, the spiritual 'assets' it had acquired through benefactions, foundations of chantries and charitable activity. It then turns to more secular matters and provides an account of all the principal ordinances of the craft as they were in 1507, before outlining details of the company's grants of arms and charters, with particular prominence given to the prestigious, though highly controversial, charter obtained from Henry VII in January 1503.[4] Remarkable though this book is, its usefulness as a means of getting to grips with the day-to-day realities of guild regulation is open to question. First, by themselves these ordinances say very little about the process of enforcement, or about the priorities that might have been given to certain regulations at the expense of others. Other sources, such as accounts and court records, need to be used in conjunction with such legislative material if a proper assessment is to be made of the importance ascribed to particular rules and regulations. Secondly, compilations of ordinances rarely reveal much about the dialogues and debates that led to their introduction. This lack of 'context' applies equally to the numerous sets of ordinances that were enrolled before the mayor and aldermen by the crafts in the later fifteenth century, and means that one can deduce little about the wider issues which lay behind the rules and regulations, and the influence of particular economic and political factors.[5]

For the London tailors and their guild, a contrast can be drawn between the lavishly produced ordinance book of the early sixteenth century and an earlier manuscript book, known by the late 1480s as the 'Great Register' of the company. This ran in tandem with separate volumes containing the minutes of the court of assistants and was used for the recording of new ordinances as and when they were agreed. This was much more of a working document, with less importance being placed upon the physical appearance of the book. Unfortunately, only the four central leaves of the Great Register now survive, containing ordinances adopted between 1429 and 1455. The names of those who were present at the court meetings are noted, along with a summary of the reasons why each ordinance was introduced.[6] In 1450, for instance, the court expressed its concern at the difficulty of exercising 'due serche and correccion' upon 'yonge men of the seid mistiere late and newe comen fro theire apprentise hode' who, perhaps deterred by the cost of setting up a more formal business, made garments hidden away in rented attic rooms well away from the scrutiny of the company's wardens. These men were known as 'chamber holders', and in an attempt to regulate their activities, and to prevent them from producing 'untrewe and deceyvable werkmanship', the court of assistants passed an ordinance requiring each of these young freemen to serve as a covenanted servant in the household of a more established freeman. A man who failed to find employment of this kind was, in the words of the ordinance, to 'inhabite hym in the comons amonges other servauntes sowers of the seid mistiere under the good rewle and governaunce of the seid Maister and Wardeins'. More established members of the craft were then to be allowed to employ these men as covenanted servants 'for competent wages by the day or by the garment'. The solution adopted by the company seems to have envisaged the setting up of some kind of 'hiring-hall', of the kind recorded in other European towns and cities in the medieval and early modern periods. The intention, apart from the regulation of quality, was to ensure that there was a ready supply of wage-labour available for those tailors who needed covenanted servants.[7] It is not known whether this rather ambitious proposal was ever put into effect: there are no subsequent references to the plan, and it may in fact have proved impossible to impose upon those young freemen who did not wish to work for wages but preferred to try their luck outside the formalised world of the legitimate workshop. It may also be the case that many established craftsmen preferred to cut costs by drawing their wage labourers from the ranks of London's unenfranchised immigrant population, a practice that was sanctioned by the Tailors for much of the fifteenth century. Some evidence does at least suggest that the wardens of the craft made occasional attempts to locate and fine those who continued to work in their chambers: as late as 1492, for instance, Thomas King was fined 12d 'for kepyng of a chambre contrary to the ordynaunces of this crafte'. The term 'chamber holder' was thus still a very relevant one for the company, and strictures against those who 'use dayly to kepe chambers secretly in alleys and upon steyers & houses in corners and cutte & make almaner of garments' were included among the ordinances of 1507.[8]

What becomes clear from a reading of the fifteenth-century accounts and court minutes of the company, however, is that the activities of 'chamber holders' were not a priority for the masters and wardens, despite the urgency of the language used in the original ordinance of 1450. Rather, the energies of the court and its officials were directed elsewhere, at issues that were felt to be much more pressing. The hundreds of fines extracted from members of the craft in this period, and the matters discussed by the court of assistants, suggest that the company had a keen sense of the areas where intervention was a priority, and those where a more relaxed approach could be allowed to prevail.

Foremost among the concerns of the company was the regulation of access to the formal structures of the craft. This function had been delegated to the livery companies by the city government in the late thirteenth and early fourteenth centuries and given further impetus by the City's charter of 1319 which determined that admission to the freedom could only be obtained through one of the official crafts or 'misteries'.[9] Apprenticeship rapidly became the most popular route to the freedom. To control the numbers of young men who entered the crafts, the companies introduced a variety of measures such as restrictions upon the number of apprentices a master could train at any one time, a move usually welcomed by small-scale producers, and steep rises in enrolment fees. As a result, companies such as the Drapers and Mercers varied their enrolment fees during the fifteenth century, in response to changes in economic circumstances and population pressures.[10] The Tailors, by contrast, left their relatively low enrolment fee of 3s 4d unchanged for many years, a decision which seems to have encouraged the expansion of the craft during the fifteenth century. In the late 1420s, for instance, an average of 60 apprentices were enrolled each year, whereas by the 1460s the numbers had risen to 85, with several peaks of more than 110.[11] This level of recruitment appears to have been tolerated for a while, indicating that opportunities for newly-qualified freemen to establish businesses were not yet being damaged by the increase in numbers. By the mid-1480s, however, there is evidence that the market for tailoring goods in the capital may no longer have been able to sustain this expansion. As a result, the Tailors' court took the momentous decision to increase the enrolment fee from 3s 4d to 20s for freemen, while liverymen were to pay 10s to enrol each of their apprentices. This six-fold increase for freemen appears to have been highly unpopular, and their anger was doubtless increased by the concession granted to liverymen. Little is recorded of the ensuing protests and debates, but by November 1487 the freemen had got their way and a new ordinance was passed which restored the fee back to its former level.[12]

The court may have lost this particular battle, but elsewhere in the minutes there is clear evidence of attempts to reinforce hierarchical values within the company. The relationship between the economic and political fortunes of the craft appears to have been at the heart of another debate, this time over membership of the livery of the craft, the fraternity of St. John the Baptist, one of the most active and important associations of its kind founded in late medieval London. In May 1490 it was reported to the court that some of those admitted to the livery 'have bene in substaunce of goodes as it hath bene supposed' but had since been forced to seek financial assistance from the company as almsmen. Although the court decided not to introduce a property qualification, as some other guilds had done, it was concluded that admissions to the livery should take place less frequently. Exceptions were to be made for any freemen who married the widows of former masters or wardens of the company or those that 'be promoted by maryage of eny other woman oute of the felasship'.[13] Like the rise in the enrolment fees for apprentices, this measure seems to have been a reaction to a long period when admission to the formal structures of the craft was subject to relatively few financial controls. In the case of the liverymen, however, there is a clear implication that the public image of the company would be damaged unless procedures were tightened up.

Similar concerns with company self-presentation can also be discerned in the apparent tightening of control over the association established for freemen outside the ranks of the livery, known by the 1420s as the fraternity of yeomen tailors and from 1488 as the Bachelors' Company. The wardens of the Bachelors were, for instance, increasingly used by the company to collect fines and other payments, and it was usual for the clerk of the company to appear at meetings of the Bachelors to read out ordinances agreed by the court of assistants.[14] These changes occurred at a time when the company was trying to consolidate its position among the greater companies, a group later known as the 'Great Twelve'. In April 1484 a dispute between the Tailors and men of the Skinners' Company had led the mayor, Robert Billesden, to make his famous award allocating sixth place in civic processions to each company in alternate years. The origins of the rivalry are not recorded, but it is likely that it was based primarily upon status rather than specific economic interests. The similarities in structure between the two crafts made them natural rivals for the places behind the great mercantile companies: both were primarily artisan crafts, but in each case mercantile interests were coming to dominate the ranks of the liverymen.[15]

A related concern for the Tailors' Company was the public behaviour of its freemen. At a meeting of the court held in February 1490 it was reported that 'a grete cryme and defamacion renneth upon this fraternytie by cause that sum persones of this felaship excede in ther behavour and demeanyng amonges men of worship and other honest persones and namely at Blakwellhall'. By this time Blackwell Hall had become an important focus for the cloth-dealing activities of members of the company, and the two culprits who were brought before the court were each required to enter into bonds of £10 for their future good behaviour. In many of the entries in the court minutes there is an emphasis upon the need for discipline and appropriate behaviour on the part of members of the craft, and on the importance of dealing with disputes internally as far as possible. In February 1493, for instance, a breach of the City's apprenticeship regulations was deemed so serious by the master that he feared:

> the grete infamy that of lyklyhode myght have growen in tyme to com to the hoole body of the feliship ... if the said matier shuld be publisshed and com to lyght affore the Chambreleyn of this citee and ferther ... affore the mair and aldremen of the same citee.

The culprit himself faced public humiliation by being 'openly shamed with a paper over his hede', labelling him as an 'untrue citezein'.[16]

The records of the court of assistants also reveal the efforts that were made to resolve disputes between company members, whether or not these involved specific breaches of the ordinances. Arbitration was widely used by all the livery companies as a means to resolve conflict. In October 1491 a dispute between Rowland Hymeson and his covenanted servant, John Langryk, was put to arbitration after Langryk had left his master before the end of his one-year contract. The judgement acknowledged the breakdown of the covenant, and made arrangements for the servant to recover his possessions from Hymeson's house on condition that Langryk returned a pair of shears, which he had taken from a stall belonging to his former master, and paid 10s compensation for leaving his service early. The language used on such occasions was designed to promote reconciliation, or at least avoid further conflict: in February 1490 Thomas Ethell and John Copelond were required to 'take the other of them by the hande and to desyre that good love may be had bytwene them from hensforth'. Every effort was made to stamp the authority of the court upon judgements and to heighten the solemnity of proceedings at the Hall and elsewhere. Great emphasis was placed upon the principles of brotherhood and mutual obligation which underpinned membership of a craft fraternity: the status of liveryman within the Tailors' Company derived from membership of the fraternity of St. John the Baptist.[17] There were occasions, however, when the religious dimension to the arbitration process had to be underlined still further: during one particularly serious dispute the parties were required to go to the church of St. Thomas of Acon between 8 and 9 in the morning to put their cases to the arbiters.[18]

It is difficult to determine how permanent these settlements were. What can be said from the evidence of the court minutes is that very few disputes appear to have flared up again in the lifetime of the surviving records, which perhaps testifies to the effectiveness of the sanctions at the court's disposal. There are, however, several examples of cases that proved difficult to resolve from the start and tested the will of the court to its limits. The main cause of difficulties was the perennial problem of what to do when one or both of the parties were former masters or court members. The first step was to ensure that the arbiters were at least as important as those involved: Walter Povey, a former master of the company, was involved in a dispute with a draper, John Stokes, during the course of which he hit Stokes and knocked out two of his teeth. Both Povey and Stokes agreed to abide by the arbitration of two senior court members and in due course Povey was found to be the main culprit and required to pay 10s damages.[19]

The dispute between Povey and Stokes illustrates how such cases were supposed to proceed, but in the autumn of 1492 the clerk wrote a long account of a dispute that escalated into open rebellion against the authority of the court. The man at the centre of events was John Heed, master of the company in 1483–4, whose dispute with John Darby over an apprentice was heard before a meeting of the court at which they were permitted to cross-examine each other. Heed accused Darby of lying 'falsely lyke a false harlot', to which Darby replied, seizing the moral high ground, 'Sir I note and remembre in what place and whose presence that I am in. And if I were in an other place ... I wold speke as playne Englissh unto you as ye have don unto me'. The only option was to appoint arbiters, but the choice of two relatively junior assistants, neither of whom had served as master, was a mistake, for John Heed simply refused to meet them. The deadline for a settlement passed, and the master, Povey, appointed new arbiters, with Stephen Jenyns, a future master and Lord Mayor, to oversee them. This time Heed announced that he would 'seale none obligacion for none horemonger' and he was duly summoned to the Hall to explain himself. Heed's principal objection was to Jenyns, whom he alleged 'had caused hym to lose xxxvij *li.* [£37]'. The master's final option was to take over the role himself: 'Sir I most be your juge this yere', to which Heed, alluding to his own period in office 'made grete comparisons with the Maister as beyng charge in the crafte'. At this point the master seems to have lost his temper, and declared that it was a pity that Heed had ever been chosen as master; Heed replied that the master himself was far from being a popular choice. In a final effort to persuade Heed to back down, the master read out some of the ordinances of the craft, a move that was deliberately designed both to de-personalise the conflict between the two men and to emphasise the way in which the ordinances embodied the collective will of the company, mediated through precedent and tradition. He then asked Heed formally if he would obey them. Heed's answer was unequivocal: 'Sir, I know thise ordynaunces as well as ye do but I wole not abide nor fulfill theym'. At this point the master had no alternative but to submit the problem to the mayor who promptly sent Heed to prison for 5 days. On his release Heed was apparently a changed man, immediately apologising for his outbursts and agreeing to accept the arbitration of his fellow court members.[20]

This was an unusual case, given exceptional treatment by the clerk who recognised the seriousness of the challenge to the master and the court and the need to record such events in the corporate memory of the company. In general the authority of the court seems to have been respected by those brought before it, and only a very few cases had to be taken before the mayor of the city. Like ordinances, however, the court minutes have their problems, not the least of which is their preoccupation with formal structures and relationships, such as apprenticeship and the behaviour of freemen. As a result the minutes can often create a rather distorted impression of the control which the company and its officers exercised over the wide range of people who worked in the tailoring industry in London, and the degree of harmony which existed within the craft. Other sources can help to redress this imbalance, notably the accounts of the company which record the fines levied by the wardens of the craft in this period. From these it is clear that the wardens often had a clear set of priorities when it came to enforcement, and were prepared to engage with issues and debates within the tailoring industry in London that extended beyond the formalised world of work portrayed in guild ordinances.

Of particular concern for the Tailors, and for many of the other companies in London, were the activities of non-freemen, very often immigrants into the city from elsewhere in England ('foreigns'), or from other countries ('aliens'). Of the latter, migrants from northern Europe were especially prominent within the garment industry in the capital, but relatively few ever became freemen.[21] The Tailors, though able to make a distinction between English and foreign-born strangers, generally referred to all of them as 'foreigns'. The company at first adopted a flexible approach to these men and their families by allowing them to set up their own tailoring businesses as long as they confined their work to the refurbishment and retailing of old clothes. When seen in the context of the expansion of the 'formal' side of the craft in the middle decades of the fifteenth century, this policy implies that for the moment there was enough new work to go around.[22] The company made great efforts to enforce the distinction between these workers, known as 'botchers', and the freemen of the craft who were allowed to make new clothing. A large number of fines were collected, indicating that regulation of the botchers had become one of the chief priorities for the wardens and the officials of the company, as well as a useful source of revenue. Examples abound of botchers who were discovered making new clothes: men were fined 'pur faisur dun kertel', 'dun nove doublet', 'pur j peticote of new russet coton', and 'pur un dagged goun', in other words for making just about every kind of new clothing.[23] The wardens were persistent: on one occasion 'un englisch forein' was fined 20*d*, which was increased by a further two shillings when they found that he had carried on making new clothes regardless.[24] The search for foreigns and the inspection of their work came to occupy a significant amount of company time and expense: in 1429–30 the sum of 13*s* 4*d* was spent 'on various occasions for the searches of the craft and other men for warning of the labour of foreigns'. Many of these craftsmen lived alone, but others had evidently established small workshops together: on one occasion the wardens discovered a group of men who 'occupied this craft in the Dragon Inn by the Great Wardrobe'. The location may well be significant in that the Wardrobe was a liberty which lay outside the jurisdiction of the guilds and as a consequence skilled, unfree craftsmen may have chosen to live in the vicinity in the hope of finding employment opportunities denied to them elsewhere in the city.[25]

The distinction between the work that free and un-free tailors in London could undertake combined concerns about the perceived threat to the businesses of freemen with consumer protection. Ordinances forbidding the mixing of old and new materials were common among London's crafts: the Skinners in 1365, for instance, had barred their freemen from mixing old and new furs, and had even tried to prevent those who worked on new furs from trading in the second-hand skins in case they were even suspected of mixing them.[26] The Tailors' interest in the botchers was thus also a way of regulating the way in which garments were refurbished: in 1425–6, for example, a botcher was fined 2s for adding a lining of 'nove bokeram' to an old gown.[27] The activities of these men remained a priority for the company throughout the fifteenth century: in February 1488 John Williamson, botcher, was fined 20d 'for making new work', while in January the following year Herman Wilde managed to escape with a fine of 4d for a similar offence. By this time, however, this tactic of sacrificing one market to preserve another was ceasing to work. The division of the craft into new and old work, to be done by freemen and non-freemen respectively, depended ultimately upon the company being satisfied that it could afford to leave the market in second-hand clothes to non-members. However, in April 1518, less than a year after the anti-alien rioting and looting of 'Evil May Day', the company was forced to reconsider its attitude towards the second-hand garment trade in London. A formal complaint was made to the city government, not only about the numbers of botchers who continued to make new clothing, but also about the plight of older freemen tailors who, perhaps due to failing eyesight or infirmity, were no longer capable of making new clothes and were 'fain to fall to the said feat of botching' in order to make a living.[28]

The change in attitude on the part of the Tailors was part of a wider re-assessment of the role of foreigns within London's crafts towards the end of the fifteenth century, a period when London's population was beginning to expand again after a long period of stagnation. The problem was recognised by a statute passed by Parliament in 1484 that drew attention to the difficulties posed by skilled alien craftsmen arriving 'in greate noumbre and more than they have used to doo in daies passed'. Its measures included a ban on the employment of aliens by fellow aliens, and on aliens exercising any craft unless they were in the employ of subjects of the king, but these were clearly almost impossible to enforce.[29] The companies increasingly brought their concerns before the court of aldermen in London, and their petitions reveal a heightened level of anxiety about the lack of opportunities for freemen in the city, even for those who wanted to become covenanted servants prior to setting up shops on their own. Many established freemen, it transpired, employed aliens and other strangers in preference to the more expensive former apprentices from their own company. [30]

Like their role in the second-hand trade, the employment of foreigns as servants became an increasingly important issue for the Tailors. The practice had been sanctioned by the company for many years: hefty fees were charged for employing foreigns, but many freemen were prepared to pay these charges in order to have access to a cheap labour force with little or no rights of appeal to the company's court. It may also have been the case, as we have seen, that at a time when the craft was expanding many young freemen preferred to set up businesses in attics rather than become covenanted servants. [31] By the 1480s, however, things had changed, and the Tailors joined several other companies in responding to the changing labour market and to pressure from below for the interests of newly-qualified craftsmen to be safeguarded. The Tailors sent delegations to the mayor in September 1489, July 1492, and finally in April 1493, and on the latter occasion, according to the court minutes, they proposed a bill 'for the reformacion of all foreyns that they hereafter worke with no freman and citezein of this citee'. [32] By this point the company had already introduced its own restrictions on the employment of foreigns, in contrast to the more relaxed approach it had adopted previously. In the autumn of 1492 fines ranging from 4*d* to 5*s* were collected from fourteen tailors who were found to have 'sette foreyns awerke contrary to thordynaunces made therfore'. For good measure the court also fined a foreign named Peter for 'shapyng' a doublet. [33] Not all attempts to enforce these new regulations went smoothly: in December the same year the beadle of the company was sent to the house of William Tetford, to seize goods to the value of a fine imposed on him for employing a foreign. Tetford refused to cooperate and 'rebuked the said Bedell and called hym carle [*i.e.* churl] and manassed hym seiyng that he wold sette his heres on the poste at his shop dore ... if the said Bedell toke any distresse there'. His threats were reported back to the master who promptly asked the mayor to intervene, and Tetford was duly imprisoned 'unto such tyme that he knew and sobred hym self better and submytted hymself unto the M[aster] and wardeyns and to the good rules of the crafte'. On another occasion the court of assistants was subjected to the outspoken views of William Gerveys, who claimed that some members of the court itself were 'gretter maytayners of foreyns' that he ever was. [34]

The debates and changes of policy which took place concerning the role of non-freemen within the craft illustrates the way in which enforcement of ordinances was frequently directed at the interface between what one might term the 'formal' and 'informal' worlds of work in London. The success, or lack of it, of the Tailors' efforts to regulate the activities of aliens and other strangers is difficult to measure. All that we can conclude is that this was one area where the company took great pains to intervene, with tangible results in the form of fines levied on recalcitrant workers. The company also prioritised other working practices, although in a less systematic way, giving some indication of the areas of the craft in which intervention was attempted. One of the powers delegated to craft officials by urban governments, for instance, was the enforcement of prohibitions on working on Sundays and feast days. The evidence from the Tailors' records suggests that the wardens took this public duty seriously, a stance which fitted well with the religious impulses and language which underpinned many of the activities of craft organisations. The wardens did, for instance, collect a large number of fines 'pur Sonday', 'pur Whitsonday' and for other holy days, although it is interesting that fewer fines were collected from the 1440s and 1450s onwards.[35]

When it came to the production and retailing of goods, company intervention appears to have been directed towards specific offences. Most striking were fines for breaching regulations concerning the use and sale of cloth, an indication of the extent to which members of the craft were becoming involved in the domestic, and later the international, trade in this commodity.[36] Especially noticeable is a focus upon the quality of cloth that tailors were buying and selling: a number of fines refer to cloth that was sold 'unwet', a term which probably meant that it had not been fulled properly. In 1427–8, for example, two tailors were fined 20*d* and 10*s* respectively 'pur sellyng kendale unwet et autres draps'. Many similar offences were uncovered by the wardens in the years which followed: in 1463–4 John West was found with 'una pecia de unwet cloth' in his house by the wardens, who endured a torrent of 'verbis inhonestis' when they attempted to search the premises.[37] Those tailors who were not directly involved in cloth-dealing were nevertheless able to supplement their income by selling off-cuts of material left over after making garments. A ready market existed for these small pieces of cloth among purse-makers, cappers and hosiers, and the trade provided a means for tailors to maximise the revenue from a piece of cloth. Despite this the Tailors' Company seems to have frowned upon this activity, perhaps because the quality of the cloth could not easily be monitored, and so those who were caught selling off-cuts were punished. In 1427–8 Robert Brown and Richard Atkins were fined 2*s* 4*d* and 3*s* 4*d* respectively for 'sellyng de shredes'.[38]

The stated purpose of much of the legislation on guilds, and of the periodic searches conducted by their officials, was to ensure that the quality of the goods produced reached certain minimum standards. The emphasis upon quality is, however, easier to document in the legislation itself than in the way in which it was enforced. The reference in 1450 to the need to prevent 'untrewe and deceyvable werkmanship' was an admirable ambition, but how successfully could this be achieved? A number of ordinances enforced by the Tailors, as indeed by other companies, directly or indirectly sought to maintain the quality of goods that were produced. Prohibitions on working in attics or alleyways were introduced for a variety of reasons, with the inspection of workmanship often singled out as the most important; restrictions upon the hours worked by craftsmen, their servants and apprentices were implemented 'by reason that no man can work so neatly by night as by day'. In the case of the Tailors, the mixing of new and old materials and hence the defrauding of the customer was linked with the need to keep a watchful eye upon the activities of 'foreigns'.[39] Yet despite the rhetorical prominence of standards of production, there is remarkably little evidence to show that the Tailors' Company was as interested in punishing those who produced faulty goods as it was in preserving opportunities for its freemen. A rare example occurs in the accounts of the company for 1436–7 when Robert Simond and three other men were fined 6s 8d each 'pur jackes faitz unsuffisauntly'. The only concerted effort that the company made during the fifteenth century was related more to changing styles than to quality, and came in response to the sumptuary legislation of 1463 that forbade the wearing and manufacture of what were seen as indecently short doublets. The following year the company dutifully fined seven tailors for making such garments, but it is likely that this was little more than a token gesture of compliance. No further fines are recorded, and evidence from other companies suggests that there was little enthusiasm for enforcing sumptuary laws among manufacturers when this might adversely affect their economic fortunes. The Tailors' Company, like the Cordwainers and others, appears to have been able to square its emphasis upon moral regulation with a pragmatic assessment of the nature of the market for apparel. Vindication of their approach came in 1483 when a subsequent Act removed the penalties imposed on tailors for making such goods.[40]

A more general explanation for the company's apparently relaxed approach to quality-control may perhaps be found in the wider network of relationships between tailors, their customers and the guild and city authorities. In the first place, the goods produced by tailors ranged widely from the refurbished clothes discussed earlier to the finery supplied to the households of the King and the nobility. Sumptuary legislation and satirical references to styles of clothing merely drew attention to the extent to which product differentiation operated within the garment industry. As the early fifteenth-century poet, Thomas Hoccleve wrote:

> Som tyme, afer men myghten lordes know
> By there array, from other folke; but now
> A man schal stody and musen a long throwe
> Whiche is whiche: O lordes it sit to yowe
> Amende this for it is youre prowe
> If twixt you and youre men no difference
> Be in array, lesse is youre reverence.[41]

In theory at least, most customers, especially in London, would have been able to locate a shop selling clothing of a quality that he or she could afford. In terms of the market for goods this meant that there were in effect many different 'standards' in operation, and even work below the company's own minimum standard would doubtless have found some customers. At the bottom end of the market much clearly depended upon the willingness of the company to intervene, but as we have seen the Tailors seem to have been remarkably unenthusiastic about doing so.[42] Those customers who were not satisfied had two options: they could complain to the city authorities or the relevant guild, or they could simply take their business elsewhere. The evidence from London suggests that many customers were prepared to sue their suppliers in the city courts, although usually it was because the goods they had commissioned had failed to materialise. In Exeter, although apparently not in London, the guild of tailors even acted as a forum for hearing complaints from customers unhappy about the service they had received.[43]

Away from the formal environment of the courts, customers were themselves far from naïve. In a period when garment construction was becoming more and more complex, customers often seem to have brought along their own cloth to be made up by tailors. This kept the cost under control and prevented the tailor from exaggerating the amount of cloth that would be needed or charging an excessive amount for each yard of material.[44] In London, moreover, the large size of the craft meant that there was plenty of scope for competition between workshops. Price, one possible area where competition might have taken place, was often strictly regulated by urban governments: in 1350, for example, the City laid down the prices to be charged by tailors for various items of clothing, ranging from 4d for a pair of sleeves to 2s 6d for an elaborate woman's gown. Controls over the prices of goods and labour were especially important to combat the effects of depopulation from 1348–9 onwards, but throughout the Middle Ages and beyond the concept of the 'just price' meant that town governments periodically intervened to prevent excessive charging. The prices of foodstuffs and fuel were naturally subject to particularly close scrutiny, but consumer goods were not immune from these regulations.[45] In many instances, therefore, the relationship between price, the quality of the goods sold and the reputation of the craftsman lay at the heart of competition between workshops, and this combination of factors led customers to chose to patronise one shop rather than another. In a late fifteenth-century petition to Chancery, a London tailor named William Nicolson complained that he had been falsely accused by another tailor, William Geffrey, of stealing away the latter's customers. Nicolson declared that he 'never procured eny man to bryng hym werk but hadde resonable occupacion as a taillour by meanes of there own free will by reason of his demeanyng and his old aquaintance which shall be proved of good disposition'.[46] Such words must, of course, be treated with caution given the exaggeration common in the evidence presented to Chancery and other courts. Nevertheless, it would be wrong to ignore evidence that attests to the importance of intangible factors such as a craftsman's 'reputation' and the power of the consumer, and indeed it is possible that the interplay between these factors might in some cases have lessened the threat of external regulation by the companies.[47]

The court of the Tailors' Company was well aware of the nature of relations between tailors and their customers and was naturally sensitive to any slurs upon the craft's good name. Caricatures abounded of scheming craftsmen in satirical literature, and occasionally echoes of these images can be found in other sources. Writing at the end of the fourteenth century, for instance, the author of the satirical poem 'Richard the Redeles' asserted that among the tailors in the court milieu

> ther is a profitt in that pride / that I preise evere
> For thei for the pesinge / paieth pens ten duble
> That the cloth costened / the craft is so dere.[48]

Almost a century later the same sentiments were echoed in an inflammatory sermon delivered by a preacher at the church of St. Thomas of Acon in the spring of 1493, the content of which was reported to the Tailors' court. The preacher, it was alleged, had 'shewed openly affore a grete audience that many and divers taillours of this citee... be worsse extorcioners than they that lye in a wayte by a high wey side in robbyng and spoillyng the kynges liege people'. The court responded by sending a delegation of senior liverymen to reason with the preacher, perhaps in the hope of persuading him to take back his accusations in his next sermon.[49]

As well as caring about its image among customers and the great and the good of the city, the evidence from the records of the Merchant Taylors suggests that the company had a clear sense of its priorities as far as the regulation of the craft was concerned. The formal structures of the craft such as apprenticeship, admission to the freedom and to the livery, were natural places where the company could intervene to maintain the status of its members and preserve economic opportunities. The perceived limitations of this strategy are made clear by the emphasis elsewhere upon the activities of those outside the ranks of the freemen, who posed a much greater threat to the businesses of London tailors. In the case of aliens and other strangers to London a flexible and pragmatic approach was adopted, with the company at first emphasising co-existence, albeit under strict conditions, before having to retreat towards the end of the fifteenth century to a position of outright opposition, perhaps prompted by pressure from its younger freemen. In other areas, notably quality-control, the role of the company seems to have been much more limited, with the consumer almost certainly playing a greater part than the evidence of fines and ordinances would suggest.

NOTES
1. A Book of Oaths compiled in 1491 survives as GL, Merchant Taylors' Company, Anc. MS Bk. 1, f. 1.
2. M. Sonenscher, *Work and Wages. Natural Law, Politics and the Eighteenth Century French Trades* (Cambridge, 1989), p. 99. See also G. Rosser, 'Crafts, Guilds and the Negotiation of Work in the Medieval Town', *Past and Present*, 154 (1997), pp. 3–31.
3. M. P. Davies, 'The Tailors of London and their Guild, *c.*1300–1500' (unpublished D.Phil. thesis, University of Oxford, 1994), p. 195; J. Imray, '"Les Bones Gentes de la Mercerye de Londres": a study of the membership of the Medieval Mercers' Company', in A.E.J. Hollaender and W. Kellaway (eds.), *Studies in London History Presented to P.E. Jones* (London, 1969), pp. 155–78. For completion rates in the sixteenth century, see S. Rappaport, *Worlds Within Worlds: Structures of Life in Sixteenth Century London* (Cambridge, 1989), pp. 394–5; I. K. Ben-Amos, 'Failure to become freemen: urban apprentices in early modern England', *Social History*, 16 (1991), pp. 155–72.
4. GL, Merchant Taylors' Company, Anc. MS. Bk. 2. For the controversy caused by the charter, see H. Miller, 'London and Parliament in the Reign of Henry VIII', *BIHR*, 35 (1962), pp. 128–49.
5. For these ordinances, see R. R. Sharpe (ed.), *Calendar of the Letter Books preserved among the Archives of the Corporation of the City of London*, 11 vols (A–L) (London, 1899–1912), Book L, *passim*.
6. GL, Merchant Taylors' Company, Anc. MS. Bk. 9.
7. GL, Merchant Taylors' Company, Anc. MS. Bk. 9, f. 10; Davies, 'The Tailors of London', pp. 211–12; B. Geremek, *Le Salariat dans l'artisanat Parisien au xiiie–xve siècles* (Paris, 1982), pp. 126–9; Sonenscher, *Work and Wages*, p. 169.
8. The bulk of the 1507 ordinances, including these provisions, were incorporated into those approved by James I in 1613: C. M. Clode (ed.), *Memorials of the Merchant Taylors' Company* (London, 1875), p. 211.
9. See A. F. Sutton, 'The Silent Years of London Guild History before 1300: the Case of the Mercers', *Historical Research*, 71 no. 175 (1998), pp. 121–41.
10. These and other issues relating to apprenticeship are discussed by Stephanie Hovland in her forthcoming London University Ph.D. thesis, 'Apprenticeship in London *c.*1450–*c.*1520', chapter 3.
11. GL, Merchant Taylors' Company accts. i–iii; Davies, 'The Tailors of London', pp. 187, 215.
12. M. Davies (ed.), *The Merchant Taylors' Company of London: Court Minutes 1486–1493* (Stamford, 2000) pp. 31–2.
13. Davies, *Court Minutes*, pp. 158–9.
14. Davies, *Court Minutes*, pp. 24–5. For the relationship between livery and yeomanry in the later sixteenth century see I. W. Archer, *The Pursuit of Stability: Social Relations in Elizabethan London* (Cambridge, 1991), pp. 108–10.
15. CLRO, Journals, 9, ff. 50v–51; Sharpe, *Calendar of Letter Books*, Book L, p. 212. For the Skinners, see E. M. Veale, *The English Fur Trade in the Later Middle Ages* (Oxford, 1966), pp. 121–5.
16. Davies, *Court Minutes*, pp. 150, 237.
17. See M. Davies, 'The Tailors of London: Corporate Charity in the Late-Medieval Town', in R. E. Archer (ed.), *Crown, Government and People in the Fifteenth Century* (Stroud, 1995), pp. 164–9.
18. Davies, *Court Minutes*, pp. 152, 190, 207.
19. Davies, *Court Minutes*, p. 177.
20. Davies, *Court Minutes*, pp. 207–10.
21. See J. L. Bolton (ed.), *Alien Communities in London in the Fifteenth Century: The Subsidy Rolls of 1440 and 1483–4* (Stamford, 1998), esp. pp. 19–23, 136, 141.

22. For estimates of the size of the craft see Davies, 'The Tailors of London', pp. 219–21.

23. GL, Merchant Taylors' Company accts., i, ff. 244, 255v. It is probable that the term 'botcher' had already taken on derogatory connotations, although the Tailors do not seem to have used it in this way.

24. GL, Merchant Taylors' Company accts., i, f. 235.

25. GL, Merchant Taylors' Company accts., i, f. 207v; ii, f. 33.

26. H.T. Riley (ed.), *Memorials of London and London Life in the XIIIth, XIVth and XVth centuries* (London, 1868), p. 328; Veale, *Fur Trade*, p. 123.

27. GL, Merchant Taylors' Company accts., i, f. 159.

28. CLRO, Journals, 11, ff. 336–336v.

29. Bolton, *Aliens*, pp. 35–40; *Statutes of the Realm* (1101–1713) (London, 1810–28), vol. 2, pp. 489–93.

30. M. Davies, 'Artisans, Guilds and Government in London', in R. H. Britnell (ed.), *Daily Life in the Late Middle Ages* (Stroud, 1998), pp. 145–6; Sharpe, *Calendar of Letter Books*, Book L, pp. 2, 10–11, 254, 256–7, 295, 302.

31. GL, Merchant Taylors' Company accts., i–ii, *passim*.

32. Davies, *Court Minutes*, pp. 139, 200, 243.

33. Davies, *Court Minutes*, p. 226.

34. Davies, *Court Minutes*, pp. 229, 257.

35. GL, Merchant Taylors' Company accts., i–ii, *passim*. For this subject see B. F. Harvey, 'Work and *Festa Ferianda*', *Journal of Ecclesiastical History*, 23 (1972), pp. 289–308.

36. Davies, 'The Tailors of London', pp. 245–50. A bitter dispute between the company and the Drapers had occurred in the late 1430s and early 1440s after a charter granted to the Tailors allowed them rights of search at St. Bartholomew's fair: C. M. Barron, 'Ralph Holland and the London Radicals, 1438–1444', in R. Holt and G. Rosser (eds.), *The Medieval Town: A Reader in English Urban History 1200–1540* (London, 1990), pp. 160–83.

37. GL, Merchant Taylors' Company accts., i, f. 181v; ii, f. 242v. This suggests that tailors were buying up unfinished cloth, presumably in the hope that they would save money either by sub-contracting the finishing work to their own fullers and shearmen or, as it appears from these examples, simply selling the cloth on at a profit.

38. H. Swanson, *Medieval Artisans: An Urban Class in Late Medieval England* (Oxford, 1989), p. 47; GL, Merchant Taylors' Company accts., i, f. 181v. Such off-cuts were used for the manufacture of purses found in excavations in London: E. Crowfoot, F. Pritchard and K. Staniland (eds.), *Textiles and Clothing c.1150–c.1450. Medieval Finds from Excavations in London: 4* (London, 1992), pp. 176–7.

39. Riley, *Memorials*, pp. 226, 243.

40. GL, Merchant Taylors' Company accts., i, f. 278; ii, f 242v; *Statutes of the Realm*, vol. 2, pp. 399–402; A. F. Sutton, 'Order and Fashion in Clothes: the King, his Household, and the City of London at the end of the Fifteenth Century', *Textile History*, 22 (1991), pp. 269–70.

41. F. J. Furnivall (ed.), *Hoccleve's Works III. The Regement of Princes*, Early English Text Society, extra series, 72 (London, 1897), p.17, lines 442–8.

42. For the role of product differentiation in stimulating consumption see, for example, J. Thirsk, *Economic Projects: the Development of a Consumer Society in Early Modern England* (Oxford, 1978), pp. 130–1.

43. Riley, *Memorials, passim*; T. Smith (ed.), *English Gilds*, Early English Text Society, original series, 40 (London, 1870), p. 321.

44. Davies, 'The Tailors of London', pp. 243–4; Smith, *English Gilds*, pp. 321–3. For the changing fashions see S. M. Newton, *Fashion in the Age of the Black Prince* (Woodbridge, 1984) and M. Scott, *The Fourteenth and Fifteenth Centuries: A Visual History of Costume* (London, 1986).

45. Riley, *Memorials*, p. 254. On this subject see R. de Roover, 'The Concept of the Just Price: Theory and Economic Policy', *Journal of Economic History*, 18 (1958), pp. 418–34; M. Benbow, 'The Court of Aldermen and the Assizes: the Policy of Price Control in Elizabethan London', *Guildhall Studies in London History*, 4 (1980), pp. 93–118.

46. PRO, C1/78/5.

47. S. A. Epstein, *Wage Labor and the Guilds in Medieval Europe* (Chapel Hill and London, 1991), pp. 124–9. On guilds and the operation of the market see, for instance, B. Gustafsson, 'The Rise and Economic Behaviour of Medieval Craft Guilds: An Economic-Theoretical Interpretation', *Scandanavian Economic History Review*, 35 (1987), pp. 1–40.

48. M. Day and R. Steele (eds.), *Mum and the Sothsegger*, Early English Text Society, 199 (Oxford, 1936), p. 17, lines 167–9.

49. Davies, *Court Minutes*, pp. 243–4.

6.

Controlling Commodities: Search and Reconciliation in the Early Modern Livery Companies

PATRICK WALLIS

On 23 August 1645 the wardens of the Goldsmiths' Company went on search. After seizing bad wares from around London, they came to the shop of one William Walton in which they found 4 belts with suspect silver buckles. When the wardens tried to take the belts, Walton refused to allow them, saying 'noe man should meddle' with goods he had paid for; even when a constable was called to carry him before the lord mayor for 'affronting...the Company in such a high nature', Walton did not back down. Then, when one of the wardens attempted to take the items a second time 'by virtue of their Charter' and his office, Walton 'in a most high and contemptible manner' forced them with 'great violence' from the warden. As the company's minutes later put it, Walton

> lifted up his hand against him [the Warden], and shouldered him up against the wall, and would have endeavoured to have kept soe many of the Company prisoners in his shop as was there, notwithstanding the constable being present.

Despite this unruly and violent behaviour, the constable refused to 'meddle' with the belts unless Walton would expressly order him to carry them to the Goldsmiths' Hall. Eventually, however, the wardens managed to get the belts away. Outraged by his great contempt of their authority, the Goldsmiths' court of assistants summoned Walton to their hall. After ignoring their summonses for five months, he finally appeared before the Court in January 1646. When told that his buckles were bad, he disagreed, but was largely indifferent to the fine 'sayeing the workman [who had sold him the belts] should make him satisfaccion for it'. Questioned further on his behaviour, he again denied any offence, at which the Court informed him that 'it was a great offence' and he should confess, be sorry and pay a fine. Walton – having withdrawn for a while to think – then 'freely and willingly submitted himself to a fine' of 50s, and later agreed with the Court not to seek recompense from the workman. In return he was given back 20s of his fine: 'he was very thankfull for the same, promising not to offend in the like againe'.[1]

How did company regulation of crafts and trades work in early-modern London? This issue has long been at the heart of debates on guilds and companies across Europe.[2] The ability of companies to regulate and discipline their members and restrict who practised their trade is central to interpretations of their economic and social impact, while their failure – or not – to do so is an important part of discussions of their 'decline'.[3] The details of the ordinances through which companies governed the manufacture, sale and distribution of the commodities and services for which they were responsible, the binding or hiring and treatment of apprentices and journeymen, and their own internal organisation are easily available, and historians have all too frequently mistaken them as indications of what guilds actually did. However, it has become increasingly clear that it is problematic to take ordinances as anything more than nominal guides to the ideals and aspirations of towns and companies.[4] Instead, as Sosson and Davies have insisted, we must seek to understand how they were understood and implemented on a day-to-day basis.

In the case of William Walton it would seem, at first glance, that the formidable powers laid out in the ordinances of the Goldsmiths' Company were strikingly ineffectual in practice. Admittedly, the Goldsmiths' troubles in this instance were unusually severe; most offenders did not offer such resistance. Indeed, it is only because of Walton's obstinate resistance that we have such a full recording of these events in the company's court minutes. However, despite its relative singularity, this case usefully highlights a number of common features of the efforts made by early-modern livery companies to regulate their crafts and community: the weaknesses of company officers; their necessary but uncertain reliance on external authority; the negotiations and compromise involved in punishment; and their emphasis on apology and submission. A system of policing that manifests such features might seem inherently bankrupt, but before we leap to any conclusion about the worthlessness of company regulation, we need to examine the events in Walton's case in the light of contemporary behaviour in other arenas of policing, crime and litigation.

Despite the fact that the policing of trade and manufacture was a major concern of city and national government, the commercial world has largely been ignored by historians of law and crime in this period. Here, I wish to argue that to understand the manner in which companies executed their duties we need to locate them in a wider context of contemporary approaches to law and order. In companies' minutes of search and punishment, as much as in the records of the Quarter Sessions, we can discern the marks of a culture in which, as Robert Shoemaker has suggested, the punishment of misdemeanours operated in 'instrumental terms', aiming not at punitive or arbitrary justice but at regulating and defining appropriate behaviour and securing compensation.[5] Companies' actions are best understood as attempts to reform present and future behaviour and to reintegrate offenders, all of which relied on a broad range of interventions and sanctions; final judgements and heavy punishments were pursued only when the dialogue between offender and court broke down. This allowed more flexible and diverse forms of economic behaviour (and misbehaviour) than the ordinances might suggest. In part this was a pragmatic retreat in the face of both the commercial realities of early-modern London and the political uncertainties that frequently surrounded company authority. But it also reflected the ongoing importance within corporate life of an idiom of fraternity marked by compassion, confession and forgiveness, and the importance of the longer-term prospects and attitudes of freemen for companies engaged in charitable relief and dependent on fees, quarterage and gifts for their funds.[6] Interpretations which judge company regulation as either strong or weak are therefore somewhat misleading, and ignore the subtleties of contemporary approaches to policing behaviour – be it in the marketplace, workshop or elsewhere. This is not to suggest that companies' internal efforts to control their members' behaviour could not still fail. Negotiation and accommodation were only tenable strategies as part of an ongoing process of regulation, and when this broke down the limits of companies' powers could be exposed. How companies dealt with their weakness in the face of resistance raises the question of their relationships with other authorities in the city and country, and the implications this had for their regulatory autonomy and internal coherence.

Describing the process of enforcement is a difficult task. In particular, we are hampered by the lack of a distinct documentary record. In contrast to the discrete and formulaic legal documents that have allowed historians of crime to embark on long and thorough statistical analyses, in order to study ordinance-breaking we have to rely on cases described in vastly varying amounts of detail that appear intermittently among the everyday business noted in companies' court minutes. To overcome some of these problems, in the first section of this essay I discuss the common forms of policing and punishment in a range of companies, concentrating on the late sixteenth and early seventeenth centuries. This survey is balanced in the second half of this essay by a more detailed analysis of the profile of offending in two companies, the Stationers and Apothecaries. The period discussed here can be seen as a relative high-point for the London companies: their membership as a proportion of those living in the metropolis was still very high; the city, while growing, had not yet developed the massive suburban areas beyond the walls that began to cripple late seventeenth-century urban regulation; and, as the Stuart proliferation of new incorporations suggests, the crown and city continued to support and expect action by companies. It is important therefore to emphasise at the outset that the structures and practises I touch on here were not consistent between companies, and they changed over time as religious practice, business forms, the size and fortunes of trade and other factors shifted. However, I seek here to outline a system which, despite these particular differences, was largely codified by custom and imitation into a form that would be recognisable to most freemen of early-modern London.

I

How were offences uncovered and dealt with by companies? The main features of corporate policing in this period are reasonably well known.[7] To uncover the majority of offences in the marketplace and workshop, London companies relied on the process of search, a periodic perambulation to inspect shops and workplaces, which they supplemented with information from other freemen and complaints from customers and civic officials. Search was generally carried out by company officers, sometimes with the assistance of expert craftsmen to judge the quality of workmanship found. While in practice searches might be infrequent, as artisan petitions often complained, it has recently been shown that the extent and regularity of search was more wide-ranging within and beyond the walls of the City than has often been thought.[8] It is still difficult, however, to assess the regularity and efficiency with which search was carried out, as company minutes often only record information about particularly recalcitrant offenders.[9]

Those found or suspected of committing offences were generally summoned to a meeting of the companies' court of assistants, where they would be examined by the master and wardens, their guilt judged and punishments set. Company ordinances and charters generally provided for courts of assistants to fine miscreants and publicly destroy any goods found to be faulty. In practice, as in other judicial arenas, punishment was shot through with discretion and companies rarely exercised the full extent of their powers.[10] Some offenders were simply ordered to stop misbehaving, either by not working in a defective manner again or by 'putting away' an illegally-kept apprentice or journeyman. If a stronger course of action was thought necessary, fines ranging from a few shillings to many pounds were the main form of punishment utilised. Alternative measures were also employed. Bonds, for instance, could be used to restrain offenders: in 1572 the Grocers ordered that comfit makers should enter recognizances for £20 to ensure they used clean sugar.[11] Other punishments reflected the concerns of specific companies. The Goldsmiths, for example, deprived members of access to the 'assay and touch' (the hallmarking process). Companies also occasionally utilised shaming punishments, such as ritually stripping an offender of his livery gown or, in an echo of a popular measure against cuckolds, riding them through the marketplace seated backward on a horse.[12] At least for freemen, physical punishment was apparently rare. The Goldsmiths placed John Brooke, a workman, in the stocks with the bowls he had deceitfully manufactured hanging around his neck, but more commonly corporal punishment was limited to apprentices.[13] Freemen might also be committed to gaol, a measure generally reserved for moments when the norms of fraternal behaviour were breached. Edward Downes was typical in being imprisoned in the Compter for 'calleing Villayne' before the masters of his company. In the twelve months after November 1598, of the nine people the Barber-Surgeons' Company committed to the local compter, eight were being punished for disrespect and contempt to the master and assistants, and one for not bringing in a fine.[14]

A significant part of the punishment process was dealing with badly made or deceitful goods found on search. Bad commodities were normally destroyed in a manner which – like the procedures of search itself – was richly imbued with ritual forms. The way in which this was carried out also reflected other particular circumstances and aims, notably the degree to which companies wished to signal punishment publicly and officers' concern with avoiding accusations of trespass and theft. Often, when such goods were discovered, the searchers cast them into the gutter or burnt them in front of the offender's shop. On occasion, these practices might be refined to direct them more closely at the offender, as when the Grocers burnt Thomas Gardener's 'nawghty ginger' before him.[15] Although measures were sometimes taken to preserve an offender's reputation, and companies might allow them to destroy goods privately, punishment could involve significant costs of stock and reputation.[16] Despite the centrality of this kind of market regulation to their public responsibilities, legal challenges to companies' powers seem to have produced some uncertainty about the extent of their right to confiscate property.[17] When destroying bad drugs, the Apothecaries' court regularly noted that the maker consented and 'acknowledge it naught', even obtaining statements under oath that medicines were 'false'. They sometimes even made a point of mentioning that the condemned medicines' containers were returned to their owner.[18]

However, the main emphasis of most companies' courts was upon submission and apology to the court or the corporate body as a whole. An admission of guilt and desire for forgiveness by an errant artisan was often rewarded with a mitigated punishment. The treatment of cooper Roger Mason, whose fine for making defective barrels was halved to 10s 'in hope of Reformacon', or that of barber-surgeon John Mullins whose fine of 30s 'for not presenting his cure to the sayd Master', was 'upon his submission … mitigated to x s', are typical examples.[19] Despite having 'fetched blood' of the upper warden during a search, Jerome Banton's 40s fine was halved by the Basketmakers' court after he 'confessed and acknowledged his…fault and humblie upon his knee submitted himselfe'.[20] When two goldsmiths willingly brought defective wares discovered in search to the hall, the court rewarded them by reducing their fine.[21] Many fines were pardoned completely after a public apology, or in exchange for a gift, such as a contribution to repairs to the hall or a piece of plate. This was a normal part of many companies' procedures: in one year, November 1598 to November 1599, the Barber-Surgeons imposed twenty-nine fines, of which only two were paid in full; fourteen were mitigated and thirteen forgiven completely.[22] Although submission may have on occasion been a formulaic and insincere performance, company minutes do frequently record in detail emotional scenes of offenders crying or falling to their knees before the court. The vast majority of offences, like most court cases, were resolved through this reintegrative combination of fine and submission.[23]

As this emphasis on submission implies, the effectiveness of companies' enforcement of ordinances was to a large extent reliant on cohesion within the company. The relatively minor – and often mitigated – punishments imposed by companies encouraged the vast majority of those who broke ordinances to confess and admit their guilt.[24] The limitations of the court's powers could be quickly exposed when offenders refused to accept its authority.[25] This was particularly apparent when freemen challenged the powers of company searchers. As well as the abuse from William Walton, mentioned above, the wardens of the Goldsmiths experienced rough treatment on a number of occasions. On one occasion a recalcitrant goldsmith shut them within a small yard in his house. On another, when the wardens found suspicious-looking chains and bracelets in his shop, the goldsmith Thomas Clowse first violently resisted and abused the officers, and then – while they were still in his shop – had them arrested for a debt of £500 by the sergeant of the Poultry Compter. In response, the Goldsmiths sought to fine Clowse £40 and make him offer his submission to the assembled company at the hall, but eventually settled for a submission in writing and reduced the fine to £10.[26] The records of many companies reveal similar cases of searchers and wardens facing unbecoming language or violence during search or court proceedings. The honesty and skill of searchers was also subject to question. On the eve of Bartholomew Fair in 1644, for example, Thomas Berisford refused to open his stall to searchers until a constable was present.[27] Doubts over the ability of searchers to assess commodities or workmanship accurately led to the employment of experts to assist them.[28] Legal action against company officers was also a threat, and courts of assistants sometimes made orders that they would be 'saved harmless' from lawsuits incurred when carrying out their obligations.[29] In 1617 the Grocers disbursed 43s 2d to pay for Sir Stephen Soame's defence of a suit brought against him in the King's Bench for false imprisonment by an offender he had gaoled on the company's behalf.[30] Breakdowns of authority could extend beyond individual cases. Disputes between groups of artisans and the assistants of their company – and between companies and other authorities – were sometimes played out in company and national courts through the corporate language of offence and misdemeanour.[31]

To counter their vulnerability in the face of recalcitrant offenders, companies fell back on the support of other sources of authority in the City and beyond. The city and crown's devolution of power to the companies had not established separate sovereign jurisdictions reliant on their own resources. Rather, it had created a matrix of semi-autonomous authorities with recourse to support both vertically and horizontally. These were not simply crisis measures, but were a constant presence in corporate life. In order to enforce punishments and to deal with other policing problems, companies often employed Lord Mayor's Officers – whose main purpose was to 'execute the Process of the Mayors Court' – to give them added muscle, sometimes paying them an annual stipend for their services.[32] Companies also regularly pursued offenders in the Lord Mayor's Court or presented them to the Court of Aldermen, most often for non-payment of quarterage or working without the freedom. Nevertheless, it is important to recognise that even then, establishing an authoritative voice in the evaluation of commodities could be problematic. Consequently, in cases where goods were defective or it was impossible to reach an agreement on their worth, the Lord Mayor's Court often ordered an Inquest of Office, giving a jury the role of inspecting the quality of the goods and deciding whether or not to destroy them.[33]

Companies also prosecuted offenders at Quarter Sessions. Between 1612 and 1618 eight companies brought presentments to the Middlesex sessions for a variety of offences, particularly for not serving an apprenticeship or abusing company officers, often during search.[34] Some companies, particularly among the 'great twelve', might have this authority on tap: Sir Stephen Soame, who was both an assistant of the Grocers and a JP, bound over several grocers to appear at the next quarter sessions for London, even committing one of them to Newgate for breaking a recognizance.[35] Companies also employed professional informers to pursue offenders in these courts.[36] In some situations, companies might resort to taking cases to higher courts such as the Star Chamber and Exchequer.[37] At a less formal level, they often made appeals for mediation or support to the lord mayor, court of aldermen or other officials, reflecting the complex patterns of patronage and sociability that linked together companies, city and court.[38] The Goldsmiths even appealed to the lord chancellor over one liveryman who was challenging them at law.[39] Much of this external reinforcement occurred informally and is invisible in the records of the institutions and officials concerned; the lord mayor, in particular, seems often to have dealt with problematic freemen on an casual basis, leaving no trace in the Repertories of the Court of Aldermen.[40]

Company regulation was contingent upon the acceptance by freemen and others of the legitimacy of their jurisdiction. When this broke down, or when their powers were insufficient, at least in this period, companies could call upon the assistance of external bodies whose jurisdiction – and often membership – overlapped with their own to give teeth to corporate enforcement.[41] If we regard the ideal company as being an autonomous regulatory institution, this could be seen as signalling failure. However, we should not overstate the importance of some kind of quasi-judicial independence to the companies. Like other aspects of their regulatory work, their policing of freemen did not exist in a vacuum, but was intertwined with the efforts of other courts engaged in similar campaigns to control labour and trade.

II

It is worth recalling that most offences ended in an apology and perhaps a fine and promise of reformation, even in quite serious matters such as assaults or the deliberate falsification of goods. This was not primarily due to legal weaknesses in the company ordinances themselves. While several legal judgements in the early seventeenth century challenged aspects of companies' authority, particularly to restrict the use of a trade or to seize goods, the necessity of ordinances and the government of trades was generally accepted.[42] In practice, this moderation in the sentences imposed can be better explained in several ways. Firstly, if a company's judgement was seen as excessive it was more likely to be resisted. The company would then face substantial costs – of both time and money – and the risk of an adverse outcome undermining their powers if they chose to pursue a suit in an external legal tribunal. Secondly, the degree of subordination they could enforce in such a context was limited by cultural as well as fiscal constraints.[43] Like churchwardens or justices of the peace, as local agents of government company officers found that punitive punishments were difficult to pursue, since those responsible for policing were often tied to the offenders by personal and commercial bonds, particularly through networks of credit that depended on ongoing favourable relations.[44] Thirdly, in institutional terms, if a company resorted to more serious sanctions it was admitting that the concord and fraternity that lay at the centre of the guild idea, and the idiom of neighbourliness more generally, had broken down. All these factors contributed to the tension between pacification and litigation that affected companies' practices, much as it did other legal bodies.[45] Perhaps more important, however, was the attitude most freemen and officers held toward ordinances and the expectations of a regulated and ordered economy which they expressed.

The meanings that company ordinances held for those they were intended to govern is inevitably very difficult to discern. The accusations of abuses and failures to enforce ordinances which were so central to the rhetoric of disputes within and between companies are too repetitive and formulaic to carry much weight as evidence of freemen's opinions. One alternative way to assess both the stigma attached to breaking ordinances and the deterrent impact of being caught and punished is through an examination of the status of offenders within the company and the consequences that offending had for them. Although we need to recognise that exposure to punishment and the type of sanction imposed will be modified by social factors such as a person's prominence within the company, friendships or enmities between those involved, or the patronage of significant outsiders, contemporary evaluations of the prosecution process and its outcomes are nonetheless implicitly reflected in offenders' identities and patterns of offending. Unravelling this evidence is clearly a complex process, requiring both good company court records and a knowledge of the identity of the freemen, liverymen and assistants in a company. It has however been possible to carry out an analysis of two, perhaps slightly unusual, companies, the Apothecaries and Stationers. Even then, the figures set out below need to be read with a constant awareness of an unknown 'dark figure' of unrecorded offending, which does not merely consist of offences missed or ignored by officers, but also of those freemen whose offences were dealt with through more informal methods of warning and reprimand.

Between 1617, the year the company was granted its charter, and 1660, 327 offences were dealt with by the court of assistants of the Society of Apothecaries. The majority of offences concerned the possession or manufacture of bad or corrupt medicines, or the infringements of the rules relating to apprentices, particularly by failing to present or turn them over properly.[46] About 28% of all apothecaries freed between 1620 and 1640 were discovered breaking ordinances at some point either during their apprenticeship or later. The proportion rises to 38% if we include only those who bound at least one apprentice – and who were therefore definitely active in London.[47] A number of apothecaries appeared more than once; one, Edward Underwood, was accused of seven different offences. Senior members of the company featured regularly among offenders. Roughly one-third of those who were or who later became assistants or liverymen were summoned at one time or another for a fault. Presentment and punishment did not cease after a freeman took the livery, or even became an assistant. Indeed, most of the offences discovered among those who became liverymen occurred *after* they took the livery. A smaller proportion of an individual's offences were discovered after they had taken office as an assistant, and so become involved in carrying out search and enforcement, although it is difficult to discern the impact of the sample period on this.[48]

A similar pattern is apparent among freemen of the Stationers' Company over the period 1600–1640. Again, the overall rate of offending is striking, with 36% of those freed in the sample period being summoned for breaking the ordinances. Even when those whose only offence was absence from a court are excluded from this total, the rate remains very high, at 27%. Multiple offences were more common among stationers than apothecaries, with an average of 2.2 offences per person. Likewise, a few individuals among the stationers were spectacularly unwilling to be reformed, such as John Hammond who had 7 illegal presses destroyed by the company at various times. Interestingly, Table 6.1

TABLE 6.1

Offences of freemen of the Society of Apothecaries and of the Stationers' Company sorted by status[1]

Apothecaries' offences[2]	All offences	Freemen (60 individuals)	Liverymen (25 individuals)			Officers (17 individuals)		
			Before livery	After livery	All	Before Office	After Office	All
Craft	77	38	9	14	23	11	5	16
Apprentice	43	23	4	13	17	2	1	3
Behaviour	11	7	0	1	1	1	2	3
Presence	3	1	0	0	0	1	1	2
Other	2	0	0	2	2	0	0	0
Totals	136	69	13	30	43	15	9	24

Stationers' offences[2]	All offences	Freemen (80)	Liverymen (33)			Officers (20)		
			Before Livery	After Livery	All	Before Livery	After Office	All
Craft	93	43	15	10	25	8	4	25
Apprentice	97	40	15	19	34	12	1	23
Behaviour	16	7	1	2	3	2	0	6
Presence	81	31	6	20	26	8	4	24
Other	7	3	4	0	4	0	0	0
Totals	294	124	41	51	92	30	9	78

Sources: GL, MS 8200/1–2. W. A. Jackson (ed.), *Records of the Court of the Stationers' Company 1602 to 1640* (London, 1957); *London Book Trades: A Biographical Database, 1550–1830*, held at the Bodleian Library. I am grateful to Michael Turner for allowing me access to the information in this database.

[1] The table is based on twenty-one year samples of freemen (those stationers admitted freemen from 1600–1620 and those apothecaries admitted from 1620–1640 inclusive) and their offences as recorded in their companies' records over a 41 year period (1600–1640 and 1620–1660 respectively). The table is not, therefore, a count of all offences those individuals may have committed during their lifetime. Each status grouping is exclusive, so 'office holders' who were also liverymen are not counted in the livery columns, while 'freemen' held no office and did not accept a call to the livery. The organisation of the officers columns in the Apothecaries section does not include a separation between their offences as liverymen and as freemen because the Society was not granted the right to a livery until 1630.

[2] Offence categorisation: offences were divided into categories for ease of analysis: 'Craft' relate to faults in manufacture or manner of sale (such as adulterating medicines, working on the Sabbath, or printing another's books); 'Apprentice' relate largely to keeping unbound apprentices over the number allowed; 'Behaviour' relate largely to bad behaviour, such as insulting or assaulting company officers; 'Presence' relate to absences from meetings; 'Other' are the few offences left over.

suggests that liverymen offended more often than those who became assistants. Several explanations can be offered for this: possibly assistants were protecting each other and sometimes turning a blind eye to offences among themselves; it might be that holding office led to a greater observance of the rules; or that, while offending was not likely to prevent access to the livery, a bad record could make it more difficult for a freeman to reach the top of his company.

These figures are no indicator of the real frequency of offences and it is clearly very difficult to establish the activities – both in offending and enforcing – that lay behind them. However, they do suggest that movement between different levels within the company had relatively little effect upon the likelihood of being caught and punished for infringing ordinances, with the limited exception of post-appointment assistants in the Stationers. Clearly, punishment by their company's court of assistants held little force as a deterrent for most freemen, and carried low costs – either socially, politically or financially – compared to the advantages of offending. Ordinances, at least in the cases examined here, were not selectively applied by officers to regulate the mass of artisans and manipulate them for the profit of company governors. While they may have been a limited deterrent, they were at least apparently being enforced at all levels of the company. Being at the top of the corporate pile did not give a freeman a license to ignore the rules, even if we might suspect they could sometimes use their position to escape supervision. Although becoming an assistant was generally for life, the annual rotation of the offices of master and warden among members of the court assistants that was normal in most companies may have helped limit abuses of power.

Obviously the situation in these two companies is no more than suggestive evidence about behaviour in other companies, and the situation may vary substantially in larger, more diverse companies, in which, it has been suggested, enforcement was employed to subordinate artisans.[49] Indeed, it is particularly difficult to generalise from the workings of these two companies. Both had at least putative monopolies over their trades and were perhaps therefore more concerned with discovering abuses than was normal: the Society of Apothecaries, which possessed an unusual occupational homogeneity, was only recently established and in part owed its existence to concerns over abuses in medicine; while the Stationers' control of book printing employed a process of registration of publications that was unparalleled in other trades, and the craft was – like medicine – a particularly significant concern for the Crown. The little evidence available for other companies does, however, generally suggest that these two companies were not exceptional in their style of offending and punishment. For example, frequent and persistent offending was also common among freemen bakers who were fined for breaking the Bread Assizes, while Ian Archer has found that a substantial number of assistants from several other companies had previously been fined for poor workmanship.[50]

The patterns of offending among freemen apparent here carry interesting consequences for our understanding of notions of respectability and reputation among early-modern artisans and tradesmen. Possessing a good reputation appears to have been of critical importance to commercial success, as echoed in the worries of the London turner Nehemiah Wallington that any frauds he perpetrated, no matter how accidentally, would rebound severely.[51] Nonetheless, it does appear that to be discovered and punished for breaking the ordinances set by companies – even those relating to deceitful trading practices – seems to have been relatively inconsequential in the *long term*.[52] At least within the company, those who committed such misdemeanours were not permanently tarnished by their actions: wrongdoing had little if any adverse effect on their prospects for advancement. Consequently, those who were responsible for catching and punishing these offenders were liable to have broken ordinances themselves in the past, as has also been found for contemporary holders of parish offices, such as constables.[53] These findings imply that the acts that were punished were not seen as being particularly odious, at least in this limited context. We should, however, recognise that the *short-term* costs could be substantial. Some of the fines imposed, even after a reduction for submission, were hefty sums, particularly for poorer freemen, which must have been made more difficult by the limited amounts of cash available to those operating within extensive networks of debt and credit. Moreover, when punishments were made *public* – and this was at the discretion of the court – then the reaction of offenders might be closer to the fear expressed by Wallington.[54]

III

This insight into the profiles of misdemeanour within London companies offers a measure of explanation for the forms through which examination and punishment was carried out. As attempts to define minimum standards of behaviour which were in part designed to allow all freemen a livelihood from their craft, ordinances did not always require consistent enforcement. For example, those limiting apprentice numbers might be comfortably ignored in times of economic health.[55] Indeed, to break those regarding apprentices might mean no more than appropriating the privileges of others. The edges of this 'moral economy' were not black and white, but shaded between the amorality of everyday salesmanship and cost-cutting, and the darker area of deceit and imposture. Mutual interest supported the enforcement of ordinances in order to keep the trust of consumers and the privileges of corporate membership. But the attraction of individual defection rose in proportion to the success with which these ends were achieved. Slippage was easy and was treated as such. These offences, like all crime in the period, were by no means the preserve of the marginal or outcast.[56] This did not, however, mean that these areas became in effect decriminalised in the manner of certain offences in the twentieth century. For, while the pattern of offending is striking, so is the persistence of policing.

It is therefore important to emphasise that attitudes to corporate regulation were complex, and personal and institutional practice might diverge dramatically, as is underlined by the campaigns for closer regulation from disgruntled artisans within companies, and the responses of the City authorities or Crown to their petitions.[57] While I have been focusing on normal procedure here, the potential for regulation to become a point of conflict and oppression also needs to be recognised. Likewise at an individual level, although the process of enforcement was structurally biased towards reintegration, relationships between companies and freemen could and did break down, and there were ultimately limits to the discretion that companies could show. The aggregate approach employed here should not be allowed to obscure the personal attitudes and relationships that shaped encounters between officers and freemen, even if such antipathies and friendships are rarely highlighted in the available sources. Nevertheless, the everyday enforcement of ordinances was largely and necessarily a flexible and discretionary matter, undertaken with the intention – but perhaps not the expectation – of re-ordering and reforming behaviour, rather than achieving retribution for past wrongs. Parallels can be seen with the processes of minor criminal and civil litigation that was endemic in this period, when law suits became techniques in ongoing negotiations that generally ended in private compromise rather than judicial resolution.[58] The operation of company courts followed similar patterns, aiming to nudge an artisan back towards acceptable behaviour, and reinforcing this with compromises over fines and apologies.[59] Enforcement was not a matter of isolated incidents, but formed part of an ongoing relationship between freemen and their companies that stretched from the moment of entering an apprenticeship through to death, departure from the trade, or – rarely – the complete breakdown of communication.

NOTES

I would like to thank Margaret Pelling, Ian Gadd, Paul Griffiths, Joe Ward, Meraud Grant Ferguson and all those present at the 'Revisiting London Livery Companies' conference for their comments on versions of this paper.

1. W. S. Prideaux (ed.), *Memorials of the Goldsmiths' Company*, 2 vols. (London, 1896–7), vol. 1, pp. 223, 230–2.
2. R. Mackenney, *Tradesmen and Traders: The World of the Guilds in Venice and Europe, c.1250–c.1650* (London, 1993), pp. 13–14; R. S. Smith, *The Spanish Guild Merchant* (Durham, 1940); B. Gustafsson, 'The Rise and Economic Behaviour of Medieval Craft Guilds', in B. Gustaffson (ed.), *Power and Economic Institutions* (Brookfield, 1991), p. 82.
3. M. Berlin, '"Broken all in pieces": Artisans and the Regulation of Workmanship in Early Modern London', in G. Crossick (ed.), *The Artisan and the European Town* (Aldershot,

1997), pp. 75–91; M. J. Walker, 'The Extent of the Guild Control of Trades in England *c.*1660–1820: A Study Based on a Sample of Provincial Towns and London Companies' (unpublished Ph.D. thesis, University of Cambridge, 1986); J. R. Kellett, 'The Breakdown of Gild and Corporation Control over the Handicraft and Retail Trade in London', *Economic History Review*, 2nd ser., 10 (1957–8), pp. 381–94.

4. J.-P. Sosson, 'Les Metiers: Norme et Realité: l'exemple des Ancients Pays-Bas Meridionaux aux XIVe et XVe siècles', in J. Hamesse and C. Muraille (eds.), *Le Travail au Moyen Age* (Louvain-la-Neuve, 1990), pp. 339–48; M. P. Davies, 'The Tailors of London and their Guild, *c.*1300–1500' (unpublished DPhil thesis, University of Oxford, 1994); G. Rosser, 'Crafts, Guilds and the Negotiation of Work in the Medieval Town', *Past and Present*, 154 (1997), pp. 3–31.

5. R. B. Shoemaker, *Prosecution and Punishment: Petty Crime and the Law in London and Rural Middlesex, c.1660–1725* (1991), pp. 311–12.

6. A. Black, *Guilds and Civil Society in European Political Thought from the Twelfth Century to the Present* (London, 1984); N. Carlin, 'Liberty and Fraternities in the English Revolution: The Politics of London Artisans' Protests', *International Review of Social History*, 39 (1994), pp. 223–54.

7. Berlin, 'Artisans'; I. W. Archer, *The Pursuit of Stability: Social Relations in Elizabethan London* (Cambridge, 1991); J. P. Ward, *Metropolitan Communities: Trade Guilds, Identity, and Change in Early Modern London* (Stanford, 1997).

8. Ward, *Metropolitan Communities*; Berlin, 'Artisans'; Archer, *Pursuit of Stability*, pp. 126–7.

9. The Blacksmiths' Company, for example, appears to have been active in regulating its members. In 1613 they spent substantial amounts on four searches, each lasting several days, but, while fines were received during search, very few offenders appeared in person in the minutes: GL, MS 2881/2, ff. 75–120.

10. S. Hindle, *The State and Social Change in Early Modern England, c.1550–1640* (Basingstoke, 2000), p. 219; J. A. Sharpe, 'Enforcing the Law in the Seventeenth-Century English Village', in V. A. C. Gattrell, B. Lenman, and G. Parker (eds.), *Crime and the Law* (London, 1980), pp. 108–11; C. B. Herrup, *The Common Peace: Participation and the Criminal Law in Seventeenth-Century England* (Cambridge, 1987), p. 193.

11. GL, MS 11588, f. 231v.

12. GL, MS 5257/2, f. 35; S. Thrupp, *A Short History of the Worshipful Company of Bakers of London* (London, 1933), p. 93; P. E. Jones, *The Butchers of London: A History of the Worshipful Company of Butchers of the City of London* (London, 1976), p. 133.

13. Prideaux, *Goldsmiths' Company*, vol. 1, p. 113. Jones notes the decline in the use of the stocks for freemen butchers from the fourteenth century onwards, while Ian Gadd has noted that the Stationers owned 2 whips 'for refomacyon' in the 1550s, although the company does not seem to have used violence against its members: *Butchers*, p. 132; I. A. Gadd, '"Being Like a Field": Corporate Identity in the Stationers' Company, 1557–1684' (unpublished DPhil thesis, University of Oxford, 1999), p. 97. The punishment of apprentices was a complex issue. Some freemen were presented to their companies for excessive punishment, but a measure of physical punishment was used by both masters and companies, see: P. Griffiths, *Youth and Authority: Formative Experiences in England, 1560–1640* (unpublished DPhil thesis, Oxford, 1996), pp. 316, 341–7.

14. GL, MS 5257/3, ff. 6, 9.

15. GL, MS 11588/1, f. 209; Berlin, 'Artisans', pp. 80–1.

16. See, for example: GL, MS 8200/1, f. 382v; 8200/2, f. 2r. Interestingly, the Barber Surgeons ordered that no order or decree of the court should be revealed publicly on pain of a fine: GL, MS 5257/3, f. 232 (5 Feb 1607).

17. Kellett, 'Breakdown', pp. 383–4.

18. GL, MS 8200/1, f. 357v; 8200/2, f. 5v.

19. GL, MS 5602/2, ff. 135r, 136v; GL, MS 5257/3, f. 1r.
20. H. H. Bobart (ed.), *Records of the Basketmakers' Company* (London, 1911), pp. 113–14.
21. Prideaux, *Goldsmiths' Company,* vol. 1, p. 194.
22. GL, MS 5257/3. The Company was perhaps unusually active that year, taking great interest in punishing freemen for working on the sabbath.
23. J. M. Beattie, *Crime and the Courts* (Oxford, 1986), pp. 268–9.
24. Archer, *Pursuit of Stability*, p. 127.
25. Berlin, 'Artisans', pp. 83–6.
26. Prideaux, *Goldsmiths' Company*, vol. 1, p. 138.
27. Prideaux, *Goldsmiths' Company*, vol. 1, p. 223.
28. Berlin, 'Artisans', p. 79.
29. See, for example: GL, MS 11588/2, f. 599.
30. GL, MS 11588/3, f. 47.
31. For example, the Quo Warranto faced by the Society of Apothecaries in the 1630s was due in part in a challenge from a group of apothecaries to the right of the College of Physicians to search their shops and destroy bad drugs.
32. *Lex Londinensis: Or, The City Law* (London, 1680), pp. 5, 121; B. R. Masters, 'The Common Serjeant', *Guildhall Miscellany*, 2 (1967), pp. 379–89; B. R. Masters, 'The Mayor's Household Before 1600,' in A. E. J. Hollaender and W. Kellaway (eds.), *Studies in London History* (London, 1969), pp. 95–114. Examples of the companies' use of Lord Mayors officers can be found in GL, MS 11588/3, f. 220; MS 2881/2, ff. 97, 111; MS 5257/2, f. 63; MS 5257/4, f. 76.
33. CLRO, MS index of schedules; Bobart, *Basketmakers*, pp. 115–16.
34. W. le Hardy (ed.), *Middlesex Sessions Records 1612–1618*, 4 vols. (London, 1936–41), vol. 1, pp. 55, 118, 119, 318; vol. 2, pp. 10, 13, 137; vol. 3, pp. 214, 294, 295; vol. 4, pp. 111, 113, 124, 245; GL, MS 2881/2, ff. 87, 120; 8200/2, f. 49r; MS 5257/4, f. 128
35. GL, MS 11588/2, f. 588r.
36. GL, MS 8200/2, ff. 36v, 43v; Prideaux, *Goldsmiths' Company*, p. 200. The Barber Surgeons employed the Clerk to prosecute unskilful surgeons in 1600, though later had a standard informer: GL, MS 5257/3, f. 76; MS 5257/4, ff. 57, 60, 70.
37. PRO, STAC 8/26/1, 8/44/9; GL, MS 4631, f. 23v.
38. D. M. Dean, 'Public or Private? London Leather and Legislation in Elizabethan England', *The Historical Journal,* 31 (1988), pp. 525–48; I. Archer, 'The London Lobbies in the Later Sixteenth Century', *The Historical Journal*, 31 (1988), pp. 17–44.
39. Prideaux, *Goldsmiths' Company*, vol. 1, p. 119.
40. For example, the Ironmongers' Court convented Robert Stedd before the Lord Mayor between the 6 and 14 July 1630, and Thomas White between 10 and 18 August 1630; the company's Minutes record that he made orders about both men. The Repertories contain no mention of either man, although they do contain details of freemen convented before the Court of Aldermen by the Poulterers' and Brewers' Companies during this period: GL, MS 16967/4, ff. 51, 54; CLRO, Rep. 44, ff. 299–322.
41. Kellett suggests that by the late seventeenth century companies were left mostly on their own in enforcement of ordinances: 'Breakdown', pp. 354–5.
42. Ordinances were overturned in the 'Clothworkers of Ipswich Case' (1615) and Norris v. Staps (1617): *The English Reports* (Edinburgh, 1907), vol. 78, pp. 147–8; vol. 80, pp. 357–9. Coke, however, defended ordinances to regulate trade, and the custom of London that none should keep a shop without the freedom: J. F. Fraser (ed.), *The Reports of Sir Edward Coke* (London, 1826), vol. 4, pp. 383–400; vol. 6, p. 103.
43. K. Wrightson, 'The Politics of the Parish in Early Modern England', in P. Griffiths, A. Fox, and S. Hindle (eds.), *The Experience of Authority in Early Modern England* (Basingstoke, 1996), especially p. 36.

44. K. Wrightson, 'Two Concepts of Order: Justices, Constables and Jurymen in Seventeenth-Century England', in J. Brewer and J. Styles (eds.), *An Ungovernable People: The English and Their Law in the Seventeenth and Eighteenth Centuries* (London, 1980), pp. 21–46; Sharpe, 'Enforcing the Law', pp. 97–119.

45. Hindle, *State*, chapter 4; C. Muldrew, 'The Culture of Reconciliation: Community and the Settlement of Economic Disputes in Early Modern England', *The Historical Journal*, 39 (1996), pp. 915–42.

46. A crude breakdown of offences by subject is possible: 79 were apprentice-related; 180 were drug-related; 20 were non-members practising as apothecaries; 9 were illegally-kept journeymen; 18 were apprentices setting up shop before their freedom; 6 were failure to appear at Court; and 17 were other offences. Between 1617 and 1661, 797 individuals were made free of the Society. The figures presented here are based on name-linkage and so avoid double-counting of individuals and offences.

47. Taking those freed between 1620 and 1640 gives each member of the sample a minimum of twenty years after freedom in which to offend.

48. The sample only covers between 20 and 40 years of a freeman's working life, depending on when he was freed, and as the average time for a freemen to become an assistant was 24.6 years in the Society of Apothecaries and 18.8 years in London companies generally, it is likely that it significantly under-records offences by officers. In contrast, the average time from freedom to livery entrance was 10.2 years in the Society of Apothecaries.

49. Berlin, 'Artisans', p. 93. A similar argument for an earlier period is made by H. Swanson, *Medieval Artisans: An Urban Class in Late Medieval England* (Oxford, 1989), pp. 112–15.

50. R. M. Benbow, 'The Court of Aldermen and the Assizes: The Policy of Price Control in Elizabethan London', *Guildhall Studies in London History*, 4 (1980), pp. 107–9; Archer, *Pursuit*, pp. 104–5.

51. P. S. Seaver, *Wallington's World: A Puritan Artisan in Seventeenth-Century London* (London, 1985), pp. 129–33.

52. C. Muldrew, *The Economy of Obligation: The Culture of Credit and Social Relations in Early Modern England* (Basingstoke, 1998); Rosser, 'Crafts'.

53. J. A. Sharpe, 'Crime and Delinquency in an Essex Parish 1600–1640,' in J. S. Cockburn (ed.), *Crime in England 1550–1800* (London, 1977), pp. 94–6; J. R. Kent, *The English Village Constable, 1580–1642: A Social and Administrative Study* (Oxford, 1986), pp. 146–8.

54. I am grateful to Joe Ward for discussion of these points.

55. Walker, 'Guild Control', p. 112.

56. Sharpe, 'Crime and Delinquency', pp. 96–7, 108.

57. Search and enforcement was a major concern of external authorities: N. Carlin, 'Liberty and fraternities in the English Revolution: the politics of London artisans' protests', *International Review of Social History*, 39 (1994), pp. 223–54.

58. C. Muldrew, 'Credit and the Courts: Debt Litigation in a Seventeenth-Century Urban Community', *Economic History Review*, 2nd ser., 46 (1993), pp. 23–38; C. W. Brooks, 'Interpersonal Conflict and Social Tension: Civil Litigation in England, 1640–1830', in A. L. Beier, D. Cannadine, and J. M. Rosenheim (eds.), *The First Modern Society: Essays in Honour of Lawrence Stone* (Cambridge, 1989), pp. 357–99; J. A. Sharpe, *Crime in Early Modern England, 1550–1750*, 2nd edn. (London, 1999), pp. 65–8.

59. Archer, *Pursuit of Stability*, p. 127; Berlin, 'Artisans', p. 82.

7.

The Pewterers' Company's Country Searches and the Company's Regulation of Prices

RONALD F. HOMER

The medieval ordinances granted to the London craft guilds customarily gave them the power to oversee and control their crafts only in the city of London and its immediate environs. Only rarely did their subsequent royal charters extend these powers countrywide. So far as can be discovered from surviving records only two companies with these rights, the Pewterers and the Goldsmiths, exercised their wider remits in a significant way. Both these companies, as time went on, were able to rely not only on the authority conferred by their charters, but also on Acts of Parliament which confirmed and reinforced their powers. This chapter considers the two areas of regulation in which the Pewterers' Company stands out from most London companies – its nationwide searches and its regulation of prices – illustrating the development of its corporate powers, both in theory and practice, from the fifteenth century to their peak in the early seventeenth century, prior to their decline in the eighteenth century.

Searches

The earliest ordinances granted by the City of London to the city's craftsmen were essentially bargains struck between the craft and the city in which the craft, in return for being allowed to run its own affairs, undertook to provide products of good quality at reasonable prices. Quality was guaranteed by requiring craftsmen to serve apprenticeships to learn the necessary skills, and by ordinances which spelt out good working practices. Prices were often laid down by precept, either from within the craft or by the city authorities. Penalties were imposed by the craft on those who transgressed its rules. Makers of pewter chalices (*calisers*) are documented in London from the close of the twelfth century and these craftsmen later diversified to supply the market for domestic pewter which emerged about 1300.[1] The London pewterers obtained their first ordinances in 1348. Among other things these laid down the composition of the metal to be used: 'fine metal', a hard alloy of tin and copper, was to be used for flatware – that is plates, dishes, chargers and the like – and 'lay metal', a cheaper, softer, alloy containing lead, was to be used for hollow-ware, such as flagons, drinking vessels and measures.[2] Neither these ordinances, nor others granted before the Pewterers received their first charter in 1473–4, gave – nor could they give – the Pewterers any rights to enforce these standards outside London. Nevertheless, by some means which is not yet understood, the same standards for metal came to be adopted by a number of provincial pewterers' guilds. Thus the ordinances of the York pewterers of 1416 and those of Bristol of 1456 specify that the metal used shall conform to the 'assay of London'.[3] Indeed, the York pewterers agreed in 1416 to be bound by ordinances identical to the London ones and the preamble to these reads: 'These are the ordinances (*articles*) of the pewterers of London which the men of the craft in the city of York have agreed to keep and ordain (*ordeiner*) among themselves'.

In the late 1460s the pewterers of London began to lobby for a royal charter which was eventually granted in February 1474.[4] As only corporate bodies could own real property their desire for a charter, which specifically granted this right, was in part probably motivated by the wish of the expanding craft to build their own hall, a project which they put in hand immediately after the grant. The charter also gave the Pewterers' Company the valuable right to search for sub-standard wares throughout England and Wales 'and to seize, take, and carry away as forfeited all maner of deceitful and unjust workmanships and merchandizes'. It appears likely that the rights of search that the Pewterers lobbied for and obtained were purposely modelled by them on those granted to the Goldsmiths in the latter's charter of 1462.[5] Under the terms of the Pewterers' charter the fines extracted from provincial pewterers whose wares were found to be substandard were to be shared equally with the crown, and local mayors, justices and other officials were ordered to assist the company's searchers in their task. The London pewterers lost no time in organising the first of their country searches. An English translation of the charter was made, search warrants bearing the royal seal were obtained, and parties of searchers set forth in 1474 as soon as seasonal weather conditions made travel feasible. The company's Audit Book records some of the documentation the searchers armed themselves with in 1474:[6]

Paid for the writing of our corporation [*i.e.* charter] in English	iis vid
Paid for another that Watts had in the westcountry in English	xvid
Paid to John Tyler for writing the corporation we had at 'Styerbryg' [Stourbridge fair]	xd
Paid for the letter of our powers and the copy of the ordinances	[blank]
Delivered iii patents to ride with into the country under the King's seal in white wax	

Detailed records of these earliest searches have survived. Their extent is impressive: one search party ventured as far west as Exeter, calling at numerous towns on the way, another travelled as far north as Lincoln and others explored the Midlands and Kent. In all, during the years 1474 to 1477, no less than 36 towns were visited and over 50 pewterers' shops were searched, some more than once. A considerable number of the country pewterers were cajoled or threatened into parting with significant sums of money, typically 20 shillings, to become members of the London company and a list headed 'These be the brethren that be of the country sworn to the King and the craft' contains 31 names. What advantage membership of the company and the associated freedom of London could confer on these individuals, some in places as far away as Exeter, Taunton and Coventry, is far from clear. It is hard to believe that they would have any worthwhile business connections in the city which would justify their voluntary investment in such a dubious privilege. The long lists of seized wares also give us a fascinating and valuable insight into the wide range of wares then being made in many provincial towns. These included 'great' and 'middle' plates, dishes and saucers, a variety of styles of salts, and tavern pots from a pottle down to half-pint in size. Many of the seized wares were lodged in the safe-keeping of the local bailiffs or constables, but their ultimate fate is not disclosed.[7]

The proceeds of these early searches were farmed for a time, the crown settling for 30 shillings a year.[8] This proved to be a distinctly bad bargain for the crown, though it reserved the right to increase the farm, since the company's accounts appear to show that the fines extracted in 1475–6 alone would have provided the crown with a half share of over £20. However, a certain – and possibly deliberate – lack of clarity in the accounts makes them difficult to interpret.

Unfortunately, save for a search in 1569, little evidence survives of subsequent country searches after the end of the fifteenth century until the 1620s, but a detailed record of the later searches survives in an essentially complete series of Search Books which begin in 1636 and continue until 1702.[9] These later and sometimes informatively annotated records include a mass of uniquely valuable information about English provincial pewtering during the period when the production and usage of pewter was at its peak. They contain the names and locations of almost 700 provincial pewterers in over 200 towns and cities and often provide comprehensive lists of the wares they were making or factoring.[10] Since the records frequently name the makers of bought-in wares found in an individual's shop they also give valuable information about marketing patterns.[11] The searches cover the whole of England west to Penzance, north to Newcastle and Kendal, and east to King's Lynn, and tend to follow set itineraries along the main trunk roads out of London calling at all the market towns along the way, and frequently branching off to visit towns lying on side roads. The searches took place between April and October when roads were at their most passable and were often timed to coincide with major fairs which were also searched. The fairs at Trowbridge, Stourbridge (Cambs.), Modbury (Devon), Stony Stratford, Wallingford, Thame, Banbury, Exeter and Probus (Cornwall) are but a selection of those visited. On one occasion, in 1677, the searchers dared to venture into Wales, visiting Wrexham, Welshpool and Montgomery, but apparently without finding any pewter in the latter two places.

The parties of searchers, five or six strong, normally included the master, the wardens, the clerk and several senior company members. They were away from London on the search for several weeks at a time. For example, one search which set off from London on 3 April 1641 called at 29 places: Odiham fair, Alton, Winchester, Southampton, Salisbury, Blandford Forum, Dorchester, Sherborne, Montacute, Chard, Honiton, Exeter, Launceston, Lostwithiel, Penryn and Looe on the outward leg and returned by way of Plymouth, Tavistock, Ashburton, Taunton, Bridgwater, Wells, Bath, Bristol, Gloucester, Chipping Norton, Oxford, Abingdon and Reading before arriving back in London almost six weeks later on 11 May. No wonder the account of one such search ends with the heartfelt words 'So came we all safe to Pewterers' Hall'. Not infrequently the searchers split into two parties which went on separate short itineraries along side roads before meeting up again after a day or two. This prolonged absence of the company's officers resulted in long gaps between court meetings during the summer months.

The thought of well-heeled London citizens groping their way around rural Cornwall in 1641 makes one wonder about their reception and whether they needed the services of an interpreter. Certainly, there is evidence that the searchers sometimes recruited – or pressed – local pewterers to assist them to find their way and to identify where pewterers' shops were to be found. Sometimes, however, the searchers relaxed for a while and a note appended to the 1702 search in the Bristol area reads: 'Being Sunday ... after evening sermon we rode with Mr Harvey our landlord over the water common and saw the Severn, but the tide was out, and about 7 at night we drank cider and ale at a house on the common'. On the same search they had breakfast with the Bristol pewterers at the Bull Tavern from which they did not depart until 11.30 a.m.

Expense accounts that survive for some of the searches show expenditure on entertaining mayors and other officials that no doubt helped to smooth the way among reluctant locals. These fascinating accounts also include the costs of accommodation for men and horses and such incidentals as barbers' bills and wear and tear on clothing. The following extract, concerning a 1677 search by a party of six, illustrates a range of expenses:[12]

	[£ – s – d]
Kidderminster 2 nights and a day	02–06–10
Shrewsbury a night and near 2 days	02–06–06
Whitchurch and on the road	16–05
For the hire of 6 horses, 24 days	18–00–00
Spent with the mayor of Worcester	00–08–08
Paid the barber	00–02–06
Paid to four persons for wear on apparel	04–00–00
Reimbursed the several members pocket expenses	02–15–07

Total outgoings for this search amounted to £72 6s 1½d and receipts came to £95 13s 10d showing a profit of £18 7s 8½d. However, this does not include money received for the sale as scrap metal of any condemned wares. The search had included 42 shops in seventeen towns and covered a distance of some 500 miles.

In 1503 the Pewterers' Company had lobbied for, and obtained, an Act of Parliament that further extended their authority.[13] The Act required makers country-wide to put their marks or 'touches' on their pewterware 'to the intent that the makers of such wares shall avow the same wares by them to be wrought'. This gave the searchers another ground on which to condemn a pewterer's goods and many references are found to the seizure of 'untouched ware'. It also enabled them to identify the makers of wares retailed by others. The same Act required the Justices of the Peace in every county and the authorities in every city or borough to appoint local searchers for pewter. In the 1550s the bailiffs of Ludlow seized unmarked wares at a fair in the town and in 1562 the city of Exeter appointed a searcher.[14] Similarly, a century later, at the Warwick Quarter Sessions in 1664, a panel of local pewterers was empowered to 'enter into and make search in the daytime in the house, shop, cellar, warehouse or other place of or belonging to any pewterer.... in the county of Warwick' and seize anything made of deceitful metal.[15] Interestingly, this 1503 Act also gave the Pewterers' Company and the locally appointed searchers a right to search for substandard brassware in addition to pewter, a power that the company exercised at certain fairs in the sixteenth century, although they seem not to have pursued to any extent at a later date.[16] The same Act laid down that the pewter alloys had to conform to the standards of London. It also prohibited the selling of pewter and brassware by itinerant hawkers and pedlars. All selling was to be done either at open fairs and markets or from the pewterers' own premises, a provision designed to simplify control over it. Subsequent legislation in 1512 reiterated these provisions.[17] As a result of further lobbying, an Act of 1533 strengthened the company's position even more by banning imports of foreign pewter and preventing any 'stranger born out of this realm' from practising the craft of pewterer.[18] These powers were later confirmed and extended by an Act of 1541.[19]

Despite their extensive coverage, visits by the London searchers to many provincial towns were infrequent and can have provided little real deterrent to the transgressions of local pewterers in these places. The extent to which locally appointed searchers filled the gaps between the London searchers' visits is uncertain. Clearly the local searchers could face conflicts of interest when searching the premises of fellow pewterers whom they would have known and had dealings with. Quite probably they only exercised their powers when there was a complaint from an aggrieved purchaser. For obvious reasons no searches were carried out by the Pewterers' Company during the massive dislocation caused by the civil war, or during the Commonwealth period when the Royal Writ did not run. In the 46 years between 1636 and 1702 when the searchers were active, extended country searches were mounted in at least nineteen years. Some of the major pewtering centres were visited quite frequently: Bristol twelve times and Reading thirteen times – sometimes more than once in one year, perhaps in an attempt to catch the local pewterers unawares – and Oxford, Gloucester and Salisbury ten times each. However, other quite important but perhaps less accessible pewtering towns were visited more rarely: Worcester six times and Coventry five times, York twice and Shrewsbury only once. Many smaller towns received only one visit during the years 1636–1702. Against this analysis, the company's exercise of its statutory powers may appear less impressive; some provincial pewterers must have gone through their working lives without ever seeing the men from London. Nevertheless, the overall picture does remain remarkable, particularly bearing in mind the difficulties and hazards of travel, the sometimes advanced age of the company's officers, and the problems inherent in running the company during the officers' absence from the capital for periods of several weeks.

The searchers assayed the metal being used in the shops they searched by melting down a sample of the wares of which they were suspicious, or else by sampling the pewterer's melting pot, and casting a standard sized pellet in an 'assay mould' which resembled a musket-ball mould. This pellet was then weighed. Since lead is heavier than tin an overweight pellet indicated that the alloy had been adulterated with lead, a tempting option for the pewterer since lead was very much cheaper than tin. They also assessed the quality of the workmanship, seizing wares that they judged to be insufficiently robust, badly soldered or improperly finished. Seized wares were defaced, and later disposed of for melting down and refining. Quite often they were sold to a trusted local pewterer, for example, in Exeter in 1636, 'all the bad wares that was seized was delivered unto Abell King and it was praised at v*d* the pound and it wayed 1cwt 3qrs 22lbs waight and so was received for it the sum of foure pounds twelve shillings and foure pence'. The price of 5*d* per pound is a scrap price which represents only a fraction of the new price which was then 13*d* or 14*d* per pound.

The incursions of the searchers were frequently resented by the local pewterers, and this resentment increased with the passage of time. Sometimes it seems that news of the searchers' coming preceded them and the Search Books note that wares had been hidden and shops shut, though this was not as frequent as might be expected: news may have travelled slowly and the searchers often covered considerable distances in remarkably short times. Additionally, they sometimes arrived at their destination early, at 7 or 7.30 in the morning, having stayed elsewhere overnight. Individuals were occasionally uncooperative and official assistance might be called for. Thus in 1636 the searchers 'went into

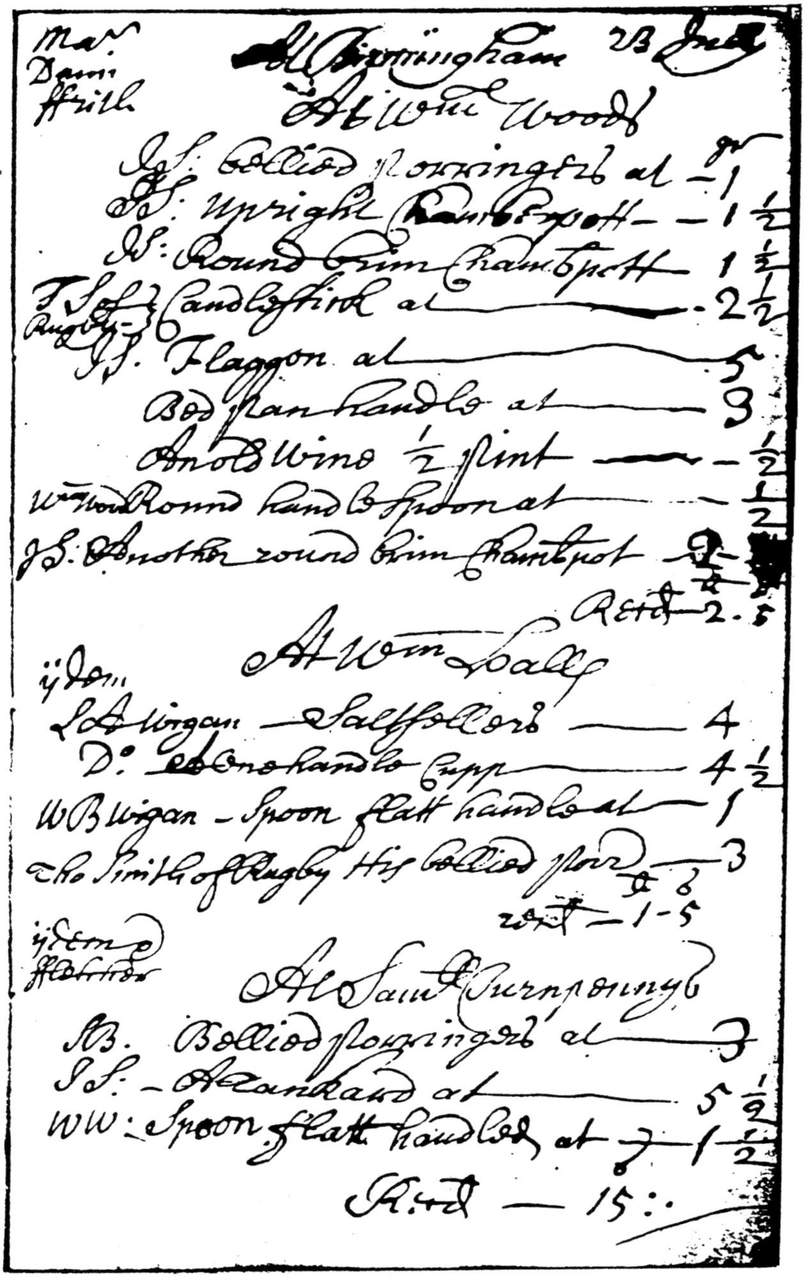

Plate 7.1. The search of the shops of William Wood, William Hall and Samuel Turnpenny in Birmingham on 23 July 1702.

The figures show the number of grains by which the weight of the assay pellet, made by melting down the suspect wares, exceeded the standard and the sums of money received record the fines levied. The names of the searchers (the Master and Dunn, Frith and Fletcher) are also noted as is the identity of the makers of bought in items. From GL, MS 22198.

(Courtesy of the Worshipful Company of Pewterers)

Ronald Speed of Blandford with a constable to search, but he would not let us search but denied us the search'. Similarly, in Hereford in 1640 William Lee 'took away our say [i.e., the assay mould] and was very troublesome in both speech and action'. Less resistance was offered by Thomas Cropp of Winchester who in 1641 concealed some of his substandard stock in a locked room:

> Our Master desired that he might go into it, but Thomas Cropp told him that his maid had gone forth and that she had the key of it with her, but we stayed till the maid came home. She had none of the key, but Thomas Cropp at length found the key and in the room was hid as follows, 26 wine pints, 9 wine quarts, 23 chamber pots, 3 candlesticks and they ben all defaced and broke.

The authority of the searchers to summon local assistance is shown by their search of a barge in the river at Gloucester in August 1636. This was carrying a barrel of pewter consigned by Thomas Nichols of Worcester when 'the sheriffs of Gloster caused the barill which this wayre was packed up in to be brought to the Kinges warehouse and there they caused it to be broke open and when it was broke open they desired us to search, and so we did' – various items were seized.

By the early years of the eighteenth century the company's right to search in the provinces was being called into question, particularly its power of entry into private premises. In 1722 counsel's opinion was sought on the legality of the searches and his advice was not encouraging.[20] The last full scale country search was in 1702, although in the face of serious complaints about the poor quality of Bristol pewter a search was mounted there in 1723.[21] Thereafter the company limited its searches to London where its influence was still unchecked.

The motive behind the searches is unclear. There was no over-riding requirement with pewter, as there was with gold and silver, to maintain alloy standards for fiscal reasons. It is difficult to believe that the London company was driven by altruism to protect the populace at large from dubious goods. The profit received from fines and from the sale of seized metal was probably a prime reason for mounting what must have been a time consuming and indeed an onerous activity. This impression is reinforced by the fact that many wares were seized when, it was alleged, they fell short of the assay of London by a margin of only half a grain (32mg) in the weight of the standard pellet cast in the assay mould which held 183½ grains (11.7g) of fine metal. Bearing in mind the crude nature of the assay, this margin is clearly below anything which could have been reliably or reproducibly measured and it appears to have been an excuse to levy a fine on the flimsiest pretext. To put this half a grain in context, really bad metal could fall short of the assay by twelve or sixteen grains or sometimes even more. In fairness it should be noted that the searches carried out in London several times a year also condemned wares which fell short of the assay by the same half grain margin. Rather strangely this dubious precision appears not to have been challenged and those fined accepted the searchers' verdict, though doubtless frequently with bad grace. A further motive for the country searches was probably to prevent the sale of poor quality goods made of debased metal at prices which would undercut those of London-made wares.

Prices

Implicit in the medieval ordinances granted to the craft guilds of London was a requirement to supply goods at what was known as a 'just price', one that was acceptable in the purchaser's eyes and which provided a reasonable profit for the craftsman. The 'just price' for a piece of pewter depended on two factors: the weight and quality of the metal in it; and the cost of production. In 1438 the City of London authorities laid down the minimum weights for a wide range of pewter flatware ranging from chargers to small saucers, for vessels of various sizes and for a range of salts.[22] Subsequently, the Pewterers' Company produced from time to time its own 'sizings' that set out in great detail the weights to which every conceivable type of item should conform. The last of these appeared as late as 1772 as a printed booklet which lists almost 300 items and in addition stipulates which alloy shall be used for many of them.[23] As we have already seen, the quality of the metal to be used was defined as early as 1348 and this remained essentially unchanged over the centuries, though antimony replaced copper as the hardener in fine metal – now called 'Hard Metal' – in the latter part of the seventeenth century. The pewterers' products were therefore governed by tight specifications (and also by regulations prohibiting certain 'short cut' manufacturing techniques that were held to be undesirable) and these constraints stifled any move towards competitive innovation. The earliest record we have of prices appears in the ordinances of 1455.[24] These specify, for example, 3-quart pots at 2s each, pottles at 16d, quarts at 10d, pints at 8d and half-pints at 5d; salts were to be sold at 2½d and 3½d each, and trenchers at 3d. Labour costs were also set out, for example, the charge for making round pots and salts for those in the craft was 7s 6d per hundred (probably meaning hundredweight) while those outside the craft paid the higher price of 9s per hundred. Because old pewter had an intrinsic value and was traded in for recycling the price to be paid for this was also specified: either 2d or 2½d per pound depending on whether it was the leady lay metal or lead-free fine metal.

In 1583 a committee of twelve was appointed from among the assistants, the livery and the yeomany 'to syt and determyne as well of the pryces of ware as also of any other matter which they shall find necesary and good for the company'.[25] The Court promulgated a schedule of wholesale and retail prices for a long list of wares in 1615 and fixed a fine which could be a high as 40 shillings for non-compliance.[26] From 1639 there survives in the company's records a remarkable document personally signed by some 120 members of the yeomanry and livery who agreed to be bound by it.[27] This imposed fixed wholesale and retail prices for a range of wares, and set out the discounts to be allowed to the 'country chapmen' who sold the wares outside London, for example, 'flagons [at] 16 pence the pound by retail, 15½d to chapmen; basins [at] 14 pence the pound and not under; stills 14 pence the pound, 13 pence to chapmen'. For old metal traded in for recycling, 11d per pound was to be paid for fine metal and 8d for lay metal. The regulation of differential provincial and London selling prices for its own members had been presaged by an order in 1560 that any person going to a market or fair to sell his wares was not to sell them for less than a halfpenny a pound more than they would cost in London unless he was facing competition from a country pewterer; one Robert Somers was fined for offending.[28]

As well as selling pewter, pewterers hired it out in large amounts to institutions such as livery companies for their election dinners and to the Lord Mayor for his banquets. As early as 1425, the Brewers' Company hired eighteen dozen of pewter vessels for their feast at a cost of 10 shillings. In 1551, Alderman Richard Lambert hired 30 garnishes for the mayor's feast, while the stock book of the pewterer John Shorey records no less than 92 hundredweight of 'loan stock' in 1708.[29] The 1639 edict set the price for hiring to outsiders at 2 shillings a garnish, and at 16 pence between one pewterer and another. A very revealing provision prevented a pewterer bargaining with his customers and also banned the disclosure of the existence of any price-fixing agreement: 'No man shall say that he will abate 2 pence or 3 pence or more whereby to get custom, neither shall any say that it is so ordered and therefore he cannot do it, but being metal it grows dear and wastes much therefore he cannot afford it'. Even the rate of interest to be charged for credit was fixed by this decree. For flatware in general there was a uniform price of 14 pence per pound, but it was ordered that 'whosoever shall give credit to a merchant for three months shall not sell under 14¼ pence and at six months for 14½'. This represents an interest rate of about 7% per annum. Such a rigid framework which left no room for competition was motivated to a large extent by the company's ambition to enhance its reputation and promote consumer confidence in the high quality and uniform prices of its members' wares.[30]

It is clear from this that a cartel was well established by the early seventeenth century and probably long before then. Whatever pewterer's shop in London a customer visited, the asking prices would have been the same. There is, however, no evidence that the company's searchers attempted to impose any fixed selling prices on the provincial pewterers whose shops they searched. Because London pewter carried a cachet and was something of a status symbol, the more affluent country households frequently bought it in preference to locally made wares and thought its reputation made any additional expense well worth paying. For example, the 1573 probate inventory of John Davy of Manchester valued his 'pewter of London metal' at 6*d* per pound while his 'pewter vessels [of] Wigan metal' were entered at 4*d* per pound. Ten years later another Manchester inventory gives values of 8*d* per pound and 6*d* per pound respectively.[31] These probate valuations suggest that at least some of the difference was due to a perceived superior quality of the London metal.

To complete the picture of the dominant position which the Pewterers' Company enjoyed, it is perhaps necessary to touch on another aspect of their control over the market. Pewterers were the main users of tin in this period and were naturally much concerned with its quality and price. Both of these could in principle be controlled since the marketing of tin was a tightly organised royal monopoly. It nevertheless seems that much adulterated tin was coming out from the stannaries, either by purposeful addition of cheap contaminants or due to incomplete refining. As early as 1444, the London pewterers were therefore granted by the mayor and aldermen a perpetual right to search and assay all the tin coming into London to discover 'the grete multitude of Tynne which is untrewe and deceyvable [which] is brought to this Citee and here is solde as dere as the best Tynne'.[32] At the same time they were to have a pre-emptive right to a quarter of all tin coming into the capital for their own members' use. From the early fifteenth century the company had established a close liaison with the Cornish tin industry by granting freedom of the craft to some of the more prominent Cornish tin merchants, such as John Megre (d. 1420) of Truro and London whose daughters married into the powerful stannary families of Erchedeken and Nanvan. John Dogow, the owner of substantial cargoes of tin landed at Southampton was granted his freedom in 1451, and in 1490–1 the Pewterers entertained 'the Cornysshe men' at their hall.[33] Over the years much tin was condemned and because of this the company was allowed in 1633 to appoint one of its members as deputy Assay Master in the stannaries.[34] From this position of strength the company was long able to bargain with the Duchy of Cornwall or with the tin farmers for a guaranteed supply of tin for its members at a favourable discounted price. Typically, the price was £4 7*s* per hundredweight for quantities up to 500 thousandweight annually in the period 1620–30 as against £5 on the open market. This gave London craftsmen an advantage over the provincial makers who had to buy their raw material at the higher open-market price.[35]

The company's favourable price for tin caused some resentment. In 1683, in Wigan, then the most important northern pewtering town, the local company of Pewterers drafted a proposed petition to the crown seeking a similar favourable price and complaining that 'the London Pewterers will certainly either bee partners in the farme or by agreement or some way or other, have such proportion of tin as they shall worke there and att the farmers rate'.[36] The Wigan company did not apparently pursue their petition which also included a request that they be granted the right of search in the north of England, as the London Pewterers 'by reason of their remoteness from these Northerne parts, and the great trouble and charge in travelling so farr, come seldom on this account, and are then in too much haste to rectify these abuses'. Though they justified their request on the grounds of maintaining a uniform national quality of alloy and workmanship, one suspects that this was a ploy to rid themselves of the Londoners and give them freedom to compete on their own terms without interference.

Another aspect of the Pewterers' influence in the tin trade was their monopoly of the manufacture of tin bars of the standard size allowed for export (as opposed to the massive ingots into which it was initially cast in the stannaries). During much of the first half of the seventeenth century the company obtained the exclusive right for its members to cast tin into bars for export.[37] This, they argued, provided undemanding employment for those of its members whose skills were restricted by age or disability, or who were without the financial resources to set up as craftsmen. The Pewterers' Company was perhaps unique among the livery companies in not only controlling the finished products of its trade, but also in its commanding position in respect of the raw material required for it.

By the latter part of the eighteenth century the pewterers' traditional domestic market in household wares had faded in the face of competition from increasingly available cheaper decorated pottery, glass, tinplate and brassware. The remaining production of beer mugs, public house measures and institutional pewter for prisons, workhouses, hospitals and the armed forces became concentrated in 'manufactories', increasingly located in new provincial manufacturing centres such as Birmingham. Moreover, in the later eighteenth century the metalworkers of Sheffield, skilled in the manufacture of Sheffield plate, applied these techniques to a new type of pewter they named Britannia Metal. This was fabricated from rolled sheet and stamped out by machine in imitation of the fashionable – and increasingly ornate – silver styles, rather than being made by the labour-intensive traditional method of casting in a mould followed by hand finishing on a lathe. The over-regulation and conservatism which had inhibited innovation and competition within the traditional pewterer's craft had left most of the old-style craftsmen unable to compete in the new industrial world. The company was bypassed and by the end of the eighteenth century its influence over its trade was at an end.

NOTES

1. R. F. Homer, 'The Medieval Pewterers of London *c.*1190–1457', *Transactions of the London and Middlesex Archaeological Society*, 36 (1985), pp. 138–9. For general reference, see: J. Hatcher and T. C. Barker, *A History of British Pewter* (London, 1974); R. F. Homer and D. W. Hall, *Provincial Pewterers* (Chichester, 1985); and J. Hatcher, *English Tin Production and Trade before 1550* (Oxford, 1973). For the later tin trade, see M. Mizui, 'The Interest

Groups of the Tin Industry in England *c*.1580–1640' (unpublished Ph.D. thesis, University of Exeter, 1999).

2. For the English version enrolled later in the company's records, see: C. Welch, *History of the Worshipful Company of Pewterers of the City of London*, 2 vols (London, 1902), vol. 1, pp. 2–5; for a variant translation, see: H. T. Riley, *A Memorial of London and London Life* (London, 1868), pp. 241–4.

3. M. Sellers (ed.), *The York Memorandum Book*, Surtees Society 120 (Durham, 1911) (translated from the French in Homer, 'Medieval Pewterers', p. 153); H. H. Cotterell, *Old Pewter, its Makers and Marks* (London, 1929), pp. 7–8 and Plate III.

4. Welch, *Pewterers*, vol. 1, pp. 37–9, and vol. 2, Appendix I for the full text in English.

5. R. F. Homer, 'The Pewterers and the Goldsmiths and their Metals – A Family Resemblance', *Journal of the Pewter Society,* 13 (2000), pp. 10–12.

6. Pewterers' Company, Audit Book, 1473–4, GL, MS 7086 (spelling modernized).

7. Audit Book, 1473–1477, GL, MS 7086.

8. *Calendar of Fine Rolls 1471–85* (London, 1961), p. 107.

9. Pewterers' Company, Court Book, GL, MS 7090/2, 4th September 1569 (the record of this search is uniquely (and anomalously) recorded in the Court Book and hence survives); Pewterers' Company, Search Books, GL, MS 7105/1 (1635–41), 7105/2 (1669–83), 7106 (1689–91), 22198 (additional searches and miscellaneous papers 1660 onwards).

10. R. F. Homer, 'A list of the names and locations of all those provincial pewterers whose shops were searched by the searchers of the Worshipful Company of Pewterers, 1474–1723', *Journal of the Pewter Society,* 11 (additional issue) (1998), pp. 55–64.

11. Hatcher and Barker, *British Pewter*, pp. 255–63, survey the marketing patterns as revealed by the 1640 searches.

12. GL, MS 22198.

13. 19 Hen. 7, c. 6. This Act and those of 1512, 1533 and 1541 (see below) are printed in C. A. Markham, *The New Pewter Marks and Old Pewter Wares*, 2nd edn. (London, 1928), pp. 20–32.

14. D. W. Hall, 'Who Enforces the Rules?', *Journal of the Pewter Society*, 10 (1996), pp. 110–11; R. F. Homer, 'Exeter Pewterers from the Fourteenth Century to about 1750', *Reports and Transactions of the Devonshire Association for the Advancement of Science, Literature and the Arts*, 127 (1995), p. 62.

15. Homer and Hall, *Provincial Pewterers*, p. 62.

16. Homer, 'Pewterers and the Goldsmiths', discusses the possible reason for the right to search for brass.

17. 4 Hen. 8, c. 7 (see n. 13 above).

18. 25 Hen. 8, c. 9 (see n. 13 above).

19. 33 Hen. 8, c. 4 (see n. 13 above).

20. Welch, *Pewterers*, vol. 2, p. 184; GL, MS 22198.

21. GL, MS 7105/2, note on last leaf. No detailed record survives though there are allusions to the search in the Court Book.

22. Welch, *Pewterers*, vol. 1, pp. 11–12, quoting Letter Book K, f. 176.

23. Pewterers' Company, *A Table of the Weights and Dimensions of the Several Sorts of Pewterwares* (London, 1772). The copy in the Guildhall Library is apparently unique and was reprinted in facsimile in the *Journal of the Pewter Society*, 4 (1984), pp. 84–99.

24. Pewterers' ordinances of 1455, GL, MS 22156 (photocopy, original at Pewterers' Hall), transcribed in R. F. Homer, 'The Pewterers' Ordinances of 1455', *Journal of the Pewter Society*, 5 (1986), pp. 101–6.

25. Welch, *Pewterers*, vol. 1, p. 290.

26. Welch, *Pewterers*, vol. 2, pp. 68–9.

27. GL, MS 22202.
28. Welch, *Pewterers*, vol. 1, p. 212.
29. G. Unwin, *The Gilds and Companies of London* (London, 1908), p. 195; R. F. Homer, 'A London Pewterers' Workshop in 1551', *Antiquaries Journal*, 79 (1999), p. 254; R. F. Homer, 'John Shorey Senior and Junior', *Journal of the Pewter Society*, 8 (1991), p. 55.
30. For a discussion of the company's motives, see: Hatcher and Barker, *British Pewter*, pp. 154, 163, 179 and 207–8.
31. T. S. Willan, *Elizabethan Manchester*, Chetham Society, 3rd ser., 27 (Manchester, 1980), p. 116.
32. Welch, *Pewterers*, vol. 1, pp. 13–14.
33. Homer, 'Medieval Pewterers', p. 143–4.
34. Welch, *Pewterers*, vol. 2, pp. 92–3.
35. Hatcher and Barker, *British Pewter*, pp. 201–2, 234–6; Welch, *Pewterers*, vol. 2, pp. 78, 94, 131–2.
36. R. J. A. Shelley, 'Wigan and Liverpool Pewterers', *Transactions of the Historical Society of Lancashire and Cheshire*, 97 (1945), pp. 10–11.
37. Hatcher and Barker, *British Pewter*, pp. 202, 236; Welch, *Pewterers*, vol. 2, pp. 18, 36, 80.

8.

Search, Immigration and the Goldsmiths' Company: A Study in the Decline of its Powers

JOHN FORBES

For seven centuries, the Goldsmiths' Company has been responsible for the assay and hallmarking of precious metal wares. During much of this time, it wielded further extensive powers to control the trade practices of not only its own members but others engaged in the manufacture or sale of such articles. For the first four hundred years of its existence, the company relied on two distinct sources for these powers: royal charter and Parliamentary statute. These powers did not remain constant throughout this period: the fortunate survival of a complete set of company minute books dating from 1334 to the present day (with the exception of a single volume covering the years 1579 to 1592) provides ample evidence of the gradual erosion of the effectiveness of its charters after the mid-seventeenth century, as the company was forced to rely increasingly on various Acts of Parliament for the confirmation of its authority to perform its duties. Two aspects of the company's activities which serve to illustrate this transition will be examined here: its periodic searches for substandard wares, and its attempts to exercise control over immigrant workers from the Continent. This decline in the company's powers appears to have mirrored the decline in the powers of the monarchy, as Parliament progressively assumed much of the authority that was formerly the prerogative of the crown. Similar problems were experienced by other London companies; however, in contrast to the fortunes of many of these companies, the Goldsmiths' Company's right to exercise its main responsibility, hallmarking (the assay and marking of gold and silver wares), was never in doubt.[1] That the Goldsmiths' powers should prove to be a special case in this instance is not entirely surprising. The trade had been closely regulated since early times, not only as a form of consumer protection but – more significantly from the sovereign's standpoint – because of the important relationship between the coinage and plate. The Mint relied largely on melted silver wares for its raw material and owners of plate could readily convert their property into money. It had therefore always been considered necessary that silver wares should be not less in fineness (a measure of the precious metal content of an alloy of gold or silver, now usually expressed in parts per thousand) than the coinage.[2]

Searches

Standards for gold and silver wares had first been laid down in 1300 by a statute of Edward I, which required them to be assayed by the wardens of the goldsmiths' guild; silver wares, if up to standard, were to be marked with a leopard's head.[3] Other statutes along the same lines followed over the next two centuries, but despite the importance of this legislation the company's powers of search were primarily provided by its charters.[4] The first royal charter was granted to the company in 1327, while further ones in 1393, 1404, 1462 and 1505 gave the company wide powers, including the right to search the premises of anyone engaged in the manufacture or sale of gold or silver wares and to punish offenders – at first in London only, but later also in other towns throughout the country.[5] Regular searches to ensure the maintenance of standards were a common activity among other livery companies, but in most cases their jurisdiction was confined to London. If wares seized during the Goldsmiths' searches were proved on assay to be below the minimum legal standard – or if other misdemeanours such as the use of defective weights or balances were discovered – the culprits were summoned to appear before the wardens at Goldsmiths' Hall in London where they would normally be fined.[6] The faulty wares were then broken. Persistent offenders were often imprisoned: the compter in Bread Street was in frequent use.[7] Offending members of the company were sometimes put in the stocks that were prominently displayed inside the Hall so that their associates could witness their disgrace.[8] The wardens were able to exercise these powers solely by virtue of the company's charter.

The company carried out its duties conscientiously during these centuries, suggesting that it was a role they accepted wholeheartedly rather than found an imposition. Its minute books contain countless records of searches with copious details of substandard articles seized by the wardens together with the names of the offenders and the fines or other punishments imposed. These searches could be extensive undertakings. In 1543, for example, one of the wardens searched in Nottingham, Derby, Lichfield, Coventry, Leicester, Worcester and other places, while in 1571, two wardens, the clerk and the beadle rode to the west country visiting Sherborne, Shaftesbury, Wells, Bristol, Bridgwater, Taunton, Exeter and Barnstaple.[9]

The company's extensive powers did not go entirely unchallenged. Following a search in Norwich in 1506, during which a number of suspect articles had been seized, the Norwich assembly sent two aldermen with two counsel to ride to London to put its case against the authority of the London company in their city. Despite their arguments, the King's Council sitting at Greenwich six months later ruled that the Goldsmiths' Company's ordinances were as valid in the city of Norwich as they were in the city of London. This decision, along with the successful prosecution of a goldsmith from Bridgwater who had defied the wardens' search, evidently provided useful precedents, for the company's authority was seldom challenged during the next hundred years.[10] Indeed, the Norwich search was possibly undertaken as a test, coming one year after the company had been granted a new charter, and in spite of the fact that the provincial city had been granted its own 'touch' (assay) in 1423.[11] By the early seventeenth century, however, the wardens began to meet resistance, not only in the provinces but also within London itself. Occasionally, they were even impeded by senior members of the company. In 1622, for instance, they had to go to the unusual extent of calling on the Lord Mayor to assist them in bringing to heel one such recalcitrant member, William Ward of Cheapside, a longstanding member of the Court of Assistants who was openly defying their authority.[12]

Such resistance prompted the Goldsmiths around 1630 to seek the means to prevent future challenges and to strengthen its powers in general. Deciding that the best method would be by statute, the company's efforts focused on promoting a Parliamentary Bill to include the right to search as well as other provisions.[13] Like a number of other companies at this time, the Goldsmiths' Company was beginning to sense that the authority it derived directly from charters granted by royal prerogative was increasingly questionable and inadequate, and that it would have to turn to Parliament if it was to retain its powers. Although in its endeavour to obtain Parliamentary legislation it would face endless frustration, nonetheless, for more than a hundred years the company tenaciously stuck to its purpose, demonstrating the importance it attached to obtaining new legislation. Charles I's personal rule in the 1630s obviously offered no opportunities to acquire statutory support, but in January 1640, encouraged by the imminent recall of Parliament, a committee of eighteen – interestingly, representing all grades of membership – was appointed by the company's court of assistants. The committee met repeatedly over the next two years to formulate proposals.[14] The resulting draft Bill was ready to be introduced in the House of Lords when the civil war intervened.[15] A further company committee was appointed in 1650 and met on a number of occasions, but again no new legislation proved forthcoming.[16]

After the restoration of the monarchy in 1660, another comprehensive Bill was drafted.[17] After much discussion and amendment, during which it was trimmed until it concentrated mainly on securing the company's powers of search, it was presented to Charles II in December 1664 together with a petition for a new charter. Although a confirmation charter was obtained two years later, no new legislation followed. The frustrations of some members of the company seem to have heightened in the ensuing years, and in 1668, some dissatisfied junior members petitioned the Privy Council, complaining amongst other things that the wardens were not carrying out enough searches.[18] As a result, these members felt that they were being subjected to unfair competition from aliens and others who were not complying with the minimum legal standards. In its counter-petition, the company admitted that it had been neglecting its searches and partly blamed this on the opposition it faced from persons refusing to let the wardens carry out their duties. A number of recommendations for reforming abuses in the trade were put forward by the company – together with a reminder that it had already presented 'a humble petition to His Majesty with a Bill to be passed into an Act of Parliament'.[19] In drafting and presenting these measures, the company called upon some of its most influential members, such as Sir Thomas Vyner, his nephew Sir Robert Vyner, Francis Meynell and Edward Backwell, all wealthy goldsmith bankers, but to no avail.[20]

Tensions within the company continued, and in March 1678, some of its trade members submitted another formal complaint against the wardens to the Privy Council. Accompanied by Sir John Shorter, Edward Backwell, several members of the court of assistants, the wardens and their legal adviser appeared before the Council to answer the charges.[21] As a result, the Attorney General was asked to prepare a draft document for Charles II with a view to strengthening the wardens' powers of search. With raised hopes, the wardens presented to the Attorney General copies of the petition (slightly amended) and the Parliamentary Bill that had been presented fourteen years earlier, but were told that it was not convenient to introduce a Bill in the House of Lords at that time owing to pressure of business. The company still hoped, however, that the King might issue a proclamation or grant a stronger charter. Disappointingly nothing was achieved. In the meantime, to avoid confrontations while ensuring some form of search was maintained in the provinces, the wardens began to pay others to purchase suspect wares on their behalf instead of searching in person. If these goods were found on assay to be substandard the offenders were summoned to London and arbitrarily fined.[22] They usually attended and paid the fines without argument, knowing they risked prosecution if they failed to do so. In contrast to the wardens' earlier searches, this practice resulted in some much needed income for the company at a time it was facing considerable financial problems following repeated demands from the sovereign (forced loans), the civil war and, more recently, the great fire, as well as relieving the wardens of making long and hazardous journeys.

In and about London and Westminster, however, the wardens continued to make regular searches in person, relying on the terms of their charter. Even here, it was apparent that they were becoming increasingly uncertain of their authority – although not of the need for the search in the first place. For example, when making their usual search at Bartholomew Fair and the surrounding district in 1682, they took the precaution of first obtaining warrants from the Lord Chief Justice authorising them to seize substandard wares from certain specified dealers whom they anticipated might refuse them access to their stock.[23] After the end of the seventeenth century, the wardens were even more frequently resisted, signalling the continued and steady erosion of their powers, and making it all the more apparent that the powers conferred by the company's charters were inadequate. New charters or confirmation of existing ones had been granted by successive monarchs (with four exceptions) since 1327, but the last grant the company received was from James II in 1685.[24]

Increasingly concerned about the legality of its procedures and faced by growing resistance, the Goldsmiths' Company took legal advice in 1716 on several matters, among them the right to search.[25] It was advised by counsel that the wardens had no authority under the terms of its charter to search the premises of persons living outside the City boundaries without their consent if they were not members of the company, nor to make seizures or fine them; although the company's own members were obliged to obey its by-laws, non-members were not. The company was also advised that the only way in which penalties could be recovered from offenders who were not freemen of the company was by action in the courts under the relevant statutes. This was unwelcome advice: having to sue for penalties was a far from lucrative business. Following this, searches in and around London were only maintained for another seven years, during which they became increasingly difficult to carry out. In 1720, the wardens reported that they had been 'reviled in a rude and indecent manner', and during their final search on 1 October 1723 they met with fifteen refusals.[26] After this date, no searches are mentioned in the minute books. A month later, the company decided that in future persons selling substandard wares would be dealt with only by prosecution under the existing law: the maker or seller of a substandard ware was liable to forfeiture of the ware or its value, which was recoverable by court action, one half of the proceeds going to the Crown and the other half to the person who sued. Shortly afterwards an advertisement was placed in the *Gazette* encouraging members of the public to bring to the notice of the company any offences committed in the trade. At about the same time, the practice of purchasing suspect wares from country dealers and arbitrary fining of offenders was discontinued. It was now clear to the company that its authority to search for substandard wares and fine offenders under its charter was in practice unsustainable and could only be restored by an Act of Parliament. Consequently, there was now no further attempt to obtain a new charter or confirmation of the existing ones.

Despite a number of other London companies abandoning their searches in this period, the Goldsmiths' Company drafted another Bill in 1726 that included the right to search by the wardens, this time restricted to within 20 miles of London.[27] Although it had a second reading in the House of Lords, it had not been passed by the time Parliament was prorogued. However, the attitudes of some of the members of the company had changed since the mid-seventeenth century: thirteen workers, including nine members of the company, signed a petition to the House objecting to the clause in the Bill relating to the right to search. Strikingly, nine of the objectors to the clause – among them six of the members of the company – were Huguenots. When a further comprehensive Bill was drafted by the company eleven years later, it was considered inexpedient to include any reference to searches.[28] Indeed, dropping search from the Bill reflected a broad climate of opposition to such powers. For example, in 1753 a Parliamentary Committee investigating the Framework Knitters' Company took objection to four of its by-laws, one of which concerned powers of search, stigmatising them as 'illegal and contrary to the Liberty of the subject; tending to a Monopoly; discouraging the Manufacture and destroying the Trade of the Kingdom'.[29]

The Goldsmiths' Company finally did obtain a new Act after a century of campaigning. *The Plate Offences Act 1738*, although containing no mention of the powers bestowed by charter, included all of the provisions put forward by the company in its draft Bill, among them the authority to charge for hallmarking small articles and new penalties for offences. The Act became one of the principal hallmarking statutes until its repeal nearly two hundred and fifty years later.[30] Many prosecutions in the courts were undertaken by the company under this and subsequent Acts, but the power to search was not included in any of these statutes until the passing of *The Hallmarking Act 1973*.[31] This Act, with subsequent amendments, embodies the whole of the current legislation. The company's former powers of search have to some extent been restored, as the Act authorises trading standards officers and officers of the Goldsmiths' Company or the other assay offices in Birmingham, Sheffield and Edinburgh to enter the premises of dealers and to seize any suspect wares: they have, however, no authority to fine offenders without action in the courts, nor are the compter or stocks any longer available!

Immigrant workers

From the early fifteenth century, the steady influx of craftsmen from the Continent was a source of constant irritation to the native goldsmith community. A list compiled in 1469 recorded 113 immigrant goldsmiths active in the London area alone.[32] The impact of these 'Dutchmen' or 'strangers', coming mainly from the Low Countries, the Rhineland and the Baltic ports, in the sixteenth century has been recently examined by L. B. Luu.[33] The company made a great effort to exercise control over them: a succession of ordinances were issued restricting the conditions under which immigrant goldsmiths could work.[34] Attempts to prevent strangers working altogether were unsuccessful, but the company did manage to impose the requirement that they produce a written testimonial of good character; they were also obliged to take an oath of obedience to the wardens for which there was a charge. Some were admitted as freemen of the company, usually after payment of a substantial fee and were then permitted to work on their own and to take apprentices.[35] Once again, the company relied to a great extent on its searches in order to locate alien workers and enforce the relevant ordinances. Its powers were confirmed to some extent by an Act of 1477 that ordered alien goldsmiths in London and within two miles of the City to be 'obedient to and ruled by' the wardens.[36] But after several re-enactments, this Act expired in 1572, leaving the wardens reliant exclusively on the powers contained in the company's charter. Attempts to control the influx of aliens into craft trades at this time were by no means confined to the Goldsmiths' Company; other livery companies were adopting similar measures and encountering similar difficulties.[37]

The members of the Goldsmiths' Company were vocal about these immigrants. The company's minute books contain many references to members complaining about aliens working in London and threatening their livelihoods. These complaints became more numerous after the mid-seventeenth century and, on a number of occasions, petitions were addressed to the wardens appealing for some action to be taken, suggesting that there was increasing competition within the trade.[38] The grievances were heightened by the fact that these foreign craftsmen were often more highly skilled than their native counterparts. This was particularly apparent in the case of Huguenot silversmiths who settled in London after the Revocation of the Edict of Nantes in 1685, a number of whom were granted denizenship and in the course of time accepted as members of the company.[39] Even so, from the mid-century onwards the company was finding it increasingly difficult to exercise any consistent control over aliens through its chartered powers. In a petition to the Privy Council in 1668, it entreated the king to issue a proclamation for suppressing aliens working in the goldsmiths' trade but received no response; like the Crown and Privy Council in the late sixteenth century, Charles II had considerable sympathy with Protestant refugees.[40] Faced with the ineffectiveness of its chartered powers, and subject to continual pressure from its members, the court of assistants in 1661 and again in 1676 considered taking action in the courts under the 1563 Statute of Artificers, according to which no-one was permitted to set up or exercise any craft unless they had served a seven years' apprenticeship.[41] The company was advised that it would be inappropriate for a corporation to initiate such proceedings, but it nonetheless hinted that it would support any of its members who might do so.[42] Such circumspection was probably fortuitous: in 1669 the Privy Council was of the opinion that the 1563 Statute 'though not Repealed yet has been by most of the Judges looked upon as inconvenient to Trade and to the Encrease of Inventions'.[43]

The petitioners to the Goldsmiths' Company were particularly concerned about competition from aliens working, as they put it, in 'holes and corners' – especially those making small articles that were often substandard.[44] While wares that were considered too small to bear a hallmark were required by law to conform to the minimum standard of fineness, they were difficult to control as they did not have to be sent to the assay office at Goldsmiths' Hall for testing. With regard to manufacture of larger articles, the company still had a reasonably effective means of restricting foreign workers. Such wares were subject to compulsory hallmarking, but only those submitted by members of the company, or from the end of the seventeenth century by London freemen generally, were accepted at the assay office. Thus, the only way anyone who was not a freeman could get wares hallmarked and offer them for sale legally, was to persuade someone who was registered at the assay office to submit them as if they were of his own manufacture, a practice known as 'colouring' which, despite the initial fraud, retained the quality control aspect. Unsurprisingly, it was strictly prohibited under the by-laws of the Goldsmiths' Company and punishable by a fine.[45]

However, the ability of the company to use its control of hallmarking to limit non-member goldsmiths was seriously undermined by an Act of 1700, according to which *any* person was entitled to submit articles to an assay office.[46] The significance of this act seems not to have been immediately realised by the company, probably because the purpose of the Act was to set up provincial assay offices in York, Exeter, Bristol, Chester and Norwich; the company itself was not specifically mentioned. It was only after taking legal advice in 1716 that the company accepted that the Act meant that it could no longer restrict the right to the so-called 'assay and touch' to citizens of London and that in future it would be obliged to accept wares for hallmarking from anyone: an Act of Parliament inevitably took precedence over a company ordinance.[47] A printed notice was therefore issued requiring 'all goldsmiths, silversmiths and plateworkers, both freemen and others, inhabiting within the Cities of London and Westminster, the Borough of Southwark and near the same' to enter their marks at the assay office and to bring their wares to be assayed and marked.[48]

The trade members of the company tried hard to get this decision reversed. A petition to the court of assistants signed by twenty craftsmen, all liverymen, argued that it would discourage young men from becoming 'apprentices to the mystery'. However, their primary concern was with the impetus it would give to foreign workers.[49] The petitioners were even prepared to indemnify the wardens and officers of the company in the case of any action brought against them for refusing to accept wares for hallmarking from someone who was not a freeman. They also acquainted the court with their own counsel's opinion which was more favourable to their cause.[50] At the same time, a similar petition was submitted by forty-eight journeymen members. However, the court of the company stood its ground. Its decision was amply justified in 1725 by the critical view of the Attorney General, Sir Philip Yorke (later Earl Hardwick), in his report on a case brought against officers of the company for making illegal charges for hallmarking:

It appears to me that this prosecution was commenced by the same artificers who are freemen of the said company not with a real intent to redress the mischief complained of or for any good purpose, but in order to compel the company to do another illegal act, that is to exclude non-freemen from the Touch and Assay or to take revenge on the company for not having excluded them.[51]

Faced with such a climate of opposition to corporate privileges, the company accepted that it would have to rely on the hallmarking statutes rather than its royal charter if it were to exercise any control over the trade, and that it could no longer discriminate against aliens working in Britain.

Conclusion

Although the exact reasons why the Goldsmiths' Company finally decided to abandon its searches and the fining of offenders are not recorded, it is probable that the major factor was its realisation that it could no longer rely on the powers granted by royal prerogative and embodied in its charters. However, the company's attempts to obtain the confirmation of their powers by statute were unsuccessful as such limited privileges became increasingly unpopular. At the same time, the company was becoming more divided, with opposition to searches by some of its members, while the growth of towns and expansion of trade increased the difficulties of its national jurisdiction. With an improvement in the company's finances after a difficult period in the second half of the seventeenth and early years of the eighteenth centuries, even the income provided by the fines exacted from offenders became less important. A similar pattern is apparent in its dealing with immigrant workers. The company's growing inability to maintain the control it once exercised over aliens by virtue of its charters was inevitable in view of the mounting public sympathy, shared by the Crown, for refugees from persecution in the late seventeenth century. The experience of the Goldsmiths' Company was certainly not unique – at the same period not only livery companies but also other chartered bodies suffered the loss of some or all of the powers they had once exercised – but in retaining an active role in governing its craft, the company managed something few other corporate bodies of the period sought or achieved.

NOTES

I would like to acknowledge the help given to me by David Beasley, Librarian of the Goldsmiths' Company.

1. W. F. Kahl, *The Development of London Livery Companies: An essay and a bibliography* (Cambridge, Mass., 1960), pp. 25–30; J. R. Kellet, 'The Breakdown of Gild and Corporation Control over the Handicraft and Retail Trade in London', *Economic History*

Review, 2nd ser., 10 (1957–58), pp. 381–94; M. Berlin, 'Broken all into Pieces', in G. Crossick (ed.), *The Artisan and the European Town* (Aldershot, 1997), pp. 75–91.

2. T. F. Reddaway and L. E. M. Walker, *The Early History of the Goldsmiths' Company* (London, 1975), p. xxi.

3. 28 Edw. I c. 20.

4. 37 Edw. III c. 7; 2 Hen. VI c. 17; 17 Edw. IV c. 1.

5. A number of other livery companies obtained charters during the same period: G. Unwin, *The Gilds and Companies of London* (London, 1908); Kahl, *London Livery Companies*, pp. 15–17. The more important of the Goldsmiths' Company's charters (excluding that of James II) are recorded in the original Latin and in translation by W. Herbert in *The Twelve Great Livery Companies of London*, 2 vols. (London, 1836), vol. 2, pp. 287–98.

6. The minimum standard for silver wares was 'sterling' – in the modern notation, 925 parts per thousand.

7. Goldsmiths' Hall, Goldsmiths' Company, Court Minutes [hereafter GCM], Book D, p. 268; GCM, Bk. G, pp. 3, 8, 21.

8. GCM, Bk. C, p. 146; GCM, Bk. D, f. 268.

9. GCM, Bk. G, p. 65; Min. Bk. L, pp. 74–6.

10. Reddaway & Walker, *Early History*, pp. 196–7.

11. 2 Hen. VI, c. 17.

12. GCM, Bk. P (Part 2), pp. 586, 590–3.

13. It appears that the Goldsmiths' Company had not previously sought to obtain Parliamentary legislation for its power to search; other livery companies had, but without success: see, I. Archer, 'The London Lobbies in the Later Sixteenth Century', *Historical Journal*, 31 (1988), p. 20.

14. GCM, Bk. V, ff. 33, 44–5.

15. GCM, Bk. V, ff. 46.

16. GCM, Bk. Y, ff. 163, 241–2, 260.

17. It was entitled 'A Bill for the Prevention of Stealing of Plate and Reformation of Sundry Abuses in the Goldsmiths' Trade' and was comprised of a number of clauses. The preamble referred to obstructions encountered by the wardens in their searches and included a clause authorising the breaking open of any locked chests, boxes or cases wherein any wares were concealed. It also referred to the increase in the goldsmiths' trade and a clause was included to permit the nomination of additional members of the company to assist the wardens on their searches: Goldsmiths' Hall, Goldsmiths' Company, Company Archives [hereafter GCA], G.II.2; J.V.(i),4; GCM, Bk. 3, ff. 22–3, 186–8, 191, 198; GCM, Bk. 4, f. 82.

18. GCM, Bk. 5, ff. 222–3.

19. GCM, Bk. 5, ff. 225–30; GCA, J.V.(i), 10.

20. Sir Thomas Vyner was Lord Mayor in 1653–54 and Sir Robert Vyner in 1674–75.

21. GCM, Bk. 8, f. 54. Sir John Shorter was Lord Mayor in 1687–88.

22. GCM, Bk. 10, ff. 197–9 et al.

23. GCM, Bk. 9, f. 25. Two and a half years later the livery companies received writs from Charles II to surrender their charters: see, I. G. Doolittle, *The City of London and its Livery Companies* (London, 1982), pp. 16–19; M. Knight, 'A City in Revolution: The Remodelling of the London Livery Companies in the 1680s', *English Historical Review*, 112 (1997), pp. 1141–78.

24. The exceptions were Henry V, Edward V, Richard III and Charles I. The Goldsmiths' Company received a new charter from James II in 1685 that gave him power to control the election of wardens and membership of the court of assistants; it was declared void in 1689 by statute (2 Will & Mary c. 8), but by October 1688 James II had already restored the privileges held by the livery companies before the surrender of their charters.

25. GCM, Bk. 11, pp. 343–48

26. GCM, Bk. 12, pp. 274–6. Resistance to searches was usually by refusal of shopkeepers to unlock their chests or 'glasses' (display cases).
27. Kahl, *London Livery Companies*, pp. 25–30. GCM, Bk. 12, p. 415; GCA, J.V.(i), 23. One of the main purposes of this Bill was to give the company authority to charge for hallmarking.
28. GCA, G.II.2. One of the six Huguenot objectors was the celebrated silversmith Paul de Lamerie. He was a member of the committee appointed by the company to draft the subsequent Bill and would certainly have pressed for the exclusion of powers of search.
29. Kellett, 'Breakdown of Gild', p. 392.
30. 2 Geo. II c. 26. Although the Bill was promoted by the Goldsmiths' Company, the resulting Act applied to all existing assay offices in England. The Act also contained clauses concerning makers' marks, duties of assay offices and lists of wares exempted from hallmarking.
31. 1973 c. 43.
32. GCM, Bk. A, pp. 120–1.
33. L. B. Luu, 'Aliens and their Impact on the Goldsmiths' Craft in London in the Sixteenth Century', in D. Mitchell (ed.), *Goldsmiths, Silversmiths and Bankers, Innovation and the Transfer of Skill, 1550–1750* (London, 1995), p. 35.
34. Reddaway and Walker, *Early History*, pp. 250, 263–5.
35. Reddaway and Walker, *Early History*, pp. 120–131.
36. 17 Edw. IV c. 1.
37. See: I. W. Archer, *The Pursuit of Stability: Social Relations in Elizabethan London* (Cambridge, 1991), pp. 124–140; A. Plummer, *The London Weavers Company (1600–1970)* (London, 1972) pp. 144–161.
38. GCM, Bk. Z, f. 205–6ff. *et al.*
39. A. Grimwade, *Rococo Silver* (London 1974), pp. 14–17.
40. See note 19 and Plummer, *Weavers Company*, p. 156–7; A. Pettegree, *Foreign Protestant Communities* (Oxford, 1986), pp. 262–4, 289–295.
41. 5 Eliz. I c.4.
42. GCM, Bk. 3, ff. 64, 66–7; GCM, Bk. 7, ff. 196, 217.
43. Kellett, 'Breakdown of Gild', p. 383. The Council was discussing a case brought against Francis Kidersby of Framlingham which was eventually stopped by an order of *nolle prosequi*.
44. GCM, Bk. 5, f. 210; See also W. B., *A New Touchstone for Gold and Silver Wares* (London, 1679), pp. 59–63.
45. Plate was certainly submitted in this way from time to time, although it is impossible to ascertain the extent of the practice.
46. 12 & 13 Will. III c.4. The legal standard of wrought plate had been raised by an Act of 1697 in order to discourage the melting of coins for use in its manufacture. As that Act did not mention the existing provincial assay offices, they were effectively closed. However, the authorities in those towns were not slow to complain and the offices were restored by the Act of 1700, except in Newcastle-upon-Tyne which was brought into line by an Act of 1702. It is unlikely that Parliament was purposely restricting the Goldsmiths' Company's powers by the Act of 1700; its effect in that respect was apparently not appreciated by the company until sixteen years later.
47. See note 25; GCM, Bk. 11, pp. 343–8.
48. GCM, Bk. 11, p. 359.
49. GCM, Bk. 11, pp. 360–4; GCA, J.V.(i), 16.
50. GCM, Bk. 11, pp. 378–81, 386–8; GCA, J.V.(i), 17.
51. PRO, T1/253.

9.

Informality and Influence: The Overseas Merchant and the Livery Companies, 1660–1720

PERRY GAUCI

In the summer of 1713, the liverymen of London were lectured on the awesome responsibility of their Parliamentary representatives who spoke for

> the capital of the British empire, the greatest emporium of trade in the world, and a City that has always been looked upon as a main bulwark of the liberty, as it is the main seat of the property, of the people of Great Britain.[1]

Even though pre-election fervour lay behind this impassioned claim for metropolitan greatness, few historians would dispute the pivotal role of the burgeoning capital in stimulating national development across a very broad front. However, many would question the significance of the livery system as an agency of London's success, especially as the late Stuart age has been characterised as one of general decline for the livery companies. In terms of economic regulation, they are perceived to have faced irreversible challenges, as the continuing expansion of the metropolitan suburbs rendered their chartered powers ever more obsolete. The great fire was also particularly damaging for their cause, forcing many of them to allocate already-stretched resources towards the rebuilding of the livery halls.[2] Given these major difficulties, it is easy to see why some analysts have assumed inexorable decline for these once-proud institutions as the citizens of Georgian London looked elsewhere for the services once provided by the company system.[3] While there can be little dispute that the company system struggled to come to terms with these fundamental challenges, this brief study will suggest that their appeal for influential Londoners did not disappear overnight, and that they remained important foci for City society in the late seventeenth and early eighteenth centuries. Through a study of their relationship with London's overseas traders, it can be shown that the company system could still adapt to the needs of a dynamic metropolitan élite. In particular, the role of the companies as informal centres of association ensured them the continuing interest of many of the City's leaders.[4]

In common with our City patriot of 1713, historians of late Stuart politics have recognised the continuing significance of the liverymen after 1660. As the qualification for the vote in parliamentary elections, the livery retained a key importance during an age when embryonic party warfare ensured an ever-higher premium on the support of the City electorate. Most notably, Gary De Krey's exhaustive study of the metropolis under William and Anne highlighted the importance of the corporate institutions of the square mile for the development of Whig and Tory groupings, and bore further testimony to the rich political culture of the City. His work has been bolstered by the researches of Henry Horwitz and Nick Rogers, whose analyses of City associations have illuminated the workings of the complex organisms of City life.[5] Inspired by their findings, this study seeks to broaden our understanding of City politics by examining the socio-political role of the companies, and asks whether historiographic concentration on the franchise has failed to do justice to the wider impact of the company system.[6] As London's richest occupational group, the merchants studied here cannot represent the overall experience of London's citizenry, and their relationship with the companies was necessarily different from that of the retailers and artisans to be found elsewhere in this volume. However, their elevated position demonstrates the potentially far-reaching influence of the companies within the social and political life of the capital. By adopting the perspective of a metropolitan élite, rather than of a party manager, it can be shown that the services of the companies were very much in demand, and that, alongside many other traditional features of the City landscape, they could adapt to an era of economic and political upheaval. This approach thus attempts to appreciate the holistic role of the companies in City life, rather than assess their political significance merely by the standard of the occasional City poll.[7] The relationship between the companies and the overseas merchant is especially interesting because in strictly business terms they offered little overt benefit to international dealers. The overseas merchants had no livery company of their own, and (at least in theory) their professional interests were furthered by the likes of the East India Company and other chartered trading companies, or by the fluid associations of the unregulated mercantile sector. Nevertheless, in 1700 merchants were still joining livery companies in droves, and their reasons for so doing re-emphasise the dynamism of the City's institutional heartland as it continued to cater for both individual and corporate needs.[8]

In order to appreciate the broader role of the livery companies, it is necessary to acknowledge the general importance of City associations for the advancement of business. The following account of 1675 pays ample testimony to the informal politicking which enlivened metropolitan commerce:

> Some men's business lies abroad, and cannot be so well managed at home, and ... these meetings of societies are advantageous to them. As first, merchants, by these clubs and meetings, have intelligence of ships going out and coming in, and also of the rates and prices of commodities, and meet with customers by accident, which possibly might never make inquiry at their homes or warehouses. The like excuses all men of business and trade pretend.[9]

This lively portrait of the merchant as a sociable, ever-alert man of business was not meant to be flattering, but it serves to highlight the essential importance of association for the overseas trader. The author in fact castigated the trader for haunting taverns and coffee-houses, and exhorted him to stick to a more regular orbit, arguing that 'the Exchange is appointed for the merchant's intelligence, and his warehouse is his shop'. However, the very unpredictability of their profession ensured that successful merchants could not restrict themselves to these two arenas, and they sought opportunity and protection through a wide sphere of contacts. In essence the overseas trader was the middleman par excellence, and his business diary would centre on the maintenance of productive relationships with customers, suppliers and creditors (both at home and abroad). The management of these networks demanded personal attention, not to mention considerable reserves of time and effort. Facing these multifarious demands, traders predictably sought their advancement through connections of varying degrees of formality. Economic historians have emphasised the pivotal importance of the family as the primary focus of a trader's economic and social perspective, and its significance reflects the commercial priority of securing trustworthy associates. However, in reality international commerce could not have functioned as a completely atomised set of mercantile businesses, and merchants readily appreciated the utility of collective action.[10] The challenges of overseas trade, particularly to far-distant lands, would simply have overwhelmed traders who lacked the support of trading associations and government-backed organisations. The early modern town could provide the physical environment for business, in the form of the afore-mentioned exchanges for dealing and warehousing for storage, but the increasing competitiveness of international commerce demanded ever more of the resourcefulness of the individual, and ineluctably forced him to rely on greater associations, and ultimately the state itself.[11]

Recognising the importance of commercial networks, historians have been quick to study formal merchant organisations, prompted not least by contemporary concern about their impact on the development of English trade, and even on Augustan party politics.[12] This exciting research has highlighted the potential sophistication of the political machinery available to merchants, even though concentration on party affiliation has largely precluded a more searching examination of mercantile associations during the age of commercial 'revolution'. Recent studies have also alerted scholars to the potential effectiveness of informal politicking within the City. As Alison Olson has shown for London-based colonial traders, the City's social and commercial environment was geared to serve commercial interests, whether formally via the walks of the Exchange, or informally through the establishment of coffee-houses dedicated to the indulgence of specific trading groups.[13] In this respect there may well be many forms of association whose importance has yet to be uncovered, for instance the City's county feasts or its pot clubs. Although these assemblies were overtly apolitical, contemporaries remarked on their widespread importance, and apologists argued that such conviviality was essential for advancing business. Given the fluid bonds within the unregulated trades, such organisational foci could have played a significant role in advancing general commercial interests, although it is notoriously difficult to pinpoint their precise influence.[14] The livery companies represent one such City structure, each of them a forum providing the 'institutional' informality attractive to both regulated and unregulated traders. The electoral privileges of the liverymen have alerted historians to their parliamentary significance, but their socio-political character must also be recognised, particularly as their brand of corporatism could respect the competing mercantile priorities of independence and influence. The appeal of the companies can be linked to their maintenance of a direct political role as commercial lobbyists, but they also provided more subtle services that ensured their continuing popularity with merchants well into the eighteenth century.[15]

The most obvious test of the continuing significance of the livery companies within the City rests with their ability to recruit businessmen into their ranks. In general, it appears that the companies were struggling to attract members from the mid-seventeenth century onwards, with declining overall rates for admission to the City freedom, which remained a prerequisite for company entrance.[16] Contemporaries expressed due concern at these developments, but closer inspection of recruitment patterns suggests that the livery companies still managed to recruit the greatest merchants after 1660, and remained central to the organisation of City public life. Taking a sample of 850 merchants active in the 1690s, it can be shown that at least 51% of them took up the freedom of the City, and that at least 321 of them (or 38%) became liverymen; figures which suggest that the perceived 'flight from the freedom' was not the mad panic that is sometimes portrayed.[17] In fact, these figures are even more impressive when limited to British-born merchants, of whom three-quarters were free of the City. There was no reason for complacency on the part of company governors, however, for it does appear that these recruitment rates represented a decline from pre-civil war levels. In particular, the freedom proved less attractive to foreign merchant-settlers, of whom only a fifth became free. Nevertheless, this failure should not mask the general importance of company and civic life to the merchant.[18]

Membership of a livery company was clearly not a prerequisite for prominence within the trading world, but large numbers still enlisted, most evidently as a boost to business and reputation. The fiscal and legal advantages of the freedom of the City were an obvious incentive, and historians have rightly concentrated on the growing importance of the livery as a means to gain the parliamentary vote.[19] However, the significant differential between freemen and liveried merchants suggests that attitudes towards the companies were far from tied to the simple issue of the franchise, and freeman-merchants were even ready to incur heavy fines to avoid the livery. For instance, in 1678 French trader Abraham Caris offered to pay the Leathersellers £25 for the privilege of remaining a simple freeman of the company.[20] It was not absolutely necessary for an overseas trader to ascend the corporate ladder after gaining the freedom of the City, and this element of choice must be recognised, since it reflects the appealing flexibility of these traditional City institutions. The corporate commitment expected of the individual was far from uniform, and we must be aware that the system could accommodate a heterogeneous membership.[21]

When attempting to ascertain the motivations of those merchants who took up the livery, it is impossible to ignore the vagaries of individual choice, and we must recognise that they would assess its advantages against a highly personalised set of circumstances, ranging from family connections to business prospects and political ambitions.[22] However, these individual decisions reflected common perceptions concerning the role of the liverymen within City life, and overall patterns of recruitment can provide significant insights concerning the general appeal of the livery to an important sector of London society. The distribution of our 321-strong sample of mercantile liverymen is analysed in Table 9.1, which also distinguishes their mode of admission by patrimony, apprenticeship and redemption. Altogether, merchant members were found in twenty-seven companies, and the most popular sixteen are represented here.[23]

The general preference of merchants for the most prestigious of the City livery companies conforms to traditional recruitment patterns. In particular, the premier livery company, the Mercers, had long been associated with London's commercial élite, and its membership reflected its pre-eminent status.[24] However, while reputation was keenly sought by the overseas trader, the heavy concentration of merchants in the 'great twelve' companies cannot be attributed to status considerations alone. When deciding whether to enter a City company, there were evidently several factors playing on each merchant's mind. For certain trades, most notably those governed by the Levant, Eastland, Russia and Merchant Adventurers Companies, the freedom was an unavoidable requirement, and there would be pressure on the wealthy trader to assume a prominent role within a livery company commensurate with his general City standing. On the other hand, each individual had to balance against this confirmation of status the costs of admission and livery fees, as well as the likelihood of corporate responsibilities. Thus, livery companies had to provide some attraction for wealthy merchants who, although having no livery company of their own, could choose to spend their time and energies as members of other City associations.[25]

Most interestingly, there is much evidence to suggest that certain livery companies were successful in attracting recruits from particular spheres of trade, whether of a specific geographic or commodity area. For instance, when Anthony

TABLE 9.1

Merchant membership of the livery companies (1690s sample)

Company	Total	Method of Admission			
		Patrimony	Service	Redemption	Unknown/Uncertain
Mercers	57	7	33	12	5
Haberdashers	30	3	20	5	2
Drapers	28	6	12	8	2
Merchant Taylors	26	3	17	5	1
Grocers	25	1	9	2	13
Fishmongers	22	0	12	8	2
Clothworkers	18	4	11	1	2
Vintners	15	2	5	3	5
Skinners	12	3	4	3	2
Ironmongers	10	1	8	1	0
Dyers	10	0	7	1	2
Shipwrights	10	0	0	7	3
Salters	8	1	2	0	5
Embroiderers	8	1	2	1	4
Leathersellers	6	2	3	1	0
Weavers	5	0	2	0	3
Others (11 companies)	31	1	2	11	17
Total (number)	321	35	149	69	68
Percentage		11	46	21	21

Cornwall sued for his freedom in June 1689, he chose not to enter the Clothworkers' Company, to which his master belonged, 'but dealing in tobacco desires his freedom in the Company of Grocers', the current home of five leading Virginia traders. For their own part, it is clear that the Grocers' Company were keen to enlist the leading specialists in their sphere of commerce, going out of their way to poach a well-connected future MP from the Haberdashers in the early 1690s. Other companies reveal similarly suggestive clusters of merchants. A third of the Merchant Taylors of our sample can be linked to the Iberian and Madeiran wine trade, while at least a third of the Fishmongers were cloth merchants. Most significantly, nearly half of the mercantile Mercers were also members of the Levant Company, thereby reinforcing both the superiority of the premier livery company, and the distinctiveness of the Turkey traders. Merchants such as Caleb Hooke were willing to pay fines of £50 to switch from his company of apprenticeship (the Haberdashers) to the Mercers. The fact that at least a fifth of the merchants in the table were prepared to pay higher redemption fees to enter companies is illustrative of the careful deliberation which accompanied the merchant's choice of company, as well as the flexibility of the system in general. Many factors would be involved in his selection, but membership patterns do suggest that civic ties could bolster trading associations, helping to bring together smaller groups of merchants united by commercial, ethnic or familial interests. Thus, while it is impossible to segregate all the mercantile livery into neat geographical or commodity areas, they do appear as an important source of political connection in the mercantile sphere.[26]

The aforementioned movement between companies is highly significant, but general admission patterns indicate that the choice of company was still heavily influenced by the young merchant's master. Nearly half of the liveried merchants were made free by service, simply following in the civic footsteps of their mercantile tutor, and these personal bonds clearly promoted the concentration of specialists in certain companies. Very often there existed a familial tie between master and apprentice to render the company even more attractive, and the livery hall could indeed become a home-from-home for certain merchants. While familial connection is a predictable feature of choice of company, admission patterns also highlight the importance of ethnic ties, with several companies appearing popular with immigrant merchants, most notably the Shipwrights, Dyers and Embroiderers. The presence of several trading dynasties in these companies is highly illustrative of the potential sociability of merchants within City institutions, which bolstered the more assured bonds of marital ties within their circle. An excellent example concerns the extended Huguenot network of the Houblons, Lethieulliers, Denews and Carbonnels, all of whom could boast members of the Dyers' Company. Livery membership undoubtedly reinforced ties between four of the leading lights of the Threadneedle Street congregation, even though the French Church took priority over the company as the topographical hub of Huguenot life. Nevertheless, like the halls of all the leading merchant companies, the Dyer's hall was sufficiently close to the Church for overseas traders to involve themselves in its activities. The company halls were also used extensively for private and group celebrations, which could only have helped to cement professional and personal ties within trading circles still further.[27]

While membership patterns suggest that the livery halls did provide a semi-formal associational focus for merchant groups, it is important to stress that the companies did not play an overt role in the politics of overseas commerce. John Brewer has highlighted the importance of the livery companies for promoting the parliamentary campaigns of artisan and retailing groups, but their significance for the interests of overseas traders is far harder to discern.[28] On the one hand, it is clear that merchants could share common commercial interests with the domestic traders in their livery companies, but surviving records do not indicate that merchants used the companies as a platform from which to champion such causes. This reticence reflects the perceived institutional responsibilities of the livery companies, since ministers and parliamentarians expected them to comment on their restricted sectors, and turned to the overseas companies or unregulated traders for specialised comment. However, given the clustering of merchants in certain companies, it would be naïve to suggest that leading liverymen were not enjoined by their brethren to act on behalf of mercantile interests, as well as on behalf of artisan and retailing members. Predictably, the less prestigious companies appeared very keen to curry the favour of leading mercantile members. For instance, when Sir John Fleet moved from the Coopers to the Grocers in 1692 in order to qualify himself for the mayoralty, the former commissioned his portrait 'in perpetual memory of so honourable and worthy a member'. The maintenance of informal personal influence was probably the most potent form of livery political activity. Voting preferences have been readily studied by psephologists, but the socio-political role of the livery companies has yet to be explored for the later seventeenth century, and they may well have provided informal meeting-places for merchants to discuss matters of state away from the Exchange, trading company headquarters, local tavern or coffee-house. It would have been particularly odd for the halls not to have evolved as such forums when they were essential elements of the formal structure of City politics.[29]

Less doubt surrounds the general appeal of the livery companies to the over-worked businessman. The hierarchical distinction between liverymen and the lesser freemen, journeymen or yeomanry was suited to flatter the pretensions of any wealthy trader to elevated City status, and overseas merchants were in general rich enough to be promoted into the upper strata of the companies with little effort. For their own part, companies appeared concerned not to overburden merchants with yet more offices, and many traders were able to rest content with the political and fiscal rights of the freedom and livery.[30] It was clearly in the interest of the Merchant Taylors' Company to show sympathy to busy MP Sir Henry Ashurst, who was allowed to postpone his tenure of the mastership on four occasions when he was 'concerned in public business' and thus 'could not in person attend the affairs of this company'. Demonstrating a more general concern for the pressures on its leading members, the company ruled in 1681 that no new motions could be entered in the court of assistants after noon so that officers could 'go to the Exchange about their several and respective concerns'.[31] Given the potential burdens involved, it is all the more significant that at least 74 of the sample (23% of the identified livery merchants) were prepared to undertake office within the companies, and 36 of these liverymen served in their highest offices. Several wardens and masters were also the leaders of other City institutions, and their willingness to accept livery office speaks volumes for the continuing prestige of the companies.[32] The example of colonial trader Robert Bristow is particularly interesting in this regard, for in July 1692 he agreed to serve as warden of the Grocers, even though professing himself to be 'wholly a stranger to the company's affairs'. The high profile of the companies within the civic calendar, especially at the time of elections and inaugurations, was an understandable incentive, giving livery officials the opportunity to preside over an influential group of their fellow citizens. However, it is more likely that at root the real attractions of the livery hall centred on the contacts to be made there, rather than the pomp of its ritual ceremonies.[33]

The kaleidoscope of connections that might be mediated through the livery system did not accord the company hall a greater significance than the immediate foci of the merchant's counting-house or the floor of the Royal Exchange. Nevertheless, when personal association was so important for the advancement of business, there is no doubt that a large cross-section of City merchants found company activity to their advantage, and historians need to appreciate the resilience and versatility of these 'declining' institutions. To this day, the commercial hub of national life has been criticised for having too 'clubbable' a feel in certain quarters, and that the golf course or old school tie can bar advancement to all but the favoured few. Such inequalities clearly existed in early modern London, and were preserved in institutionalised forms. Not every liveryman gave slavish devotion to his company, and as with any association various degrees of commitment could be espied among the membership. However, beyond the pomposity of civic ceremony there remained an informality in which businessmen could indulge their passion for networking in a convivial but controlled atmosphere. Undoubtedly there were individuals who found livery life stuffy and uncongenial, but many more thrived in its surroundings, and secured advancement on many personal fronts thanks to this fluid form of political association. All in all, membership did have its privileges.[34]

NOTES

I would like to thank the Oxford University Press for permission to use extracts here from my *The Politics of Trade* (Oxford, 2001).

1. *Advice to the Liverymen of London, showing that it is for their Interest and Honour to choose Merchants in Trade for their Representatives in Parliament* (London, 1713), pp. 1–2.
2. J. R. Kellett, 'The Breakdown of Gild and Corporation Control over the Handicraft and Retail Trade in London', *Economic History Review*, 10 (1957–8), pp. 381–94; T. Reddaway, *The Rebuilding of London after the Great Fire* (London, 1940), esp. chapter 9.
3. Note in particular Peter Clark's recent argument asserting the dominance of new forms of voluntary association in eighteenth-century society: *British Clubs and Societies, 1580–1800* (Oxford, 2000), pp. 23–4, 35, 154. For the political travails of the liveries, see M. Knights, 'A City Revolution: The Remodelling of the London Livery Companies in the 1680s', *English Historical Review*, 112 (1997), pp. 1141–78.
4. For a more positive view on the role of the seventeenth-century livery company, see J. P. Ward, *Metropolitan Communities: Trade Guilds, Identity and Change in Early Modern London* (Stanford, 1997). B. G. Carruthers has also recently noted their 'considerable organizational vigour' – *City of Capital: Politics and Markets in the English Financial Revolution* (Princeton, 1996), p. 185. Their views in general accord with the work of M.

J. Walker: 'The Extent of the Guild Control of Trades in England *c*.1660–1820: A Study Based on a Sample of Provincial Towns and London Companies' (unpublished PhD thesis, University of Cambridge, 1986).

5. G. S. De Krey, *A Fractured Society* (Oxford, 1985); H. Horwitz, 'Party in a Civic Context: London from the Exclusion Crisis to the Fall of Walpole', in C. Jones (ed.), *Britain in the First Age of Party* (London, 1987), pp. 173–94; N. Rogers, *Whigs and Cities* (Oxford, 1989). In common with all historians of the City, they are indebted to the pioneering work of Valerie Pearl on the workings of City politics in the Stuart age: *London and the Outbreak of the Puritan Revolution* (Oxford, 1961).

6. The potential rewards of livery studies have been highlighted by recent histories of the companies, which have sought to contextualize individual companies within broader social and political developments: I. Archer, *The History of the Haberdashers' Company* (London, 1991), esp. chapters 9 and 10; I. Doolittle, *The Mercers' Company, 1579–1959* (London, 1994).

7. For a stimulating discussion of the diverse and important role of the medieval guild in mediating economic relationships, see Gervase Rosser, 'Crafts, Guilds and the Negotiation of Work in the Medieval Town', *Past and Present*, 154 (1997), pp. 3–31.

8. For a survey of the relationship between the merchant and politics in the seventeenth century, see R. Grassby, *The Business Community of Seventeenth-Century England* (Cambridge, 1995), chapter 7. Concentration here on the overseas traders (as distinct from inland/domestic merchants and wholesalers) has been recommended by recent research and contemporary observation. The growth of England's international commerce in the seventeenth century appears to have promoted a more distinct cadre of overseas specialists, who were increasingly fêted by the press. Domestic traders still continued to deal directly abroad, especially in provincial towns, but by the early 18th century the term 'merchant' was generally reserved for an overseas trader – see my *The Politics of Trade*, chapters 1 and 4.

9. R. T., *The Art of Good Husbandry, or The Improvement of Time* (1675), reproduced in J. Thirsk and J. P. Cooper (eds.) *Seventeenth-Century Economic Documents* (Oxford, 1972), pp. 97–9.

10. The best survey of the workings of an international firm remains H. Roseveare, *Markets and Merchants of the Late Seventeenth Century* (Oxford, 1987).

11. Peter Clark has recently provided a tantalizing glimpse of the huge range of commercial clubs in the late seventeenth century, and notes that a contemporary defined 'club' as a group designed 'to promote trade and friendship': *British Clubs and Societies*, pp. 9–12, 53–4. For more general discussion of the inter-dependence of urban residents, see J. Barry, 'Bourgeois Collectivism? Urban Association and the Middling Sort', in Barry and C. Brooks (eds.), *The Middling Sort of People: Culture, Society and Politics in England, 1550–1800* (London, 1994), pp. 84–112.

12. Although concentrating on the joint-stocks, the best general account of corporate activity remains W. R. Scott, *The Constitution and Finance of English, Scottish and Irish Joint-Stock Companies to 1720* (Cambridge, 1919). For a brief, although illuminating, account of the development of the companies in the post-Restoration period, see C. Wilson, *England's Apprenticeship, 1603–1763*, 2nd edn. (Harlow, 1984), pp. 172–6. For published company histories covering the Augustan period, see A. C. Wood, *A History of the Levant Company* (Oxford, 1935); K. N. Chaudhuri, *The Trading World of Asia and the English East India Company* (Cambridge, 1978); L. S. Sutherland, *The East India Company in Eighteenth-Century Politics* (Oxford, 1952); K. G. Davies, *The Royal African Company* (London, 1957); R. W. K. Hinton; *The Eastland Trade and the Commonweal* (Cambridge, 1959); W. E. Lingelbach, 'The Internal Organization of the Merchant Adventurers of England', *Transactions of the Royal Historical Society*, n.s., 16 (1902), pp. 19–67; E. E. Rich, *The History of the Hudson's Bay Company 1670–1870* (London, 1958–9); J. Carswell, *The South Sea Bubble* (London, 1960).

13. A. G. Olson, *Making the Empire Work: London and American Interest Groups, 1690–1790* (Cambridge, Mass., 1992). For an excellent example of the impact of 'private' commercial combinations on overseas trade, see H. Roseveare, 'The Damned Combination: The Port of London and the Wharfingers' Cartel of 1695', *London Journal*, 21 (1996), pp. 97–111.

14. Thirsk and Cooper (eds.), *Seventeenth-Century Economic Documents*, pp. 97–9; J. Macky, *A Journey Through England in Familiar Letters* (1714), vol. 1, pp. 189–90. For the political impact of the London county feasts, see N. Key, 'The Political Culture and Political Rhetoric of County Feasts and Feast Sermons, 1654–1714', *Journal of British Studies*, 33 (1994), pp. 223–56. For more formal organizations, see N. Rogers, 'Clubs and Politics in Eighteenth-Century London: The Centenary Club of Cheapside', *London Journal*, 11 (1985), pp. 51–8; H. Horwitz, 'Minutes of a Whig Club', *London Record Society*, 17 (1981); D. Allen, 'Political Clubs in Restoration London', *Historical Journal*, 19 (1976), pp. 561–80. For a recent reappraisal of the role of the coffee-house, see S. Pincus, 'Coffee Politicians does Create: Coffee-Houses and Restoration Political Culture', *Journal of Modern History*, 67 (1995), pp. 807–34.

15. For the role of the livery companies as lobbyists, see J. Brewer, *The Sinews of Power: War, Money and the English State, 1688–1783* (Oxford, 1989), pp. 237–42. For a brief survey of the constitutional development of the livery companies in this period, see I. Doolittle, *The City of London and its Livery Companies* (Dorchester, 1982), pp. 1–20.

16. Ian Doolittle has shown that the number of freeman admissions doubled after a crackdown by the London corporation in 1712, but fell again shortly afterwards. The overall admission rate in the eighteenth century was only two-thirds that of the preceding century: 'The Government of the City of London, 1694–1767' (unpublished D. Phil. thesis, University of Oxford, 1979), pp. 29–48.

17. The sample is based on the returns from the poll tax assessments of the 1690s at the Corporation of London Records Office, which have been collated in a database held at the Centre for Metropolitan History, Institute of Historical Research, Senate House, London. The sample is restricted to merchants resident within the City. The only other major survey of Augustan merchants traced 42% of a sample of 1,339 traders as liverymen: De Krey, *Fractured Society*, pp. 128–9.

18. Immigrant merchants constituted 181 (21%) of the sample, with significant numbers of French, Dutch and Jewish traders settling in the capital after 1660. Their presence was a significant factor behind the declining freeman rate within the sample: born pre-1642 (130 traders), 74.6%; born 1642–59 (316 traders), 61.7%; born post-1660 (125 traders), 60%. Immigrants would have to obtain naturalized or denizen status before becoming members of the companies, and thus they were unlikely to recruit foreign merchants who wished to spend a limited time in England.

19. For a contemporary account of freeman privileges, including exemptions from tolls in other English towns, preferential rates for local port duties, and the right to be tried in local courts, see *The Freeman of London's Necessary and Useful Companion* (London, 1707).

20. Leathersellers' Hall, Leathersellers Company, Court Minutes, 27 May 1678. Although the freedom and livery were key stages on the civic *cursus honorum*, it cannot be assumed that freedom-taking reflects a burning political ambition, since only 120 of our sample (i.e. 28% of the freeman-merchants) achieved civic office.

21. Remarking on the increasingly diverse occupational profile of the Haberdashers' Company, Ian Archer queried whether livery life would have retained the same attraction for members in the Stuart period: *Haberdashers' Company*, pp. 125–36. Such variety was not necessarily a disincentive for the mercantile middleman, especially in terms of securing business contacts.

22. The paucity of merchant archives is particularly frustrating in this context. However, personal records can misrepresent an individual's commitment to the companies (or any

other association). In particular, wills present many problems, since even very active livery officials often made no reference to their companies in their last testament.

23. The vast majority of livery company records can be found in the Guildhall Library, although several companies still retain their archives, most notably the Mercers, Clothworkers, Leathersellers and Drapers. The London poll books of 1710 and 1713 are also very useful for identifying liverymen. A further 113 (13%) of our merchant sample can be identified as City freemen, but have not be linked to a City company.

24. For excellent studies of the prominence of the Mercers' Company, see Doolittle, *Mercers' Company*; J. Imray, *The Mercers' Hall* (London, 1991).

25. Ian Archer has demonstrated that the costs of livery membership could be high, especially in terms of providing dinners and paying fines to avoid office. For instance, the early Stuart officers of the Haberdashers' Company might have had to supply as much as £100 p.a. for hospitality, while the fines for the court of assistance were as high as £40 in the late seventeenth century: *Haberdashers' Company*, pp. 53–4, 93, 126–8. Quarterage dues for liverymen were generally much more modest (only 9–16*d* per quarter in the Ironmongers' Company), but often evaded: GL, MS 16986/5.

26. Freeman petitions can be found at the CLRO, esp. CF1/23, no. 166; History of Parliament 1690–1715 section, draft biography of Edmund Boulter. I. Doolittle noted a rise in freedom redemptions after the 1690s, and linked it to the desire of 'outsiders' to participate in City politics: 'Government of the City of London', pp. 31–2. Olson sees political significance in the fact that active colonial traders accounted for 22% of the liveried merchants in the 1690s (according to De Krey's figures): *Making the Empire Work*, p. 33.

27. The Merchant Taylors' Hall appears to have been in great demand for musical events and feasting: GL, MS M F331, *passim*. Of published works, note in particular Imray, *The Mercers' Hall*, which provides a fulsome account of the multi-faceted uses of the livery halls, including the three-day celebrations at Drapers' Hall for the nuptials of Sir John Frederick's eldest son in 1676: pp. 261–2. By way of contrast, the large overseas trading companies do not appear to have fostered a clubbable attitude on the basis of their essential business unity: K. G. Davies, *The Royal African Company* (London, 1957), p. 162.

28. Brewer, *Sinews of Power*, pp. 237–42. Chartered artisan and retailing companies provided less than 6% of the 1,174 petitions submitted to the Commons concerning mercantile matters in the 1690–1714 period.

29. W. Foster, *A Short History of the Worshipful Company of Coopers of London* (Cambridge, 1944), p. 129. A suggestive example of the subtle influence of livery ties on business dealings relates to the company for winding fine silk. The company was founded in 1692, and three of first investors were John Barkstead (its governor), John Franks and Humphfrey Simpson, all of whom had become Mercers in 1690: *CSPD*, 1691–2, pp. 302–3. Livery links can also be espied in the lists of witnesses to brokers' bonds, although common interests in overseas trade appear a more obvious focus for collective activity: CLRO, BR/P.

30. The reluctance of merchants to serve as company officers probably helped to prevent too obvious a polarization between greater and lesser members of the companies, which has been seen as a source of tension in the early seventeenth century: G. Unwin, *The Gilds and Companies of London* (London, 1908), chapter 17. No evidence has been found to suggest that merchants used the companies as a means to dominate their domestic suppliers and customers.

31. Ward, *Metropolitan Communities*, pp. 83–5; GL, MS M F331; Merchant Taylors' Company, Court Minutes, November 1681, 19 July 1689, 27 July 1691, 29 June 1692, 17 July 1696. In July 1698 Ashurst fined for £80 to avoid the office 'by reason of his living at distance in the country' (i.e. Oxfordshire).

32. For the propensity of Tudor and early Stuart merchants to rise through parish, livery and civic ranks, see F. F. Foster, *The Politics of Stability: A Portrait of the Rulers in Elizabethan*

London (London, 1977), chapters 4 and 7; R. Brenner, *Merchants and Revolution* (Princeton, 1993), chapter 2.

33. GL, MS 11588/6, p. 6. At the same time as Bristow's election, two other merchants each paid £25 to escape office as wardens. Alongside other evidence, the surviving portraits of liveried benefactors highlight the essential link between the companies and the City hierarchy.

34. On the variety of commitment evident in the livery companies, see Ward, *Metropolitan Communities*, pp. 145–6.

10.

The Shaping of a Family Trade: The Cordwainers' Company in Eighteenth-Century London

GIORGIO RIELLO

Despite being one of the oldest medieval metropolitan companies, the London Cordwainers' Company never acquired the status associated with the twelve major livery companies.[1] The trade was considered unattractive because of its low profit margins, while cordwainers (shoemakers who were members of the Cordwainers' Company) were often not distinguished from other artisans who made shoes in the metropolis.[2] The low profile of the Cordwainers' Company and the shoemaking trade has been paralleled by the lack of interest that historians have paid to the guild.[3] This chapter investigates one of the classic themes of historical studies of guilds in early modern Europe: the relationship between a guild's structure and the associated trade. It focuses in particular on the structural and functional innovations introduced to the trade by the Cordwainers' Company during the eighteenth century as it attempted to retain control over its members and craft. In addition, I seek to draw attention to the place of the urban family in the craft, and to examine how the family unit responded to the company's actions as part of a complex and constantly changing social and economic web. Research on proto-industry, Jan de Vries's 'industrious revolution', and the history of the domestic economy has found the family system a useful structure around which to construct interpretative models of economic change.[4] However, all these models are based on rural situations: in analyses of urban environments, the family has tended to be overshadowed by other social systems. My aim is to locate the three central characters of company life – the apprentice, the journeyman and the master – within a family context. Through this analysis I show how changes that occurred during the eighteenth century affected not only the destiny of the trade, but also the actions of the company itself and its relationship with the familial dimension of the trade.[5]

The relationship between the activities of guilds and the organisation of crafts and trades in the eighteenth century has generally been considered in the light of the declining role that guilds were playing in urban economies. The century has often been perceived as witnessing the final collapse of already weakened companies. In this view of the pre-industrial economy, guild regulations were synonymous with economic stability, limited competition and old-fashioned productive methods.[6] The argument is straightforward: until the end of the seventeenth century, the interests and actions of trade and guild in England existed in harmony, but the expansion of internal and international markets in the early eighteenth century created an opportunity for different productive activities to develop in the countryside (proto-industry) and towns. From about 1700, guilds found themselves unable to govern a growing economy, and trades began to develop freely outside the guilds' regulations. Apprenticeship and formal mastership declined, while new forms of labour organisation appeared in the urban economy.[7] As other kinds of productive organisation became increasingly influential in structuring the economy, guilds limited themselves to social, rather than economic, functions. This narrow view of guilds, perpetuated in numerous studies, has helped sustain a vision of the industrial revolution as the birthplace of modern economic growth. The suppression of sclerotic institutions such as the metropolitan companies has thus been presented as one of the necessary conditions for economic 'take off'.[8] With the separation of trade and guild, occupations became 'modern' productive systems though not only technological and organisational changes, but also the removal of their corporate bonds. It is not surprising, therefore, that the relationship between guilds and other social and economic agents has been considered central to understanding the transformations of the eighteenth-century economy.

While some version of this argument cannot be denied, historical research on guilds has not yet provided a sufficient explanation of the mechanisms and agents of such changes. As Cissie Fairchild has observed with regard to the guild system of eighteenth-century Paris, most research has 'paid more attention to the guilds' political and ideological dimensions than to their economic roles'.[9] Indeed, the lack of knowledge about the process through which guilds lost their traditional economic roles seems to be, at least partially, a product of the theoretical structure used to analyse the guild system rather than the available archival sources. Research on guilds mainly operates along a 'vertical axis', focusing on the state and its actions and studying how companies sought to acquire protection from internal and external competition by regulating access to the trade. These were political issues: the state or local authorities had to agree with the company's policies and regulate their application. Much less research has been carried out along a 'horizontal axis', examining the relationships between different companies, or on an endogenous level, looking at the connections between the structures of the company and the trade.

As the aim of this chapter is to analyse the complex relationship between trade, guild and family during the eighteenth century through the case of the London Cordwainers' Company, the first element to consider is the extent of the power that the company could wield over the trade. It has been argued that only the systematic and continuous control of the trade by a guild could stop the development of productive activities outside the company's bounds.[10] If so, the degree of association between guild and trade should reflect the power of a company. However, the fragility of the political power of the Cordwainers' Company is striking, even though there appears to be a dialectic confrontation between the structuring power of the company – which still had substantial control over most of the trade at the beginning of the century – and the new economic needs of the shoemakers. There is hardly any evidence of an internal oligarchy able to direct the interests of the company.[11] The company made only a few, weak political interventions; its most notable effort was in January 1769 when it campaigned for the prohibition of leather export and the encouragement of the domestic leather trades by the introduction of a bounty on its import.[12] On this occasion, as on many others, complaints were made about the difficulty of even writing a company petition, with the company eventually relying on the Tanners for the formulation of a joint text.[13]

In such a period of limited corporate power, it would be easy to assume the presence of opportunities for a separation between the shoemaking trade and the Cordwainers' Company. Indeed, the lack of information in the court minutes about trade matters suggests the company was not enforcing its ordinances. As with other London livery companies, a substantial problem was the geographical extent of company authority. During the eighteenth century it was still able to act effectively throughout the city and Southwark, but not in the suburbs. While this had been a marginal problem in the early seventeenth century, the economic importance of London suburbs had increased massively by the eighteenth century.[14] The problem became more acute during the second half of the eighteenth century as the centre of London shifted from the City to the western part of the metropolis.[15] Although the company was theoretically involved in the prosecution of 'several persons for illegally carrying on the trade of a cordwainer' during the century, it did not possess the power, authority or financial resources necessary for continuous enforcement.[16] The costs of prosecution could be prohibitively high: when Charles Wood was prosecuted in July 1789 for illegally practising the trade, he was found guilty and fined £2, but the company paid £60 in legal expenses.[17] The company gained little even when it won a case.[18] It is not surprising, therefore, that the cases in which the company intervened were those with a strong symbolic value. For instance, the company decided to prosecute George James and Samuel Sapson at the Court of King's Bench in 1739 and 1742 respectively. The defendants had not only worked as shoemakers without being freemen, but more importantly had accumulated large debts in their activities. In these two cases, the principal aim of the company appears to have been to protect the respectability and solvency of company members.[19] In contrast, although there were numerous examples of curriers, leathersellers and cobblers working illegally as shoemakers, only occasionally did the company decide to intervene.[20]

The spatial dimensions of corporate control and the tensions between companies over the boundaries of trades are traditional subjects for investigations of a guild's power. Such studies follow what I have already described as the vertical and horizontal axes of analysis of the guild system. In the Cordwainers' case, neither the geographical extent of their control nor their relationship with other trades is sufficient to explain why a close relationship between guild and trade continued in shoemaking for most of the eighteenth century. Instead, the notion I seek to employ here is that of guilds as 'communities', or *communautés* (as Steven Kaplan has put it), institutions which aspired to embrace a wide part of the political and economic life of a state, and whose possible decline – or perhaps 'transformation' – during the eighteenth century has to be linked to the birth and empowerment of other kinds of social institutions.[21] The ability of the guilds to evolve in response to economic and social change was mediated through systems of power, control and identification.[22] Masters, journeymen and apprentices could belong to different social systems, in particular, different neighbourhoods and different parishes, making the notion of 'brotherhood' a fundamental concept in the creation of an occupational identity. However, companies were not always able to supply a trade with a cohesive and united identity.[23]

Apprenticeship

Apprenticeship has long been considered one of the fundamental mechanisms through which livery companies were able to govern their trades. The Statute of Artificers of 1563 established a seven-year minimum apprenticeship period in order to qualify for mastership. However, well before the its repeal in 1814 apprenticeship was in decline and, in London as well as in the provinces, trades were often not complying with the statute. The decline of apprenticeship has frequently been taken as an indicator of the degree of association between trade and guild. Historians have suggested different datings for the decline: at the start of the twentieth century George Unwin suggested a date as early as the sixteenth century, the Hammonds postulated that it coincided with the first industrial revolution, while O. J. Dunlop and R. D. Denman cautiously put it between 1720 and 1780.[24] More recent studies of apprenticeship based on the quantification of companies' records have highlighted the seventeenth and early eighteenth century as the critical period, leaving scope for variations among the different trades.[25] Diverse reasons for decline have been offered. The classical interpretation considered the fall in the number of apprentices as a tangible sign of the crisis in the corporate system. The more recent and pessimistic view of Phelps Brown and Hopkins proposed falling real wages in the eighteenth century as one of the main causes for early terminations of apprenticeships and the general reduction in the numbers of apprentices.[26] In contrast, Styles has offered a more optimistic thesis, pointing to the expansion

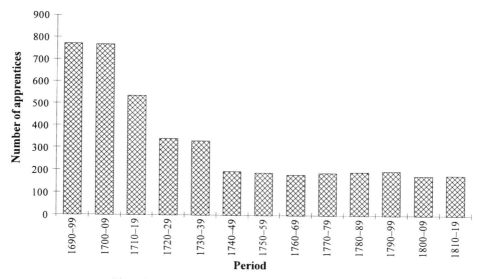

Fig. 10.1. Cordwainers' apprentices, 1690–1819
Source: GL, MSS 7357/2 and 24139.

of the consumer goods' market in Britain during the eighteenth century as
having led to the development of production outside the companies which
offered better opportunities than the corporate system.[27]

The Cordwainers provide a distinctive case for both the timing and causes
of apprenticeship's decline. The fall in the number of cordwainer apprentices
was a relatively late phenomenon, beginning only after 1710. The number of
cordwainers' apprentices enrolled in each decade fell from 770 in the 1690s to
340 in the 1720s; by 1740, rates of enrolment had settled at around 170 to 190
apprentices per decade (Fig. 10.1). The Cordwainers present a pattern of
decline in the number of apprentices that was not only late compared to many
other London companies, but also relatively long in duration, stretching over
three decades. Moreover, I would suggest that the assumption of a
straightforward relationship between declining apprenticeship and decreasing
company participation in the trade's affairs should be questioned. There is a
qualitative dimension that the simple counting of apprentices cannot assess.
Moreover, there is a significant problem with these figures: a cordwainer's
apprentice was not always bound to learn the trade of shoemaking. He could
be apprenticed to a master who, although registered as a member of the
company, was in fact practising another trade. By the late eighteenth century,
this phenomenon was quite common. From 1765, the 'Register of Apprentice
Bindings' began to distinguish between the occupation exercised by a master
and his membership of the company. Moreover, in order to avoid confusions in
the cases of masters with multiple occupations, it was also stated which
occupation the apprentice was going to learn. For example, when in 1797 an

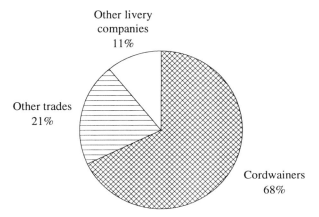

Fig. 10.2. Cordwainers' apprentices' training, 1765–1801
Source: GL, MS 24139.

apprentice was bound to a Buckinghamshire grocer and cordwainer who was also a freeman of the London Cordwainers' Company, it was specified that the apprentice was to learn the trade of a cordwainer.[28] The register therefore allows us to estimate the proportion of apprentices who were being trained in the craft. As Figure 10.2 shows, a considerable proportion (68%) were still learning the shoemaker's trade; 21% were training in trades not organised into companies; and only 11% were going to learn trades which had their own London companies. These are impressive figures. This dimension of apprenticeship has not yet been fully investigated in relation to other companies. Although the proportion of non-shoemaking apprentices was increasing during the second half of the century, the Cordwainers' Company figures suggest that even at this late date some London companies were more homogenous than has sometimes been thought.[29]

However, in order to discuss how the decline of apprenticeship affected the destiny of the company and its control over the trade, we need to consider other changes occurring in the profile of cordwainers' apprentices. By taking samples of apprentices over the century it is possible to identify shifting geographical and social patterns in their backgrounds.[30] As Table 10.1 shows, from the 1730s onwards a high percentage of apprentices, many of them sons of cordwainers, were coming from the metropolis and adjacent counties. In part this reflects a general trend affecting most of the London trades as the development of urban economies in the provinces created alternative local markets with opportunities for apprentices that rivalled those of the metropolis.[31] However, if we compare this pattern with the contemporary figures compiled by William Kahl for the Grocers', Goldsmiths' and Fishmongers' companies or the data provided by Wareing or Glass, we find that the proportion of cordwainers' apprentices from London was unusually high in all the periods considered.[32]

TABLE 10.1
Places of origin of cordwainers' apprentices

	1710–11	1738–41	1759–64	1778–83	1797–1802
	%	%	%	%	%
London	32	52	40	48	55
Middlesex	11	20	23	16	30
Surrey, Kent and Essex	14	13	16	21	2
Other counties	43	15	21	15	13
Total number in sample	85	103	87	104	105

Source: GL, MS 24139.

That London trades not only attracted shrinking numbers of apprentices, but also that most of them were fairly local, has traditionally been interpreted as a further sign of the crisis of apprenticeship in this period.[33] However, this inference can be questioned, particularly when the geographical dimension of apprenticeship is considered alongside the intergenerational links within the trade apparent in the occupation of apprentices' fathers. The father's occupation can be used to measure both social origin and the level of occupational mobility within shoemaking. If we look at the most common occupations of apprentices' fathers (Table 10.2), the relative absence of fathers with high-status or high-income occupations is obvious; the bakers, coopers,

TABLE 10.2
Selected occupations of cordwainers' apprentices' fathers

	1710–11	1738–41	1759–64	1778–83	1797–1802
Baker	2	3	3	6	2
Carpenter	2	3	6	4	4
Chandler	1	2	4	3	0
Cooper	4	2	1	1	2
Cordwainer	*15*	*22*	*9*	*17*	*18*
Craftsman	6	1	0	1	0
Gentleman	0	2	6	7	6
Husbandman	7	1	7	2	3
Labourer	4	3	2	1	3
Taylor	4	4	5	0	0
Victualler	0	7	0	1	6
Watchmaker	0	1	1	6	0
Weaver	3	4	1	2	1
Yeoman	6	6	7	4	0
Other occupations	31	42	35	49	60
Total number in sample	85	103	87	104	105

Source: GL, MS 24139.

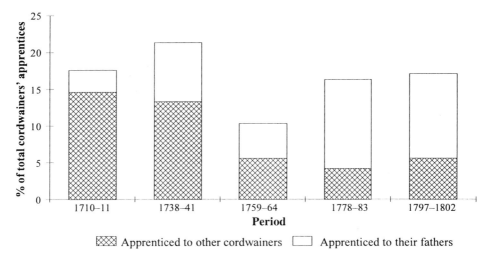

Fig. 10.3. Apprentices from shoemakers' families
Source: GL, MS 24139.

tailors, weavers or labourers who are most prominent among apprentices' fathers were employed in the commonest and often the humblest trades in eighteenth-century London. Perhaps most striking is that, although there were few apprentices from families involved in other parts of the same chain of leather production, such as butchers, tanners, curriers, saddlers or leatherdressers, by far the largest occupational group among apprentices' parents were cordwainers.

An appreciation of apprentices' backgrounds allows us to reassess some common arguments about apprenticeship's decline in the eighteenth century. In the Cordwainers' case, even in a situation of numerical decrease, apprenticeship was not characterised by a simple decline; instead, we find an increasing family dimension to the trade. Throughout the century, apprenticeship remained the main method of communicating 'skills and experience' from one generation to another.[34] Eric Hobsbawm, in his examination of European shoemaking at the end of the *ancien regime*, underlines the existence of just such an intergenerational continuity in London shoemaking, something not present in other European cities.[35] Continuity within families was achieved through the company: about 15 to 20 per cent of all cordwainers' apprentices had a father whose occupation was cordwaining (Fig. 10.3).

The practice of apprenticing sons to their father's trade was widespread within the lower metropolitan trades and cordwaining was no exception.[36] It was normal when the son was supposed to succeed his own father in the family business. An alternative, in which the parental willingness to continue his business in future generations was linked to the expansion of skills, was to apprentice a son to another cordwainer.[37] By entering another's workshop a shoemaker's son could learn new techniques and eventually transmit them back to his father. Through these mechanisms of apprenticeship, shoemakers found in the Cordwainers' Company a useful means of ensuring that their business passed successfully from one generation to the next.[38] However, we should not paint too rosy a picture. In the course of the eighteenth century, an increasing number of young workers were employed in the shoemaking trade outside the company, especially in the East and West parts of London. Even remaining with one's father to learn the trade was not always successful. James Lackington recorded his unfortunate experiences as an apprentice cordwainer with his father in his *Memoirs*: 'I continued with him several years, working when he worked, and while he was keeping Saint Monday'. He finally gave up the occupation, becoming rich and famous as the owner of the *Temple of Muses*, the circulating library in Finsbury Square.[39] Despite these problems, the company continued to prosper within the more traditional sections of the trade where the family was the 'productive unit'. It was perhaps the increasing economic difficulties facing such family workshops in an expanding marketplace that explains the company's eventual problems in controlling the trade as a whole.

Freemen, Journeymen and Women

During the eighteenth century, the decision to enter one of the livery companies increasingly became a sign of social status rather than a requirement to follow an occupation.[40] Membership not only implied social distinction, but also granted the right to attend the meetings and feasts of a company, elect the Mayor and Sheriffs of the City and its Members of Parliament once a liveryman, and sometimes gave access to additional charitable assistance in old age or poverty.[41] Over the same period, apprenticeship decreased in importance as a means to gain the freedom, while patrimony and redemption, claiming the freedom as son of a freeman and paying the company for the freedom respectively, became more common. It should be underlined that these changes in how people acquired the freedom and in what it meant to be a freeman, although connected, did not happen simultaneously or evolve in the same way within different companies. As William Kahl has shown, such changes varied between companies, something which he attributed to their different social standings, as well as to the economic motivations associated with each occupation.[42] In the Cordwainers' Company, as we saw above, admission centred on apprenticeship for a longer period than in other companies, and as a consequence most freemen still worked as shoemakers. In 1756, 75 per cent of Cordwainers followed the cordwaining trade; only in the Butchers', Feltmakers', Innholders' and Brewers' companies did Kahl note higher proportions practising the company craft.[43] The unusual degree of occupational homogeneity in the company is best explained by the cordwainers' social status.[44]

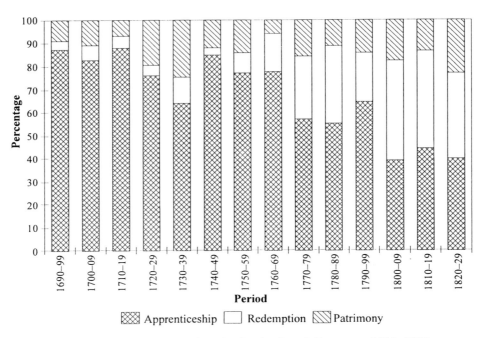

Fig. 10.4. Methods of entering the Cordwainers' Company, 1690–1829
Source: GL, MS 24140.

The changing social and economic environment of eighteenth-century London reduced the authority and control exercised by the City companies over their respective trades.[45] Even in cordwaining, as elsewhere, access to the occupation was becoming easier as redemption and patrimony became increasingly common routes into the company (Fig. 10.4).[46] Cases of sons – and sometimes daughters – joining the company this way are common occurrences in this period. Redemption only became widespread after the 1780s. Even a completed apprenticeship did not guarantee entrance to the trade: numerous difficulties could beset individuals between the end of the period of apprenticeship and the moment at which the shoemaker was able to become a member of the company or set up a business. Financial problems and family conflicts could influence the destiny of an apprentice finishing his term, sometimes forcing him to become a journeyman rather than a master shoemaker.

Only in the 1770s does a dissociation between membership of the company and the practice of the trade become evident. Before that time, an Act of Common Council forbade non-freemen to trade at the City markets and to set up their own shops, although such rules were applied with a certain degree of flexibility by the Cordwainers' Company who welcomed foreigners in periods when production was expanding.[47] Different measures undertaken by the Cordwainers' in the second half of the eighteenth century suggest that it was making great efforts to retain its control over the trade. Recognising that it could no longer force all producers into its fold, in November 1750 the company instituted special licences for non-freemen under which they could be hired as assistants and craftsmen by freemen.[48] Similarly, in 1771 the company again tried to extend its control over the trade: instead of punishing those producers who did not respect their rules, a more relaxed solution was proposed in which the company sought instead to make all London shoemakers become members of the company, with a £5 fine for infraction of the rule.[49] The mixing of old prerogatives with new needs was to a certain degree contradictory, and the establishment of a different mechanism just a few years later suggest that these attempts had proven unsuccessful.

The introduction in 1776 of the 'Right to the Trade' (a certificate attesting the right to exercise the occupation) can be interpreted as a revival of the system of licensing established in the 1750s, albeit in a modified form. It gave an opportunity to those who did not comply with the traditional requirements to work in the trade under the company's jurisdiction but without becoming members. Applications for certificates of 'Right to the Trade' were received especially from London shoemakers who had either served apprenticeship to non-members of the company or gained experience of the craft outside its jurisdiction, both in London and throughout the whole of Britain.[50] We should note, however, that the 'Right to the Trade' neither implied nor led to admission to the freedom.[51] Its introduction created a *legal* break between the membership of the company and the exercise of the trade. On the other hand, such a measure was the only possible course of action available to the company if it were to supervise the increasing number of producers who did not meet the requirements for membership. At the same time, the 'Right to the Trade' gave the company the opportunity to test the skills considered necessary for a shoemaker, as in order to acquire this right a shoemaker had to produce a 'proofe worke' consisting of a pair of boots and shoes.[52] Although not a completely new idea for the company, in this case the 'proofe worke' became the means to secure minimal skills and competence for those who were willing to work within the company's jurisdiction, but who lacked formal training.[53]

As these efforts to retain control over cordwainers suggest, the company was keen to prevent the trade disintegrating into the hands of thousands of unregulated, legal or semi-legal producers, which would have resulted in higher competition in a market where profit margins were already very low. A particular problem they faced in this regard was the curriers' practice of selling small pieces of leather rather than whole hides to 'middling and poorer' shoemakers.[54] According to an enquiry by the House of Commons in 1738, there were less than five hundred London shoemakers who could afford the £10 price of an entire hide, most of them masters and members of the Cordwainers' Company.[55] During the first decades of the eighteenth century, curriers started selling small pieces of leather for as little as two shillings, enabling journeymen to buy the exact quantity needed to produce a pair of shoes for the market on their own account, instead of working for a master who provided their raw materials.[56] With the profit from just a couple of pairs of shoes or boots, journeymen were able to sustain their families and buy another two shillings-worth of leather.[57] Unsurprisingly, large shoemakers opposed the creation of a small shoemakers' market in order to discourage competition and the diversion of labour from the 'virtuous trade'; in this they were supported by the company.[58] In 1738, the company petitioned the House of Lords for the enforcement of an Act of James I preventing curriers from selling small pieces of leather, as they were 'executing the trade of a shoe-maker by cutting leather'.[59] However, the company was not united. Many poorer cordwainers and most of London's small shoemakers supported the curriers' counter-petition, arguing that:

> It is plain that the drift of the rich shoe-maker is to engross the business of shoe-making in the hands of a few to the prejudice not only of the publick, but of thousands of their own trade, who will, in all likehood, be under the necessity of leaving their families to their respective parishes, to travel foreign countries for bread, to the great detriment of the British nation.[60]

The opposition of the curriers and small shoemakers was so strong that Parliament, after a long hesitation, decided to pass a bill in 1739 that repealed the earlier statute, leaving small and large producers to co-exist as best they could.[61]

This picture of journeymen trying to exercise the trade as small independent shoemakers illustrates some of the problems and contradictions associated with their status. Under the family system of production, the journeyman was a member of a close social and affective environment as well as an economic unit.[62] Traditionally, a journeyman was not simply a wage earner but a member of both the trade and, with his master, a community of tradesmen.[63] To understand their shifting roles in production as well as in the labour market, we need to remember that the status of journeyman had traditionally been a transitional phase between apprentice and master.[64] However, this situation was rapidly changing in the mid-eighteenth century. In 1747, the Lord Mayor of the City decided to license all London masters to employ journeymen who had not been formally apprenticed. These workmen, coming in particular from the 'liberties' of the metropolis, were to fill a shortage of skilled labour.[65] This measure seems to have been the formal recognition of an already widespread phenomenon. On average, only one-third of cordwainers' apprentices between 1690 and 1800 completed their apprenticeships and entered the company, meaning that over a century or so only 1500 men could have legally practised as shoemakers in the City of London and two miles outside it. Such small numbers explain why it became necessary to employ journeymen who had not been apprenticed. The expansion of the metropolitan market also meant that many journeymen were employed outside the workshop – unsupervised but still dependent on their masters.[66] This 'out-work system', which flourished from the mid-eighteenth century onwards, allowed the appearance of new forms of business, such as warehouses or wholesale dealers selling ready-made shoes, in direct competition to the traditional system centred on the small workshop that the Cordwainers' Company promoted.[67] As a result of these developments, journeymen were no longer masters-in-waiting. The importance of journeymen's wage disputes during the last quarter of the eighteenth century reflect their increasing concern about an issue that, contrary to established traditions, now influenced not just the first few years of their career, but possibly their entire working lives. When in June 1766 journeymen shoemakers combined to raise their wages, their protests were so acute that the officers of the company had to intervene to restore order and reconcile journeymen and masters.[68]

The increasing difficulties faced by journeymen seeking to rise up the occupational hierarchy were not the only changes in eighteenth-century London shoemaking. Women were also being increasingly marginalised.[69] The shoemaker's craft had long been dominated by men, with women, normally wives or daughters, helping in complementary jobs inside the family business, such as sewing uppers.[70] Women very rarely ran a shoemaking business on their own; Leonard Schwarz's study of insurance registers for 1775–87 shows that of a total of 529 master shoemakers only nine (1.7%) were women.[71] Only twelve women entered the company in their own right during the period 1690–1860, half of whom were daughters of cordwainers.[72] The lack of female master cordwainers was matched by the absence of female apprentices in the trade. At the beginning of the eighteenth century, only 2%–3% of apprentices were women.[73] This percentage fell to 1% after 1710, and women completely disappear from the registers after 1760. The 'Register of Apprentice Bindings' entries show that, on the occasions that they were not cordwainers' daughters, these women apprentices normally came from outside London and had humble origins: the two sisters, Mary and Wilhelmina Vernall, who were bound apprentices to Mary Newark in 1710, were typical in being daughters of a yeoman in Hertfordshire.[74] It was more common for young girls to be apprenticed by a male master but their backgrounds were similar: for instance, Mary Richardson, the daughter of a Nottingham stocking weaver, was bound apprentice to a man in 1739.[75]

Such figures give us an impression of a decline in the importance of women in the occupation. This was not a new phenomenon, having probably started in the medieval period.[76] However, do the figures also reveal a decrease of female participation in boot and shoe production? Recent research has suggested that women continued to make an important contribution generally to the workforce in eighteenth-century Britain.[77] There is, it seems, a dichotomy between the dynamic role of women in the proto-industrial household economy, as highlighted in de Vries's concept of the 'industrious revolution', and women's marginalisation in the organisation of metropolitan craft production.[78] During the eighteenth century, women's roles changed; they lost what remnants of authority they had occasionally possessed and assumed an even more limited role inside the family productive system, either providing additional income or assisting their husbands, sons and brothers 'to bind shoes of all kinds, and to sew quarters together of those that are made of silk, satin and stuff'.[79] Women were no longer independent participants in the trade, even if only on the margins of the company. Their position shifted from the public to the domestic world.[80] However, inside the family, the work of wives and daughters remained important in providing both flexibility and low costs of production.[81]

Conclusion

This paper has sought to show how the demise of the corporate system was, in the case of the Cordwainers' Company, neither straightforward nor unchallenged. When considering how trade and guild interact, the Cordwainers' Company provides a particular and complex example. This relationship appears even more complicated when the relevant actors are placed within the setting of a traditional family-centred system of production. The trade became increasingly reliant on apprentices who had, through their families, stable connections with the occupation. This created a self-perpetuating and increasingly closed system and, by the late eighteenth century, the company was still dominated by cordwainers. However, the corporate system was still under pressure from forces for change.[82] Faced by the same influences, the family also adapted: journeymen found it increasingly harder to become masters and so started to set up businesses outside the company's jurisdiction and their masters' households. At the same time, the role of women changed as they retreated completely into an 'inclusive productive sphere' within the household.[83]

The Cordwainers' Company applied different strategies in trying to resist losing control over the trade. On the one hand, it recognised in the family structure a safe environment in which it could continue to exercise control, retaining it as a corporate and productive ideal; on the other hand, the company tried repeatedly to maintain its authority by developing flexible and responsive measures rather than through direct confrontation. It promoted supervised access to avoid being overwhelmed by unregulated producers. However, this strategy did not ultimately prove successful, as the market shifted away from London and its environs, where the limited efforts of a company could still hope to influence events, towards a national network of production and distribution. In the second half of the eighteenth century, the growth of London presented new opportunities for the trade outside the corporate system. The import of shoes from Yorkshire, Staffordshire and Northamptonshire created a clear division between production and retailing, a separation that the Cordwainers' Company had been resisting for several decades.[84] This new distributive and productive structure could not be contained either inside the boundaries of small-scale family businesses or within the guild system. Paralleling the experience of other companies, by the end of the eighteenth century the Cordwainers' Company had retreated to a defensive rather than an active economic role.[85]

NOTES

I would like to thank Richard Butler, Giovanni Luigi Fontana, Ian Gadd, Perry Gauci, Negley Harte, Julian Hoppit, Gabriella Lombardo, Denise Valerio, Patrick Wallis and Joseph Ward for their help in researching and writing this paper.

1. It has been argued that the concentration on the Twelve Great Livery Companies 'has furnished an eccentric view of guild experience': M. J. Walker, 'The Guild Control of Trades in England, c.1660–1820' (Paper circulated at the Economic History Society Conference, Loughborough, April 1981). See also M. J. Walker, 'The Extent of the Guild Control of Trades in England, c.1660–1820: A Study based on a sample of Provincial Towns and London Companies' (unpublished Ph.D. thesis, University of Cambridge, 1986).
2. On the social and political difference between a cordwainer and a shoemaker, see E. M. Green, 'The Taxonomy of Occupations in Late Eighteenth-Century Westminster', in P. J. Corfield and D. Keene (eds.), *Works in Towns 850–1850* (Leicester, 1990), pp. 176–7.
3. There are two official histories of the Cordwainers' Company, both commissioned by the company itself: C. H. Waterland Mander, *A Descriptive and Historical Account of the Guild of Cordwainers of the City of London* (London, 1931); J. Lang, *The History of the Worshipful Company of Cordwainers of London* (London, 1979).
4. J. de Vries, 'Between Purchasing Power and the World of Goods', in J. Brewer and R. Porter (eds.), *Consumption and the World of Goods* (London, 1993), pp. 85–132; J. Rule, *The Experience of Labour in Eighteenth Century Industry* (London, 1981), pp. 42–4. Volume 6, part 2 (2001) of the journal *The History of the Family* is dedicated to 'family enterprise and family life'. See in particular, T. K. Haveren and A. Plakens, 'Introduction: Family Enterprise and Family Life', pp. 143–5.
5. M. C. Howell uses the useful concept of 'family production unit': *Women, Production and Patriarchy in Late Medieval Cities* (Chicago, 1986), pp. 27–8.
6. For a recent critique see C. R. Hickson and E. A. Thompson, 'A New Theory of Guilds and European Economic Development', *Explorations in Economic History*, 28 (1991), pp. 127–68. See also J. R. Farr, *Hands of Honor: Artisans and their World in Dijon, 1550–1650* (Ithaca, 1988); S. L. Kaplan, *The Bakers of Paris and the Bread Question, 1700–1775* (Durham, 1996).
7. L. D. Schwarz, *London in the Age of Industrialisation: Entrepreneurs, Labour Force and Living Conditions, 1700–1850* (Cambridge, 1992), pp. 11–30; D. R. Green, *From Artisans to Paupers: Economic Change and Poverty in London 1790–1870* (Aldershot, 1998), pp. 1–14; D. Barnett, *London, Hub of the Industrial Revolution 1775–1825* (London, 1998), pp. 1–11.
8. The general historiography has underlined the role of guilds as coercive structures, using economic theory in a 'constraint related environment', with problems of free riding, individual behaviour and monitoring: E. Lindberg, 'Urban Privileges and Corporate Groups in

Stockholm, 1820–1846' (Paper presented at the ESTER Seminar, Lisbon, February 2000), pp. 4–5.

9. C. Fairchilds, 'Three Views on the Guilds', *French Historical Studies*, 15 (1988), p. 688.

10. This should be true in particular for manufacturing and service trades, but not for distributive trades. See K. D. M. Snell, *Annals of the Labouring Poor: Social Change and Agrarian England, 1660–1900* (Cambridge, 1985), pp. 238–9.

11. P. N. Sutton, 'Metropolitan Artisans and the Discourse of the Trade, *c.*1750–1825' (unpublished PhD thesis, University of Essex, 1994), p. 50.

12. *The Present Situation of the Leather Trade with Respect to the Tanner, Currier, and Complete Manufacturer, Fairly and Impartially Stated by the Cordwainers' Company of the City of London* ([London], 3 Jan 1769).

13. PRO, T1 463/331 and 333; *A State of the Agreement Between the Cordwainers and the Tanners* (London, 1769).

14. V. Pearl, 'Change and Stability in Seventeenth-Century London', *London Journal*, 5 (1979), pp. 3–34; M. Berlin, '"Broken all in Pieces": Artisans and the Regulation of Workmanship in Early Modern London', in G. Crossick (ed.), *The Artisan and the European Town, 1500–1900* (Aldershot, 1997), pp. 78–9; C. Harvey, E. M. Green and P. J. Corfield, 'Continuity, Change and Specialization within Metropolitan London', *Economic History Review*, 2nd ser., 52 (1999), pp. 469–72.

15. R. Finlay and B. Shearer, 'Population Growth and Suburban Expansion', in A. L. Beier and R. Finlay (eds.), *London 1500–1700: The Making of the Metropolis* (London, 1986), pp. 44–6.

16. GL, MS 7353/6, f. 28.

17. GL, MS 7353/ 8, ff. 104–5.

18. T. K. Derry, 'The Repeal of the Apprenticeship Clauses of the Statute of Artificers', *Economic History Review*, 1st ser., 3 (1931), pp. 69–70.

19. GL, MS 14318, additional folios.

20. W. M. Stern, 'Control vs. Freedom in Leather Production from the Early Seventeenth to the Early Nineteenth Century', *The Guildhall Miscellany*, 2 (1968), pp. 438–42.

21. S. L. Kaplan, 'The Luxury Guilds in the Eighteenth Century', *Francia*, 9 (1981), p. 257.

22. J. P. Ward, *Metropolitan Communities: Trade Guilds, Identity, and Change in Early Modern London* (Stanford, 1997), p. 3. See also S. L. Kaplan and C. J. Koepp (eds.), *Work in France: Representations, Meaning, Organization and Practice* (Ithaca, 1986); R. MacKenney, *Tradesmen and Traders: The World of the Guilds in Venice and Europe, c. 1250–1650* (London, 1987).

23. Ward, *Metropolitan Communities*, p. 3.

24. G. Unwin, *The Gilds and Companies of London* (London, 1908); J. L. and B. Hammonds, *The Town Labourer* (London, 1917); O. J. Dunlop and R. D. Denman, *English Apprenticeship and Child Labour: A History* (London, 1912). See also Snell, *Annals*, pp. 228–9.

25. J. R. Kellett, 'The Breakdown of Gild and Corporation Control over the Handicraft and Retail Trades in London', *Economic History Review*, 2nd ser., 10 (1957–8), pp. 381–94; W. F. Kahl, 'Apprenticeship and the Freedom of the London Livery Companies, 1690–1750', *Guildhall Miscellany*, 7 (1956), pp. 17–20; D. V. Glass, 'Socio-Economic Status and Occupations in the City of London at the End of the Seventeenth Century', in A. E. J. Hollaender and W. Kellaway (eds.), *Studies in London History* (London, 1969), pp. 373–89.

26. E. H. Phelps Brown and S. V. Hopkins, 'Seven Centuries of the Prices of Consumables Compared with Builders' Wage Rates', *Economica*, 23 (1956), pp. 296–314; E. H. Phelps Brown and S. V. Hopkins, *A Perspective of Wages and Prices* (London, 1981), pp. 16–61.

27. J. Styles, 'The Goldsmiths and the London Luxury Trades, 1550–1750', in D. Mitchell (ed.), *Goldsmiths, Silversmiths and Bankers: Innovation and the Transfer of Skills, 1550–1750*

(London, 1995), pp. 113–14. For a longer perspective, see J. R. Farr, *Artisans in Europe, 1300–1914* (Cambridge, 2000), p. 49–56.

28. GL, MS 24139 (1797).

29. Another problem derives from duplications among the entries. The transfer of an apprentice from one master to another can be recorded as an addition to the entry registering the initial contract between the apprentice and the master, but in some cases there is a wholly new entry for the year of the transfer, stating that the apprentice was previously apprenticed by another master. Such difficulties could in part be overcome through nominal data linkage.

30. A total of 4184 cordwainers' apprentices were enrolled between 1690 to 1820. I have taken five samples, which cover in total about 500 apprentices and 24 of the 130 years. The cases where an entry does not state either an apprentice's geographical origin or the occupation of the father, along with the cases of apprentices registered in the Cordwainers but learning another trade, have not been included in this analysis.

31. C. Brooks, 'Apprenticeship, Social Mobility and the Middling Sort, 1550–1800', in J. Barry and C. Brooks, *The Middling Sort of People: Culture, Society and Politics in England, 1550–1800* (London, 1994), p. 72; J. Wareing, 'Changes in the Geographical Distribution of the Recruitment of Apprentices to the London companies, 1486–1750', *Journal of Historical Geography*, 6 (1980), p. 246.

32. For other investigations of London apprentices' geographical origins, see Kahl, 'Apprenticeship and the Freedom', p. 17; D. V. Glass, 'Socio-Economic Status and Occupation in the City of London', in A. E. J. Hollaender and W. Kellaway (eds.), *Studies in London History* (London, 1969), pp. 373–89; J. Wareing, 'Recruitment of Apprentices', pp. 244–5; M. J. Kitch, 'Capital and Kingdom: Migration to Later Stuart London', in A. L. Beier and R. Finlay (eds.), *London 1500–1700*, pp. 224–51. Glass in his sample of 1590 apprentices bound to various London trades in 1690 found that 20% were coming from London, 9.4% from Middlesex, 9.9% from Surrey, Kent and Middlesex and 60.7% from other counties.

33. In particular, lower trades such as shoemaking are deemed to attract apprentices only from a restricted area: R. S. Smith, 'The London Apprentices as Seventeenth-Century Adolescents', *Past and Present*, 61 (1973), p. 195

34. J. F. Rees, *The Art and Mystery of a Cordwainer* (London, 1813), p. v.

35. E. J. Hobsbawm, 'Political Shoemakers', *Past and Present*, 88 (1980), pp. 102–3.

36. G. Mayhew, 'Life-Cycle Service and the Family Unit in Early Modern Rye', *Continuity and Change*, 6 (1991), pp. 212–16.

37. I. K. Ben-Amos, 'Failure to Become Freemen: Urban Apprentices in Early Modern England', *Social History*, 16 (1991), p. 165.

38. On inter-generational mobility, see in particular: S. M. Cooper, 'Intergenerational Social Mobility in Late Seventeenth- and Early Eighteenth-Century England', *Continuity and Change*, 7 (1992), pp. 283–301; M. R. Hunt, *The Middling Sort: Commerce, Gender and the Family in England, 1680–1780* (London, 1996), pp. 49–53.

39. J. Lackington, *Memoirs of the First Forty-Five Years of the Life of James Lackington* (London, 1794), p. 6.

40. D. Mitchell, 'Innovation and the Transfer of Skills in the Goldsmith's Trade in Restoration London', in Mitchell (ed.), *Goldsmiths, Silversmiths and Bankers*, p. 20.

41. P. H. Ditchfield, *The Story of the City Companies* (London, 1926), p. 271.

42. Kahl, 'Apprenticeship and the Freedom', p. 17.

43. W. F. Kahl, *The Development of London Livery Companies: A Historical Essay and a Select Bibliography* (Boston, 1960), p. 28.

44. J. Dacres Devlin, *The Shoemaker* (London, 1839), pp. 3–4.

45. Kellett, 'The Breakdown of Gild and Corporation Control', p. 381.

46. Kahl, 'Apprenticeship and the Freedom', p. 19.

47. GL, MS 24964, ff. 1–3.

48. Kellett, 'Breakdown of Gild and Corporation Control', pp. 383, 388. This was a particularly important decision, extending the company's influence also to large producers and retailers, characterised by complex productive structures of 'putting out' and sub-contracting.

49. *Commons Journals*, 31 (8 March 1771), pp. 237–8. See also Waterland Mander, *Guild of Cordwainers*, pp. 90–1.

50. GL, MS 14321.

51. Guildhall Library, *Catalogue of Manuscripts of the Worshipful Company of Cordwainers* (London, 1994), p. 67.

52. This introduction of the so-called 'proofe worke' came very late in comparison with other European guilds. In Venice, for instance, the *prova* was introduced in 1553 for all the new members expect masters' sons: A. Vianello, *L'Arte dei Calegheri e Zavateri di Venezia tra XVII e XVIII Secolo* (Venice, 1993), pp. 5–6. In London the 'proofe worke' was quite similar to the sample journeymen carried with them when going 'occasioning', that is to say looking for a job in a shop.

53. GL, MS 24964. Some historians regard the proof work as a social, rather than economic, practice by which newcomers were initiated as members of a community: C. Brooks, 'Apprenticeship, Social Mobility and the Middling Sort', p. 75.

54. GL, MS 7360; *The Case of the Middling and Poorer Sort of Master Shoe-Makers: Humbly Set Forth to the Honourable House of Commons* (London, 1738).

55. *Commons' Journals*, 23 (3 May 1738), pp. 176–7.

56. GL, MS 24963; R. Campbell, *The Complete Tradesman* (London, 1747) p. 217.

57. GL, MS 7353/4, ff. 108–9; Rule, *Experience of Labour*, p. 34.

58. Waterland Mander, *Guild of Cordwainers*, pp. 89–90; GL, MS 7361, ff. 17–42. In eighteenth-century England, the 'virtuous trade' was the part of shoemaking still controlled by the Cordwainers' Company.

59. 1 Jac. I, c. 22 (1603); *The Case of the Cordwainers in Behalf of Themselves, and Other Manufacturers of Leather in this Kingdom: Humbly Offered to the Right Honourable the House of Lords* ([London?], 1738). See also M. D. George, *London Life in the XVIIIth Century* (London, 1925), p. 197. The London Cordwainers' Company sought help from various provincial guilds and societies of cordwainers to support their petition to Parliament. Many provincial groups, however, did not support the London Company.

60. *Case of the Middling and Poorer Sort.*

61. 12 Geo II, c. 25, sect. 7; GL. MS 7353/5 (30 April 1739). See also Stern, 'Control vs. Freedom', pp. 441–2.

62. Smith, 'Apprentices as Seventeenth-Century Adolescents', pp. 157–61.

63. I. Prothero, *Artisans and Politics in Early Nineteenth Century London* (Folkstone, 1979), p. 4.

64. Ben-Amos, however, underlines that since the fifteenth century an increasing number of journeymen did not become masters: 'Failure to become freemen', pp. 154–72.

65. Brooks, 'Apprenticeship, Social Mobility and the Middling Sort', p. 73.

66. R. S. Duplessis, *Transitions to Capitalism in Early Modern Europe* (Cambridge, 1997), pp. 272–3. In London, shoemakers' journeymen were allowed to employ as many apprentices as they could feed, cloth and house. These apprentices provided cheap labour, and, without parental financial assistance or the possibility of accumulating sufficient capital to set up their own business, it was very unlikely that any would become masters. George, *London Life*, p. 201; P. Earle, *A City Full of People: Men and Women of London, 1650–1750* (London, 1994), p. 69; P. Sharpe, 'Poor Children as Apprentices in Colyton, 1598–1830', *Continuity and Change*, 6 (1991), pp. 253–70.

67. G. Riello, 'Shopping for Walking: Structures and Practices in Footwear Retailing, 1750–1850' (Paper presented at the Institute of Historical Research, London, October 2000).

68. Sutton, 'Metropolitan Artisans', p. 54; GL, MS 7353/6, ff. 301–310. The company intervened again in May 1777 (MS 7353/7, ff. 121–24), March 1792 (MS 7353/8, f. 55),

January 1798 (MS 7353/8, ff. 231) and May 1825 (MS 7353/10, ff. 160–4). See also A. Aspinall, *The Early English Trade Unions: Documents from the Home Office Papers in the Public Record Office* (London, 1949), pp. 83–4; C. R. Dobson, *Masters and Journeymen: A Prehistory of Industrial Relations, 1717–1800* (London, 1980), pp. 24–5; Schwarz, *London*, p. 196; D. R. Green, 'Lines of Conflict: Labour Disputes in London 1790–1870', *International Journal of Social History*, 43 (1998), pp. 203–33.

69. On the role of women in eighteenth-century business, see M. R. Hunt, *The Middling Sort*, pp. 125–46

70. In 1690, out of 1590 new freemen of the City of London only twelve were women: Glass, 'Socio-Economic Status', pp. 385–6.

71. Schwarz, *London*, p. 21.

72. GL, MS 24139.

73. P. Earle, 'The Female Labour Market in London in the Late Seventeenth and Eighteenth Centuries', *Economic History Review*, 2nd ser., 42 (1989), pp. 328–53; I. K. Ben-Amos, 'Women Apprentices in Trades and Crafts of Early Modern Bristol', *Continuity and Change*, 6 (1991), p. 228.

74. GL, MS 24140 (1710).

75. GL, MS 24140 (1739).

76. Howell, *Women*, pp. 27–32.

77. P. Sharpe (ed.), *Women's Work: The English Experience, 1650–1914* (London, 1998).

78. J. de Vries, 'The Industrial Revolution and the Industrious Revolution', *Journal of Economic History*, 54 (1994), pp. 249–78; J. G. Coffin, 'Gender and the Guild Order: The Garment Trades in Eighteenth-Century Paris', *Journal of Economic History*, 54 (1994), p. 769. See also B. Hanawalt (ed.), *Women and Work in Pre-Industrial Europe* (Bloomington, 1986); M. Berg, 'Women's Work, Mechanisation, and the Early Phases of Industrialisation in England', in P. Joyce (ed.), *The Historical Meanings of Work* (Cambridge, 1987), pp. 63–96.

79. *The Book of Trades, or Library of Useful Arts, Part II* (London, 1804), p. 90. See also J. Greenfield, 'Technology and Gender Division of Labour in the Boot and Shoe Industry, 1850–1911' (unpublished PhD thesis, University of Warwick, 1998).

80. Ben-Amos, 'Women Apprentices', p. 228.

81. See C. Crowston, 'Engendering the Guilds: Seamstressers, Tailors, and the Clash of Corporate Identities in Old Regime France', *French Historical Studies*, 23 (2000), pp. 339–71.

82. Ben-Amos, 'Failure to Become Freemen', p. 165.

83. For the seventeenth and early eighteenth century, see R. Grassby, *Kinship, and Capitalism: Marriage, Family, and Business in the English-speaking World, 1560–1740* (Cambridge, 2001).

84. As early as 1747, Campbell wrote that 'The Country Shoe-Makers supply most of the Sale-Shops in Town, the Price of making being too large to allow these Shop-keepers to employ *London* Workmen': *The London Tradesman*, p. 219.

85. See G. D. Ramsay, 'Victorian Historiography and the Guilds of London: The Report of the Royal Commission on the Liveries Companies of London, 1884', *London Journal*, 10 (1984), pp. 155–66.

Responses

11.
Guildwork

Mark Jenner

Since the heyday of their historiography in the early twentieth century, the guilds and livery companies of London have occupied a curiously marginal place in early modern English social and economic history.[1] Their rich records have consistently attracted researchers on topics ranging from sermons to secrecy and from government to gardens.[2] There have been many histories of individual companies, but few volumes have centrally concerned themselves, as this one does, with the guilds' position in the history of the early modern metropolis.[3] What conclusions, then, emerge from this collection, and, more importantly, what questions and what further lines of research does it suggest?

First of all it is clear that historians have not reached a consensus on how best to emplot the companies' history between the sixteenth and nineteenth centuries. The usual shorthand by which to characterise their fortunes has been 'decline', but the authors in this collection agree neither on the chronology of any decline, nor on the utility of the term as a way of understanding guild history.[4] Archer, Forbes and Homer all argue that the power of companies declined precipitately from the mid-seventeenth century, with Archer emphasising that the Fire was an economic disaster for the companies. Riello and Gauci, however, suggest (like Joseph Ward's *Metropolitan Communities*) that livery companies were remarkably adaptable institutions and that some of them remained vigorous into the eighteenth century. Even if their powers of search and their control of apprenticeship became less important, their feasts and other meetings were useful occasions for mercantile sociability and their committees were often important lobbies for economic regulation.

One reason for such different emphases is clearly the sheer diversity of livery companies. Some companies were relatively homogeneous, others so riven by disputes between the livery and the journeymen that it is difficult to write of "the company" at all.[5] Moreover, as Riello demonstrates, smaller companies like the Cordwainers retained a significant correlation between company and craft into the second half of the eighteenth century, whereas membership of the larger companies was largely a means of gaining the freedom and had little connection with their nominal trade.[6] Another reason is the extreme difficulty of generalising about every sector of the London economy.[7] In high-cost, high-skill sections of the economy, companies like the

Clockmakers and Spectaclemakers seem to have retained a degree of effectiveness in the regulation of their trade in the second half of the seventeenth century.[8] By contrast the regulatory authority of guilds connected with construction work apparently collapsed with particular rapidity in the same period. Unfree immigrants like the companions of the Quaker, Benjamin Bangs, quickly found work rebuilding the City after the fire, when Parliament temporarily suspended freemen's privileges in order to assure an adequate supply of labour.[9] Companies like the Carpenters and the Masons continued to campaign in favour of their control over their trade, but the most recent study of the 'speculative building world' of late-seventeenth-century London concluded that guild regulation was 'of little consequence'.[10]

It is important to note the role of *political* factors in shaping the livery companies' fortunes rather than to assume that their culture was inevitably doomed by purely economic developments, what Roy Porter revealingly termed 'capitalist realities'.[11] Recent writing on European artisan culture has rejected or at least greatly qualified the tradition of free market economic thought (itself highly political) which saw guilds as necessarily inhibiting innovation and thus producing economic stagnation.[12] Other studies have shown that their fortunes were entwined with national policies and politics with regard to social and economic regulation. In late seventeenth-century France, for instance, guilds of various kinds became *more* important with Sully's reforms, and as James Farr has recently reminded us, in many areas of Europe 'the importance of corporatism *per se* in terms of status and politics should not be underestimated'.[13] Moreover, in London as elsewhere, the power of individual guilds always depended on gaining patronage and political favour – upon mobilising *extra-urban* sources of authority and social power.[14] If we are to understand guilds' histories it is vital to attend to *these* day-to-day practices as well as the quotidian exercise of power rightly highlighted by Davies and Wallis.

To take one humble example – the Paviours' power of search, for instance, was undermined during the seventeenth century not only by the growth of the suburbs but also by a bitter and expensive dispute with one William Hart, who Charles II made 'Master Paviour-General' with power over all public paving work and a monopoly of a new form of paving.[15] An inhabitant of Westminster, Hart was particularly dangerous to the company. He declared that they 'were all cheatinge knaves', that they had engrossed supplies of paving stone, and that they 'had noe power nor authority at all', and also encouraged paviours to refuse to pay their dues.[16] Crucially he was able to mount this challenge because he had been recommended for his position by the Commissioners for Highways and Sewers set up to improve the metropolitan (and especially West End) paving in 1662, and because he could count upon the support of Sir John Denham, Master of the King's Works.[17] Not only did Denham imprison some company officials in Marshalsea and place others in the stocks, but he and the other commissioners were able to convince Charles II that a salaried royal appointee would regulate the city's streets more effectively than the craft.[18] As a result of this, the Paviours were driven into litigation, and had to initiate an enormously expensive (and ultimately inconclusive) campaign for a charter, which left them impoverished and politically weakened.[19]

Yet paradoxically such campaigns provided a powerful political and commercial *raison d'être* for some London livery companies in the eighteenth century.[20] As John Brewer noted a decade ago, in the first half of the eighteenth century the Distillers and the Brewers, the Goldsmiths, the Gold and Silver Wire Drawers and the Curriers all showed themselves to be energetic and resourceful lobbyists of Parliament.[21] Forming special committees, they showed that they were more than able to adapt to the politics of print and coffee house even if they could no longer maintain an effective search.

It is rarely, if ever, easy to adjudicate between different emplotments of the same events, but adjudicating between these varying accounts is particularly difficult because there are larger issues at stake than the fortunes and adaptability of the livery companies. Debates about their role parallel those about the significance of the wardmotes, the freedom and other distinctive aspects of the City's citizen culture.[22] These disagreements in turn mirror wider debates about the periodisation of both London and English history, not to mention those about the onset and nature of modernity.[23] Did the mid-seventeenth century (the period, say, from the outbreak of the civil war to the great fire) mark a significant discontinuity in metropolitan history and the emergence of a new mentality, in which '[t]he conservative and corporate nature of the livery companies was contrary to the individualist spirit of the age'; or was the transformation more gradual, completed only after the Financial Revolution or not until the first half of the eighteenth century? [24] Should we endorse eighteenth-century commentators who presented the City and the "cit" as often comic irrelevancies to the life of the Town and the new dominant culture of politeness; or should we, like Rosemary Sweet and Jonathan Barry, stress the vitality of civic forms of culture up to the early nineteenth century?[25] It is certainly striking how the City's political culture retained remarkable national prominence in the eighteenth century, even though it contained only a minority of the inhabitants of the metropolis.[26] Susan Brown has suggested that in the late eighteenth century members of the Corporation presented themselves in ways which fused civic traditions with a vocabulary of the commercial interest.[27] Did the companies present their activities in similarly hybrid ways?

There are many possible ways of approaching these issues. One might be to examine the livery companies through the combined prisms of social *and* intellectual history, to explore when the companies' regulatory powers ceased to be presented as a desirable way of organising production or disciplining youth and were instead denounced as a monopolistic and illiberal abuse, and to investigate the identity of those who penned such denunciations.[28] This would involve tracing what might anachronistically be termed the social history of political economy. For the rights which guilds were granted by virtue of their charters could certainly be seen as examples of the 'exclusive privileges of corporations...which restrain, in particular employments, the competition to a smaller number than might otherwise go into them', which Adam Smith criticised as 'a sort of enlarged monopoly'.[29] He was far from the first to voice such sentiments – more than twenty years before the publication of *The Wealth of Nations* a committee of the House of Commons condemned the 'vexatious Prosecutions' initiated by the Company of Framework Knitters and denounced the rights granted them by their Charter of Charles II because they were 'hurtful to the Trade and tend to a Monopoly'.[30] It would be helpful to map the complex ways in which terms like monopoly were deployed in debates about guilds and other chartered corporations through the seventeenth and eighteenth centuries.[31] Such an enterprise would have to examine not only the press and parliamentary debates but also the judgements of the courts. It is particularly striking that in their articles both Forbes and Homer highlight the role of legal advice and judgements in curtailing the Pewterers' and the Goldsmiths' searches, and it would be most valuable to discover more about the opinions of the judiciary about the companies' powers in the late seventeenth and the eighteenth centuries. We should not assume that it was an uncomplicated story of progressive economic liberalisation. Douglas Hay's recent detailed study of Lord Chief Justice Kenyon has, for instance, shown how some of the judiciary strongly upheld traditional Tudor economic regulations up to the end of the eighteenth century.[32]

Another way of exploring some of these issues might be to start unpacking the affective culture of the livery company, examining the nature of individuals' identification with or psychic investment in a particular guild or the image of a City structured by the freedom.[33] Wallis and Davies, for instance, both stress the language of amity, fraternity, even of love, which suffused many of the rituals and the records of the companies between the fifteenth and seventeenth centuries. More particularly, Robertson suggests that migration to London and the desire to be a freeman of the City could be fired at least in part by identification with particular (semi-fictional) figures such as Sir Richard Whittington or with an imagined civic *cursus honorum*. Gadd, meanwhile, asks whether the development and long continuation of a market for catalogues itemising the livery companies and for broadside tables of engravings of their coats of arms in the sixteenth and seventeenth centuries was a form of civic nostalgia in the face of rapid urban expansion.

Historians have frequently suggested that livery companies were one of a number of 'overlapping communities' – including neighbourhood, parish and ward – to which individual Londoners belonged. They have generally analysed sentiments such as loyalty to a company functionally, exploring how far they contributed to social cohesion and the prevention of economic and generational conflict.[34] Alternatively, within the historiography of the labour movement there has been great interest in how the solidarities of artisans' groups fed into early trades unionism.[35] It would be revealing also to investigate these issues *ontologically*, asking whether and how, for instance, a particular individual or group belonged differently to neighbourhood and guild, and seeking to develop a language and a set of categories with which to describe and to compare such structures of feeling over time. Questions of gender are clearly crucial for such inquiries, for the livery companies were strikingly homosocial institutions: Merry Wiesner's work on Germany has shown how the fraternalism of early modern journeymen's associations could produce distinctive forms of masculinity in tension with many of our assumptions about the norms of patriarchy.[36] Such research would also force us to focus on what we might term guildwork, the myriad of cultural and material practices, ranging from the sending out of summonses and invitations to feasts, to the keeping of records and the management of property, by which livery companies have remained in process and in being.[37]

NOTES

I wish to thank Patricia Greene for reading and commenting on drafts of this article and for so much more.

1. For this period of study: G. Unwin, *Industrial Organization in the Sixteenth and Seventeenth Centuries* (London, 1904); G. Unwin, *The Gilds and Companies of London* (London, 1908).
2. P. Seaver, 'Laud and the Livery Companies', in C. Carlton with R. L. Woods, M. L. Robertson and J. S. Block (eds.), *State, Sovereigns & Society in Early Modern England* (Stroud, 1998), pp. 219–34; P. Griffiths, 'Secrecy and Authority in Late Sixteenth- and Seventeenth-Century London', *Historical Journal*, 40 (1997), pp. 925–51; B. M. U. Boardman, 'The Gardens of the London Livery Companies', *Journal of Garden History*, 2 (1982), pp. 85–116.
3. J. Ward, *Metropolitan Communities* (Stanford, 1997) is an important exception. More usual has been the practice of devoting one or two chapters of a larger study of London life to social relations within the livery companies.
4. This is most powerfully brought home if you examine the index entries under 'guild' in general histories of London such as R. Porter, *London: A Social History* (London, 1994) or S. Inwood, *A History of London* (London and Basingstoke, 1998). For a introductory survey of some of the ways in which decline might be understood, see P. Burke, 'Tradition and Experience: The Idea of Decline from Bruni to Gibbon', *Daedalus*, 105 (1976), pp. 137–52.
5. N. Carlin, 'Liberty and Fraternities in the English Revolution: the Politics of London Artisans' Protests 1635–1659', *International Review of Social History*, 39 (1994), pp. 223–54; I. J. Prothero, *Artisans and Politics in Early Nineteenth-Century London* (Folkestone, 1979), pp. 36–7.
6. See also J. R. Kellett, 'The Breakdown of Gild and Corporation Control Over the Handicraft and Retail Trade in London', *Economic History Review*, 2nd ser., 10 (1957–8), p. 390n. For

more on the contrasting fortunes of the great and smaller companies in the eighteenth century, see I. G. Doolittle, 'The Government of the City of London 1694–1767' (unpublished DPhil thesis, University of Oxford, 1979), chap. 7, esp. pp. 168–70.

7. For a stimulating discussion of the relationship between varying investment in guild culture and the nature of different sections of the clothing trade, see H. Deceulaer, 'Guildsmen, Entrepreneurs and Market Segments: the Case of the Garment trades in Antwerp and Ghent (Sixteenth to Eighteenth Centuries)', *International Review of Social History,* 43 (1998), pp. 1–29.

8. M. Berlin, '"Broken All in Pieces": Artisans and the Regulation of Workmanship in Early Modern London', in G. Crossick (ed.), *The Artisan and the European Town* (Aldershot, 1997), pp. 82–3. For the Clockmakers' later regulatory policies, T. K. Derry, 'The Repeal of the Apprenticeship Clauses of the Statute of Apprentices', *Economic History Review,* 3 (1931–32), pp. 70–1.

9. B. Bangs, *Memoirs of the life and convincement of that worthy Friend, Benjamin Bangs, late of Stockport in Cheshire* (1757), p. 12; T. F. Reddaway, *The Rebuilding of London After the Great Fire,* 2nd edn. (London, 1943), pp. 115–21.

10. E. McKellar, *The Birth of Modern London: the Development and Design of the City 1660–1720* (Manchester, 1999), p. 97. For more on the companies involved in the building trade: Ward, *Metropolitan Communities,* pp. 36, 38 and 158 nn. 63–64; B. W. E. Alford and T. C. Barker, *A History of the Carpenters Company* (London, 1968); E. B. Jupp, *An Historical Account of the Worshipful Company of Carpenters,* 2nd edn. (London, 1887), pp. 311–15; D. Knoop and G. P. Jones, *The London Mason in the Seventeenth Century* (Manchester and London, 1935), pp. 10–12 and *passim.*

11. Porter, *London,* p. 148.

12. S. R. Epstein, 'Craft Guilds. Apprenticeship, and Technological Change in Preindustrial Europe', *Journal of Economic History,* 58 (1998), pp. 684–713; J. Farr, '"On the Shop Floor": Guilds, Artisans, and the European Market Economy', *Journal of Early Modern History,* 1 (1997), pp. 25–54; R. Mackenny, *Tradesmen and Traders: The World of Guilds in Venice and Europe, c.1250–c.1650* (London, 1987), chap. 3; S. D'Amico, 'Crisis and Transformation: Economic Organization and Social Structures in Milan 1570–1610', *Social History,* 25 (2000), pp. 1–21.

13. C. Crowston, 'Engendering the Guilds: Seamstresses, Tailors, and the Clash of Corporate Identities in Old Regime France', *French Historical Studies,* 23 (2000), pp. 339–71; D. K. Smith, 'Learning Politics: The Nîmes Hosiery Guild and the Statutes of 1706–1712', *French Historical Studies,* 22 (1999), pp. 493–533; J. R. Farr, *Artisans in Europe, 1300–1914* (Cambridge, 2000), p. 31.

14. Compare Smith, 'Learning Politics' and J. Dambruyne, 'Guilds, Social Mobility and Status in Sixteenth-Century Ghent', *International Review of Social History,* 43 (1998), pp. 31–78. For a good example of an alliance between courtly patentees and London producers, M. Berlin, *The Worshipful Company of Distillers: A Short History* (London, 1996), pp. 5–15. See also I. Archer, 'The London Lobbies in the Later Sixteenth Century', *Historical Journal,* 31 (1988), pp. 17–44; D. M. Dean, 'London Lobbies and Parliament', *Parliamentary History,* 8 (1989), pp. 341–65; D. H. Sacks, 'The Corporate Town and the English State: Bristol's "Little Businesses" 1625–1641', reprinted in J. Barry (ed.), *The Tudor and Stuart Town* (London, 1990), pp. 297–333, and Robertson's contribution to this volume, above, pp. 51–66.

15. PRO, SP29/255/74–74I; *CSPD, 1668–69,* p. 190.

16. GL, MS 181/10i, 181/13); C. Welch, *History of the Worshipful Company of Paviors* (London, 1909), pp. 43–46 prints the former with only minor inaccuracies.

17. For details of Hart's employment by the Commissioners for Highways and Sewers, see PRO, E101/623/1–10 (especially 2 & 10).

18. GL, MS 183A, larger bundle, Bill of August 5 1668.
19. GL, MS 181(12); 183A (larger bundle, unnumbered): Bill of 5 August 1668 & Petition of John Barker (n.d.). The Company also instituted a special view of all Hart's work: GL, MS 182/3, f. 88. The Paviours continued in dispute with Hart for another decade: GL, MSS 183A, larger bundle, last item; 181(26). On the Paviours' campaigns: Welch, *Company of Paviors*, pp. 46–52. The campaign cost over £166: GL, MS 181(15). It is instructive to compare this episode with the Brewers' successful campaign against Richard Drake who was granted a monopoly of beer and wine for vinegar by Queen Elizabeth: I. W. Archer, 'London Lobbies', pp. 41–43.
20. Indeed Kellett stresses how the political campaigning of the City Corporation and the companies in the mid eighteenth century greatly extended the duration of their jurisdiction: Kellett, 'Breakdown of Gild and Corporation Control'.
21. J. Brewer, *The Sinews of Power: War, Money and the English State 1688–1783* (London, 1989), pp. 237–9. On the Fishmongers' lobby see W. F. Kahl, *The Development of London Livery Companies* (Cambridge, Mass., 1960), pp. 27–8.
22. Although the presentments of the wardmote inquests had largely become minor and often ineffectual by the end of the seventeenth century, Tony Henderson has shown how even in the early nineteenth century the institutions of the ward could be used against bawdy houses with considerable effect, T. Henderson, *Disorderly Women in Eighteenth-Century London* (London, 1999), pp. 149–53.
23. For further reflections on the periodisation of London history, see M. S. R. Jenner and P. Griffiths, 'Introduction', in P. Griffiths and M. S. R. Jenner (eds.), *Londinopolis: Essays in the Cultural and Social History of Early Modern London* (Manchester, 2000).
24. Quotation from P. Earle, *The Making of the English Middle Class* (London, 1989), p. 250.
25. For the former approach: L. Klein, *Shaftesbury and the Culture of Politeness* (Cambridge, 1994), pp. 11–13. Klein elaborated this theme more fully in a paper at the conference on 'The Streets of London 1660–1870' which will appear in T. Hitchcock and H. Shore (ed.), *The Streets of London 1660–1870* (forthcoming). For the latter: J. Barry, 'Provincial Town Culture 1640–1780: Urbane or Civic', in J. H. Pittock and A. Wear (ed.), *Interpretation and Cultural History* (London and Basingstoke, 1991), pp. 198–234; R. Sweet, 'Freedom and Independence in English Borough Politics c.1770–1830', *Past and Present*, 161 (1998), pp. 84–115.
26. For example, N. Rogers, *Whigs and Cities: Popular Politics in the Age of Walpole and Pitt* (Oxford, 1989), esp. Part I.
27. S. E. Brown, '"A Just and Profitable Commerce": Moral Economy and the Middle Classes in Eighteenth-Century London', *Journal of British Studies*, 32 (1993), pp. 305–32.
28. For a superb example of this kind of interdisciplinary approach, M. Sonenscher, *Work and Wages: Natural Law, Politics and the Eighteenth-Century French Trades* (Cambridge, 1991).
29. A. Smith, *An Inquiry into the Nature and Causes of the Wealth of Nations*, R. H. Campbell, A. S. Skinner and W. B. Todd (eds.), vol. 1 (Oxford, 1976), p. 79.
30. *Commons Journals, 26* (1750–54), p. 788. See also, J. D. Chambers, 'The Worshipful Company of Framework Knitters (1657–1779)', *Economica*, 9 (1929), pp. 296–329; S. A. Mason, *The History of the Worshipful Company of Framework Knitters* (London, 2000).
31. Importantly, this investigation would have to explore early seventeenth-century denunciations of monopolists as well as later advocates of free trade. For the former theme, see D. H. Sacks, 'Parliament, Liberty, and the Commonweal', in J. H. Hexter (ed.), *Parliament and Liberty from Queen Elizabeth I to the Civil Wars* (Stanford, 1991), pp. 85–121.
32. D. Hay, 'The State and the Market in 1800: Lord Kenyon and Mr Waddington', *Past and Present*, 162 (1999). For divergent judgements as to whether company by-laws constituted a restraint of trade: I. Doolittle, 'Government of the City of London', p. 163 n. 1.

33. For some extremely stimulating thoughts on the role of identification in the formation of group identity, L. J. Jordanova, 'Medical Men 1780–1820', in J. Woodall (ed.), *Portraiture: Facing the Subject* (Manchester, 1997), esp. pp. 102–3.

34. See, in particular, I. W. Archer, *The Pursuit of Stability: Social Relations in Elizabethan London* (Cambridge, 1991), *passim*, 'quotation at p. 260'.

35. For the most recent review of some of this literature, M. Chase, *Early Trades Unionism: Fraternity, Skill and the Politics of Labour* (Aldershot, 2000), chap. 1.

36. M. E. Wiesner, 'Guilds, Male Bonding and Women's Work in Early Modern Germany', *Gender and History*, 1 (1989), pp. 125–37. See also M. A. Clawson, 'Early Modern Fraternalism and the Patriarchal Family', *Feminist Studies*, 6 (1980). For an interesting exploration of how German artisans developed a more restrictive understanding of dishonour than urban magistrates which has many parallels with Wiesner's discussion of gender, see K. Stuart, *Defiled Trades and Social Outcasts* (Cambridge, 1999), chaps. 7–8.

37. This term is an adaptation of M. Di Leonardo's notion of 'kin work' outlined in 'The Female World of Cards and Holidays – Women, Families, and the Work of Kinship', *Signs*, 12 (1987), pp. 440–53.

12.

Livery Companies: What, When and Why?

DEREK KEENE

In these chapters, I have been above all struck by the livery companies as institutions which express aspects of London's character as a metropolis: not just a capital city, but a uniquely dominant social and physical organism. By the seventeenth century, as Gadd reveals, the London companies could legitimately be attributed a prominent place in iconographic expressions of the identity of the realm. As wealthy communities with responsibility for their own affairs, the leading companies were at least equal to some provincial cities. The foundations of this prominence were deep. London was setting national standards in commerce and crafts by the year 1000.[1] In the later Middle Ages, as London's influence grew, there were many ways in which the legal, commercial and linguistic habits of its citizens became an ever more pervasive force throughout the kingdom.[2] This did not require guilds, for much of that influence was informal, as we have seen with Homer's observation on the way in which provincial pewterers came to follow the metal standards of their London counterparts. Nevertheless, the powers of search acquired and developed by London companies such as the goldsmiths and pewterers led to direct intervention by Londoners in the shops and workshops of craftsmen in many distant parts of the realm, as Forbes and Homer vividly describe. This was a strong expression of the companies' national role and of the power of London's market. The companies had a similarly widespread impact through their regulation of apprenticeship. Young potential migrants in many towns and villages in distant parts of the realm must have had a clear perception of the London companies as a means of advancement, as Robertson's examination of the Dick Whittington story makes apparent.[3] Moreover, a good many of that large proportion of London apprentices who failed to complete their terms, as Davies describes for the Merchant Taylors, presumably returned to the provinces, so that the London companies thereby made significant contributions to training and to the diffusion of knowledge and skills at a national level. As Archer points out, the companies also served in more formal ways to consolidate links between the metropolis and the provincial regions from which so many of their members came: through charity, patronage, educational provision, and memorialisation. The companies are commonly discussed in terms of their role within London. Equally important, however, was their part in articulating the complex economic, social and cultural exchanges between the metropolis and its hinterland.

As a medievalist, I urge early modernists to pay due regard to the earlier centuries of company and guild history. Indeed, some of the papers in this collection, most notably Archer's, do that in interesting ways. This will help to identify some of those company characteristics that are most deeply rooted in city life. A guild of leading Londoners can be traced back to the eleventh century, if not the tenth, but craft guilds, the ancestors of the later companies, appear to have emerged before any recognisable governing community of citizens. Craft guilds are first recorded early in the twelfth century, when they may have been of recent origin and the outcome of rapid economic growth. They derived their authority from the king, seem to have made an important contribution to the regulation of the city and its environs, and were independent, at least initially, of the communal authority that eventually emerged. The complex pattern of separate but interdependent institutions which characterised city government in the early modern period can be at least in part explained by these early developments in the structuring of power, where the lines of authority derived from the king served as the principal linking factor. Later developments, such the establishment of the crafts as the main avenue to the freedom of the city, the registration of their ordinances in civic records, their role from time to time in the election of civic councils, and the consolidation of their legal capacity by means of royal charters, have sometimes tended to obscure the dynamic contribution of the craft guilds in earlier periods. Several of the later livery companies can trace direct lines of descent from the twelfth century, and there were probably more such cases than are revealed by the surviving records. This long history, antedating the mayoralty and the community of citizens, underlines the deep-rooted nature of the crafts and associated guilds in the social and political organisation of London, and helps us understand their long survival. [4]

Such considerations raise a question that should always be to the fore in livery company history: what were these institutions for? The papers clearly demonstrate their multiple functions in the early modern period. The earlier histories of some of the companies also reveal the way in which a guild could combine a variety of craft interests, along with neighbourhood, charitable, and religious concerns. The later focus on the single craft may reflect ideals of taxonomy and social order, strengthened by statute, rather than the complex realities of manufactures and trade in the city. Indeed the later London custom whereby a citizen in one company could practice the trade of another seems to recognise that reality.[5] Thus a straightforward assessment of the guilds in terms of economic utility, while certainly valuable and thought-provoking, is fraught with difficulty, not least in any systematic attempt to factor in the social benefits as forces which, by encouraging cohesion, contribute to the economic rationale of the institution.[6] In a number of cases, the social and religious elements in the association seem to antedate the connection with a particular craft. Perhaps we should regard the ultimate coming together of the three elements as a process of maximising advantage. Cohesion may be the essential thing, with the well-known craft and commercial advantages of encouraging quality, the flow of information, and the most efficient use of the labour resource. Perhaps the very ineffectiveness of the companies in regulating their trades was an aspect of their utility in promoting cohesion. Too strong an intervention could risk fracturing the collective trust that they sought to promote, while low fines, the encouragement of apology and the tolerance of frequent offenders against regulations might serve to keep members sufficiently in line, but at the same allow them to pursue private advantage. One cannot help feeling that many of the court and other formal proceedings of the companies, as described in Davies's and Wallis's papers for example, were ritualised activities intended to promote a common ideology rather than to compel members to conform to every aspect of the ordinances. Some companies, as Riello states, clearly served to extend the familial bonds that regulated most artisan workshops, and such practices remained useful in London well into the nineteenth century and even have value today. The details of these patterns of company behaviour are worth close attention.

The survival and continued (perhaps even continuing) utility of the companies has much to do with their multi-faceted character and their capacity to provide an environment where the flexible forms of association and exchange conducive to doing business could prosper. Seen in this light, they need be no more a barrier to enterprise or technological innovation than any other institution or collection of individuals, and could positively promote such activities.[7] The seventeenth- and eighteenth-century merchants (in Gauci's paper) and instrument makers who joined companies which lacked any nominal connection to their business clearly thought in that way, and recent writing on guilds in general stresses that side of their contribution.[8] On the other hand, in the case of the London companies, there can be little doubt that their survival owes much to their endowments and charitable responsibilities, and that this has at times promoted a narrow concern with patronage, inward-looking policies and the exclusion of enterprise from their halls. The interplay of these forces and attitudes in the London companies remains a subject of abiding interest for those concerned to understand how the city has worked and continues to function. It is a topical subject too, given the current progress of 'reform' in the city and the public and civic promotion of the companies themselves (not least at the Bluewater 'shopping destination' on the outskirts of London, where images of the city's guilds and livery companies, both medieval and modern, provide programmatic ornamentation within England's largest shopping mall).

NOTES

1. D. Keene, 'London from the post-Roman Period to 1300', in D. M. Palliser (ed.), *The Cambridge Urban History of Britain, volume I, 600–1540* (Cambridge, 2000), pp. 187–216, especially, p. 204.

2. D. Keene, 'Medieval London and its Region', *London Journal,* 14 (1989), pp. 99–111; D. Keene, 'Metropolitan Values: Migration, Mobility and Cultural Norms, London 1100–1700', in L. Wright (ed.), *The Development of Standard English, 1300–1800: Theories, Descriptions, Conflicts* (Cambridge, 2000), pp. 93–114.

3. S. L. Thrupp, *The Merchant Class of Medieval London (1300–1500)* (Ann Arbor, 1962; first edition Chicago, 1948), pp. 207–10, 389–92; S. Rappaport, *Worlds Within Worlds: Structures of Life in Sixteenth-Century London* (Cambridge, 1989), pp. 76–81, 232–4; Keene, 'Metropolitan Values', figs 6.7, 6.8.

4. Keene, 'London from the post-Roman Period', pp. 204–11; C. M. Barron, 'London 1300–1540', in Palliser (ed.), *Cambridge Urban History,* pp. 395–440, especially pp. 403–6, 428–32; E. Veale, 'The "Great Twelve": Mistery and Fraternity in Thirteenth-Century London', *Historical Research,* 64 (1991), pp. 237–63.

5. Rappaport, *Worlds Within Worlds,* pp. 112–17.

6. Compare S. R. Epstein, 'Craft Guilds, Apprenticeship, and Technological Change in Pre-Industrial Europe', *Journal of Economic History,* 58 (1998), pp. 684–713.

7. Coherently argued in Epstein, 'Craft guilds'.

8. M. A. Crawforth, 'Instrument Makers in the London Guilds', *Annals of Science,* 44 (1987), pp. 319–77; G. Clifton, *Directory of British Scientific Instrument Makers, 1550–1851* (London, 1995); G. Rosser, 'Crafts, Guilds and the Negotiation of Work in the Medieval Town', *Past and Present,* 154 (1997), pp. 3–31.

13.

Livery Companies and the World Beyond the Metropolis

Joseph P. Ward

The chapters in this volume remind us of the significance of London's early modern livery companies not only for the metropolis but also for the nation and the wider world. London's economic health benefited from its location on both national and international trade routes, and its growth was made possible by steady immigration from abroad as well as from provincial England and Wales. Although some Londoners were certainly capable of expressing rather hostile attitudes towards the foreigners in their midst, throughout the early modern period London became an increasingly cosmopolitan place. These chapters provide ample evidence that the livery companies and their members played a central role in this process.

London's livery companies figured prominently in the national imagination. When, as Robertson points out, the town fathers of Exeter sought parliamentary action to create for their town a guild of merchants like London's in the 1530s, they were indicating both their awe and their ignorance of London. It is not surprising that provincial governors were unaware of the actual workings of the City and its companies, but their desire to emulate metropolitan institutions is further evidence that provincial town élites were not as insular as some historians have claimed.[1] Who could blame provincial townsmen for misunderstanding a place into which a poor boy could migrate and become rich enough to rise to the position of lord mayor on the basis of venturing his cat on an overseas voyage that reached a land overrun with mice? Surely the wide circulation of the Dick Whittington legend attests to the fascination of people from across the realm with the magical qualities of the metropolis. The same can be said for the marketing of the histories and arms of London's livery companies. Gadd makes clear that those who sold the histories and reputations of the companies to provincial audiences did not think the London institutions lacked self-esteem. To assert, as did at least one of the engravings of arms that Gadd discusses, that London livery companies were as significant as cathedral cities testified to their prominence not only in the City but throughout the realm – or, at the very least, to the artist's perception of their importance to his potential customers. Gadd is wise to raise the question of the potential audience for these works. We may never know for certain whether they were intended for metropolitan or national consumption or, perhaps, for both. In any case, their symbolic equation of the livery companies with the major provincial towns confirms the companies' national profile.

The legends and exaggerated reputations of London's livery companies likely enhanced their appeal to potential immigrants. Davies describes how by the late fifteenth century the Merchant Taylors' Company had absorbed so many immigrants, many of whom were from northern England, that its officers felt the need to take steps to control their inflow. Their efforts, it seems, were rather half-hearted. While some company members complained about the officers' inaction, others defended their right to employ such 'foreign' workers. Davies reasonably suggests that this reflected the pragmatism of the officers in the face of an endemic issue for London: how to protect the rights and interests of the freemen without discouraging the immigrants whose presence lent dynamism to the metropolitan economy. It may also have reflected the fact that many company officers had themselves once immigrated to London. They may have worked their way up the company's ranks rather than striking it rich as Dick Whittington had, but they presumably had not forgotten their provincial origins and so may have wished to be as hospitable as possible when dealing with the foreigners. For example, Stephen Jenyns (c.1448–1523) had migrated to London in his youth from Wolverhampton. Over the course of a long career, Jenyns gained prominence in the Merchant Taylor's Company and, in 1508, was chosen Lord Mayor, but he never lost sight of his home town. When he turned his attention to bestowing his considerable estates, he funded charities in both the metropolis and Wolverhampton.[2]

Jenyns was not atypical. Archer amply demonstrates that charity was essential to the social and cultural lives of the companies, enhancing company cohesion while continually connecting members to the generous benefactors of the past. These charities addressed livery company members who fell upon hard times and also contributed to the social well-being of the metropolis and the nation. Indeed, many prominent Londoners followed Jenyns's example by leaving large bequests in the care of their companies that supported both metropolitan and provincial needs in a variety of areas such as poor relief and education. For many members of early modern London's livery companies, charity began at home but extended further as well.

Their willingness to welcome immigrants and to share their wealth with provincial communities did not obviate the impression of many London freemen that they had to combat competition from craftsmen across England. Riello argues that members of the Cordwainers' Company had some success defending their traditional mode of production from provincial competition for much of the early modern period. Only after the metropolitan market for shoes and boots expanded to the point that it became profitable for shoemakers in

Yorkshire, Stafford, and Northampton to ship their products to London did the workshop replace the family as the primary unity of production. The desire to limit the effects of such provincial competition undoubtedly accounts for the effort that other companies put into gaining and exercising the right to inspect production across England. Forbes demonstrates that the Goldsmiths' Company's medieval charters empowered its officers to search goldsmiths' shops throughout the provinces, and that they took advantage of their powers into the middle of the seventeenth century, at which point their charters were considered less powerful than statute. Similarly, Homer indicates that the Pewterers' officers energetically exercised their right to search nationally throughout the early modern period because they were more successful than were the Goldsmiths' officers in having their chartered rights buttressed by acts of Parliament. It would be good to learn more about the reasons why the Pewterers' Company successfully pursued legislative confirmation for their powers to search outside the metropolis in the early sixteenth century while the Goldsmiths' officers seemed content to rely on royal charters until much later.

Homer also raises the question of why so many provincial pewterers joined the London company. This may be answered in part by the argument Wallis advances about the enforcement of company regulations in the metropolis. In addition to charity, freemen may have been able to expect lenient treatment from their company officers in the event that they were apprehended violating company rules. The slack attitude towards regulation that Wallis demonstrates may itself have been a reflection of the tacit understanding that companies would protect the well-being of their members. Rather than destroying the livelihood of members whom they caught cheating by excluding them from future participation in their trade, officers took great steps to reincorporate them into the company. For these reasons, we may speculate that provincial pewterers may have hoped that by joining the London Pewterers' Company they might receive more favourable treatment at the hands of their metropolitan brethren than would their fellow provincials.

London freemen seemed ever watchful for the encroachment of provincial competition in the metropolitan and national markets, but it is essential to bear in mind that as the early modern period progressed, some London freemen became increasingly involved in international markets. Gauci demonstrates that several livery companies contained clusters of merchants involved in overseas trade. The presence of such international traders in organisations typically considered to be focused on metropolitan markets indicates that the companies were a valuable means for the dissemination of information that would facilitate mercantile activity. In this way, the companies continued to offer resources to entrepreneurs even though their ability to protect all of their members from the effects of provincial competition may have been declining. The companies' ability to meet the needs of members in a variety of trades goes a long way toward explaining their continued viability.

For this reason, the history of the livery companies can be seen as an aspect of national and international history as well as a branch of the history of metropolitan London. The interactions of European and non-European societies in the early modern period were often arranged by many of the kinds of people we encounter in livery company archives.[3] One may therefore hope that as our understanding of London's livery companies develops, we may continue to engage with broader, rather than narrower, historiographies and methodologies. After all, Dick Whittington did not acquire his legendary fortune by bringing cats to Newcastle.

NOTES

1. For a full discussion of this historiography, see C. F. Patterson, *Urban Patronage in Early Modern England: Corporate Boroughs, the Landed Elite, and the Crown, 1580–1640* (Stanford, 1999), esp. pp. 1–11.

2. G. P. Mander, *The History of the Wolverhampton Grammar School* (Wolverhampton, 1913), pp. 1–12.

3. In addition to Gauci's work on London merchants, see R. Brenner, *Merchants and Revolution: Commercial Change, Political Conflict, and London's Overseas Traders, 1550– 1653* (Princeton, 1993) and D. Hancock, *Citizens of the World: London Merchants and the Integration of the British Atlantic Community, 1735–1785* (Cambridge, 1995). On merchants and overseas trade more generally, see D. H. Sacks, *The Widening Gate: Bristol and the Atlantic Economy, 1450–1700* (Berkeley, 1991).

Index